CONTROVERSIES ABOUT HISTORY, DEVELOPMENT AND REVOLUTION IN BRAZIL

Studies in Critical Social Sciences Book Series

Haymarket Books is proud to be working with Brill Academic Publishers (www.brill.nl) to republish the *Studies in Critical Social Sciences* book series in paperback editions. This peer-reviewed book series offers insights into our current reality by exploring the content and consequences of power relationships under capitalism, and by considering the spaces of opposition and resistance to these changes that have been defining our new age. Our full catalog of *SCSS* volumes can be viewed at https://www.haymarketbooks .org/series_collections/4-studies-in-critical-social-sciences.

CONTROVERSIES ABOUT HISTORY, DEVELOPMENT AND REVOLUTION IN BRAZIL

Economic Thought in Critical Interpretation

EDITED BY
MARIA MALTA, JAIME LEÓN,
CARLA CURTY AND BRUNO BORJA

Haymarket Books
Chicago, IL

First published in 2021 by Brill Academic Publishers, The Netherlands
© 2021 Koninklijke Brill NV, Leiden, The Netherlands

Published in paperback in 2022 by
Haymarket Books
P.O. Box 180165
Chicago, IL 60618
773-583-7884
www.haymarketbooks.org

ISBN: 978-1-64259-805-6

Distributed to the trade in the US through Consortium Book Sales and
Distribution (www.cbsd.com) and internationally through Ingram Publisher
Services International (www.ingramcontent.com).

This book was published with the generous support of Lannan Foundation and
Wallace Action Fund.

Special discounts are available for bulk purchases by organizations and
institutions. Please call 773-583-7884 or email info@haymarketbooks.org for more
information.

Cover design by Jamie Kerry and Ragina Johnson.

Printed in the United States.

10 9 8 7 6 5 4 3 2 1

Library of Congress Cataloging-in-Publication data is available.

Contents

Foreword

This collective work, edited by Professors Maria Malta, Jaime León, Carla Curty and Bruno Borja, offers a precise and innovative contribution to the History of Brazilian Economic Thought (HBET). Furthermore, by creating a foundation for a critical and committed history of ideas about development in Brazil, this book also indicates a way to renew left-wing political activity in the country. When a book can transform our understanding of the past and simultaneously contribute to the political construction of the future, it becomes a classic.

The examination of HBET presented in this work demonstrates the unequalled fertility of Brazilian social thought, flourishing throughout the 20th century amid a whirlwind of radical economic and social transformations. The work of Nelson Werneck Sodré, Caio Prado Jr, Celso Furtado, Florestan Fernandes, and other first-rate intellectuals reviewed in this volume, reveals their potency and practical relevance as opposed to purely academic achievements disconnected from people's lives. On the contrary, this book shows how the ideas of our key intellectuals stem from their deep political commitment, often at grave personal risk due to the repeated waves of political repression in the country. For decades, our authors have faced serious problems and emerging tensions in Brazil, with their political consequences and the construction of alternatives, both inside and outside the government. Their intellectual integrity stands out, and the recognition of their contribution demands a corresponding gravity in the reading of their works. Unfortunately, for a long time, until the release of this book, their work went unnoticed and did not receive the attention it deserved.

The authors read and (re) interpreted in the following chapters launched intellectual projects, converging but never identical, seeking to elucidate the dynamics of Brazilian development, its contradictions, and limitations and – most importantly to them – its points of tension, where the intervention of mobilized people could transform reality in a progressive direction. Few peripheral countries can count on two generations of brilliant, critical, original thinkers, committed to the realization of the nation's potential with its impoverished majority, continually dominated, humiliated, repressed and exploited.

•••

The dizzying transformative waves that have marked the Brazilian economy in the last century, including, prominently, import substitution industrialization and the transition to neoliberalism, were accompanied by profound social changes and serious political dramas. Despite this, the roots of national society have remained unchanged. Just as a century ago, Brazil today remains branded by its slave-owning heritage and structural racism, relentless elitism, brutal repression of the poor majority, and development generally propelled by foreign forces, and particularly subordinated to the imperialist center. The country continues to suffer from the hegemony of consumer standards imported from the North, and from the elites᾿ deliberate ignorance regarding national cultural values and expressions. The contempt for the majority, social exclusion and political repression are deeply linked to economic, social, and regional inequalities: everything revolves around the reproduction of the elites᾿ power. The continuity of these differences, inequalities and subordinate relations has been the defining characteristic of the Brazilian state, the guiding principle of public policies and the main obstacle to the construction of a democratic order and the recognition of citizenship.

Through critical analysis of the ideas, dreams, challenges, and commitments of Brazil᾿s greatest interpreters, this book offers an innovative materialistic methodology for understanding HBET. The approach developed here examines the respective roles of dominant theory, history and ideology, including the issues of population, social and productive structure (especially the relationship between agriculture and industry), organization and distribution of labor, the role of imperialism and the composition and historical role of elites and workers, peasants and middle classes. These topics, which can be summarized in the concept of production mode applied to the historical moment, that is, the accumulation system and its transformations, illuminate the discussion of socialist movements᾿ tactics and strategies and the scope for alliances between the left᾿s forces. Any form of progressive engagement with Brazil᾿s history and, ultimately, overcoming capitalism in the country must face these challenges, both in theory and in practice; that is, the character and possibilities of the Brazilian revolution.

The investigation in this work aims, then, to illuminate the unique nature of Brazilian capitalism and ways to overcome it. To this end, the essays in this book focus on relevant controversies, rather than a neoclassical emphasis on building models from arbitrary and disconnected elements. Neither does this book assume a linear evolution of thought towards a transcendent 'truth': not identifying and treating ideas in an abstract and (supposedly) 'pure' way, but in their economic and social context, and through the intellectual polemics and political confrontations from which they emerged. This approach renders theory and history inseparable, which is certainly the correct method of exposure within materialism.

•••

The Brazilian left has always faced many challenges, and its characters have often taken great risks. Many paid the highest price for their boldness. The first cycle of the left in the country revolved around anarchist and communist union activists based in Brazil`s main cities between the early 20th century and the so-called Revolution of 1930. This cycle was shattered by Vargas' repression. The second cycle emerged from mobilizations for Brazil`s entry to the Second World War and the nationalization of oil, led by the Brazilian Communist Party. This cycle lasted from the mid-1940s until it was crushed in the wake of the 1964 coup. The third cycle gradually emerges a decade later to be consolidated in the Workers' Party`s foundation in the 1980s. This cycle is vigorous, but increasingly reformist, ending between the 2013 mobilizations and the coup against President Dilma Rousseff. We are now experiencing an interregnum, from which a new form of popular mobilization must emerge, inspired by left-wing ideals – defined by the search for equality, solidarity and distribution of income, wealth and power – and organized into structures yet to emerge. It is not a question, therefore, of advocating the immediate construction of a new party, or of postulating the merger of existing organizations. As in previous cycles of the Brazilian Left, the question is to identify the national accumulation system and the corresponding working-class composition; and from there, develop representative class structures, with its peripheral and allied sectors, as they exist in concrete reality. This is not an academic challenge or a task that can be performed at conferences or activist meetings. On the contrary, it is about experiencing the class struggles that exist in reality, trying new avenues of defense and confrontation, examining the lessons of defeats, and applying the teachings of victories. The new organizational structures will not be found in the minds of intellectuals but will emerge from practical conflicts in the streets.

These fundamental lessons were captured by our authors. Despite their fine intellects, they never postulated the superiority of writing over practical action; on the contrary, their intellectual work served the urgent and practical purposes of political struggle. They engaged, worked together with many others, debated, disagreed, and learned from the humblest. Their most important lesson is that their works are subordinate to the struggle for the state and society`s democratization and the improvement of the people's living conditions. These are the ideals that also move this ongoing work. Enjoy it!

Alfredo Saad-Filho
Department of International Development, King's College London
London, November 2021

Tables

Notes on Contributors

Bruno Borja
Professor at Multidisciplinary Institute of Federal Rural University of Rio de Janeiro (UFRRJ). Researcher at Marxist Collective (Coletivo MAR / UFRRJ) and Laboratory of Marxist Studies (LEMA / UFRJ / UFRRJ). Researcher in the fields of Political Economy of Culture and Latin American Economic and Social Thought. Email: borja.bruno@gmail.com

Carla Curty
Professor at Três Rios Institute at Federal Rural University of Rio de Janeiro (UFRRJ). Researcher at Laboratory of Marxist Studies (LEMA / UFRJ / UFRRJ) and Marxist Collective (Coletivo MAR / UFRRJ). Researcher in the fields of history of economic thought, critique of political economy and history of economic and social thought in Brazil and Latin America. Email: carla_curty@yahoo.com.br

Jaime León
Researcher at Laboratory of Marxist Studies (LEMA / UFRJ / UFRRJ) and professor at Political Economy Institute at Federal University of Rio de Janeiro (UFRJ). Researcher in the fields of Brazilian socioeconomic formation, democracy and racial issues. He is also a member of the Florestan Fernandes Study Group (GEFF). Email: jaime.leon@ie.ufrj.br

Maria Malta
Professor at Political Economy Institute at Federal University of Rio de Janeiro (UFRJ). Coordinator of Laboratory of Marxist Studies (LEMA / UFRJ / UFRRJ). Researcher in the fields of history of economic thought, critique of political economy and history of economic and social thought in Brazil. Email: maria-malta@ie.ufrj.br

Filipe Leite Pinheiro
A substitute professor at Department of Economic Sciences (DeCE) at Federal Rural University of Rio de Janeiro (UFRRJ), where he participates as a researcher at Marxist Collective (Coletivo MAR / UFRRJ). Between 2009 and 2016 he participated as a researcher at Laboratory of Marxist Studies (LEMA / UFRJ / UFRRJ). Researcher in the fields of Brazilian economic thought and Marxist theory of value. Email: leitepn@gmail.com

Larissa Mazolli Veiga
Researcher at Laboratory of Marxist Studies (LEMA / UFRJ / UFRRJ). Graduated in International Relations at Unilasalle-RJ and in Economic Sciences at UFF and Master in International Political Economy at UFRJ. Her master's dissertation was about "Changes in the Brazilian agrarian structure and its consequences in economic development". Email: larissamv@gmail.com

Wilson Vieira
Researcher at Laboratory of Marxist Studies (LEMA / UFRJ / UFRRJ) and at Laboratory of Hegemony and Counter-Hegemony (LEHC), both at UFRJ, and professor at Political Economy Institute at Federal University of Rio de Janeiro (UFRJ). Researcher in the fileds of economic history of Brazil, Brazilian economy and Brazilian and Latin American economic and social thought (especially in the themes of nation and the relationship between development and underdevelopment). Email: wilson.vieira@ie.ufrj.br

Introduction and Warning to the Reader

Bruno Borja, Carla Curty, Jaime León and Maria Malta

This book is one of the results of an eight-year survey of Brazilian thinkers and their main debates throughout the republican period in Brazil (from 1889 to the present day) and the maturing of the research initiated earlier and presented in the book *Ecos do Desenvolvimento: uma história do pensamento econômico brasileiro* (2011) – Echoes of Development: a history of Brazilian economic thought. It is a collective work developed by a group of authors who build a method together to approach the history of economic thought based on a Marxist perspective and who wrote the following articles in the systematic space of group debate. This method is detailed in the first chapter of this book *Methodological elements for the organization of the history of Brazilian economic thought: the approach of controversies* written by Carla Curty and Maria Malta.

This introduction aims to take the reader through the construction of the history of Brazilian economic thought (HBET) during republican times, inviting them to travel through the main controversies that stood out for Brazilian social and economic thinkers. According to the proposed method, to understand the formation of controversies, knowledge of the historical movement that manages and incites them is fundamental. In this sense, the present introduction seeks to fulfill the role of giving the reader, who enters the universe of debates of Brazilian economic and social thought during the Republic, the path of approximation of the referred movement that will be the filling of the book in hand.

The work is presented in two parts. The first part is more theoretical and has an opening chapter presenting the method, previously mentioned, and two further chapters that discuss the origins of the History of Brazilian Economic Thought and the History of the Economy of Brazil. In both cases, the chapters present a methodological critique of the established way of building these areas in Brazil, using the Marxist point of view as the key to presenting a new perspective. The second part of the book is based on the history of essential controversies that were developed in Brazil. These debates are fundamental to understand the main reasons why the Brazilian thought about the nation and its transformations were established. The controversies explored are the Brazilian revolution, underdevelopment, dependency, structural heterogeneity and democracy. This introduction fulfills the role of stating the more relevant historical facts of these controversies, in the sense of locating the context in which they occur. With this, the intention is not to explore in depth all the historical facts of the period since the establishment of the Republic until today, but only to give a sense of the movement in which the controversies explored in this book develop.

1   An Approach to the History of the Brazilian Republic

The Brazilian Republic started with a military coup. A monarchist general, a friend of the emperor, mounted on a white horse, announced the Republic before a group of military men and removed the emperor. Few could imagine, but some certainly already wished, that this was the keynote of the history of the following 130 years: elitist schemes to keep the country always faithful to the Lampedusa paradigm in *Il Gatopardo*: "Everything must change for everything to remain the same". In fact, Octávio Ianni recalled in the 1988 *Raízes da Antidemocracia da América Latina*, (Roots of Antidemocracy in Latin America), that the history of Latin American societies is the history of successive coups d'état, always given in the name of a supposed democracy. This fact is so contradictory and so characteristic of Brazil, that countless constitutions were enacted, and the schemes took place from the beginning of the process of political independence, in the beginning of the 19th century, until the end of the 20th century.

There are many Interpreters of Brazil who see in the proclamation of the Republic and /or in the abolition of slavery the beginning of a class society and the origin of the bourgeois revolution in Brazil. Sérgio Buarque de Holanda and Florestan Fernandes are two of them. In fact, after the proclamation of the Republic, a liberal regime with very peculiar characteristics was organized, in which the fundamental reference was the American experience. The 1891 Constitution was so intensely based on the federalism of the United States of America, that even the country's first republican name was almost a copy of it: Federative Republic of the United States of Brazil. The combination of a political structure imported from abroad together with the historical form of construction of the Brazilian Republic, in which unification did not imply a broad civil war defining political positions, gave rise to a typical combination of social formations of colonial origin: a republic liberal-oligarchic daughter of a military coup.

The context of the proclamation of the Republic and the abolition of slavery, to mention some of the many changes to Brazilian society in the period, are the backdrop for the first interventions of what was conventionally called "Interpretations of Brazil". The contributions of Interpreters of Brazil are movements of analysis of the Brazilian reality and its specificities, which sought to understand the historical process of configuration of society. Thus, through the historical assessment, they have a deeper understanding of the Brazilian conjecture that they faced at their time, and they presented a proposal for a political project for the future of the country.

The first generation of Interpreters of Brazil took place in late 19th century, in this context of the proclamation of the Republic and the abolition of slavery. A second generation, perhaps the best-known Interpreters of Brazil, takes place in the 1930s, marking the modernizing transformations that Brazilian society was experiencing, in its political, economic, social and cultural spheres. In the chapter *Interpreters of Brazil: influences on the origin of Brazilian economic thought* authored by Carla Curty, Maria Malta and Bruno Borja, we have the presentation of what Interpreters of Brazil are and the analysis of some of the interpretations made by authors of the first and second generation.

We then had the first republic known, initially, as "República da Espada" ("Republic of the sword"). A Republic with a liberal constitution led by the military. It was the first "great coalition": *paulistas* and *mineiros* with republican-liberal tendencies and *gauchos* with republican-positivist influences joined forces with military personnel centered in the army, forming a republican coalition. The constitution was written by a directly elected constituent assembly and convened immediately after the coup. It could all seem very democratic, but the voters were only men, of legal age and literate, which excluded most of the newly freed enslaved and all women. That is, it excluded the expressive majority of workers, counting the clergy and military personnel without an official rank. The elected constituent met on November 15, 1890, and drafted the Constitution that it enacted on February 24, 1891, based on the project of Rui Barbosa, a liberal Brazilian lawyer and Americanist, who would be the Minister of Finance of the provisional government.

The elected constituent, Marshal Deodoro da Fonseca, was indirectly elected by the constituent representatives and had an opponent as vice president, Marshal Floriano Peixoto. Soon the first Brazilian president of more autocratic tendencies, just eight months after being elected, wanted to close the congress. With the episode of attempted closure of the congress and declaration of a state of siege, Deodoro weakened, not receiving support from the military, and receiving much criticism from Brazilian civilians, he ended up resigning on November 23, 1891. In eight months, Brazil had its first vice president governing the country. According to constitutional rules, he should call for new elections, but he did not do so fearing "political instability" and with the support of the São Paulo elites behind him he felt no need to risk further unrest. His legal argument was the article 42 of the constitution, which determined that if the presidency or vice-presidency becomes vacant, when two years have not yet elapsed, new elections should be held, however it only applied to presidents elected directly. Floriano's government was marked by military revolts.

The economic policy of the "Republic of the Sword" was characterized by the decision, still in the provisional government, to support national industry and guarantee loans to finance companies and the payment of wage earners, using the currency issuance as a mechanism for generating debt. The then slave-based economy was becoming monetized. This process, not having been accompanied by adequate control of registration and guarantees, gave rise to an increase in fraudulent activities, such as taking loans for companies that only existed on paper. The policy did not make it to the end of 1891, but it ruined many budding capitalists and left an extremely complicated mark on credit support policies financed with currency issuance.

In any case, Floriano Peixoto's term was marked by many revolts and insta-bility. The São Paulo and Minas Gerais elites articulated the succession in the name of stabilizing the Republic. The first direct elections, in 1894, saw Prudente de Morais, the first elected civilian president, ascend to the presi-dency. It is worth remembering, however, that this was an open voting process in which only literate men, over 21 years old, but who were not homeless peo-ple, clerics or military personnel without an official rank, participated. That is, only 6% of the Brazilian population at the time. A *sui generis* democracy.

The then established Republic had very peculiar characteristics and became known as the oligarchical Republic, because with an open vote it was quite simple to have control over the electoral college. There was also no electoral justice, and it was the local lords themselves who organized the elections, the same who were responsible for preparing the minutes and declaring the results. From the local level to the election of presidents of state (equivalent to today's governors) and that of the President of the Republic, agreements were often made. With regard to the presidency of the republic, the succession of presidents from Minas Gerais and São Paulo, the two wealthiest states in the country, was established as a rule. Hence the policy name "*café com leite*" (milk coffee), which derived from the most common export products of the two states, coffee and milk, expressing the political unity between the states of São Paulo and Minas Gerais.

From an economic point of view, the first Republic had to deal with major problems, such as a serious crisis of overproduction in 1893 that significantly affected its main export, coffee. Five years later, Brazilian debt was so great that President Campos Sales had to make the first deal with international creditors to receive a conditional loan: £10 million from the Rothschilds in exchange for a deflationary economic policy. The recession was established with the cut in credit and, a few years later, the deepening coffee crisis was. America responded primarily to US interests, under the Monroe Doctrine, the *Big Stick* policy and the dollar diplomacy, and coffee was not the center of this policy. While in Brazil, all economic policy movements were aimed at defending coffee prices. The situation of Brazil's economic dependence in relation to the results of this product (coffee) created a strong pressure on the need to establish an industry sector and a national economy. At the same time, fortunes from the Brazilian treasury were spent on profit guarantee policies for coffee farmers.

In this context, the generic corruption agenda was brought up as a fundamental criticism of the liberal government by its conservative detractors. Authoritarian thinkers made several allegations of corruption in the electoral process and one of the preferred arguments in defense of an authoritarian state was that the paraphernalia of the liberal political system was corrupt and expensive, so that true democracy would be in finding the right leader. In addition to authoritarian pamphlets and texts, before and from a different perspective, some popular criticisms, such as Revista Illustrada (Illustrated Magazine) and Don Quixote, edited by Angelo Agostini, contained articles and cartoons criticizing the way the political system was carried out in Brazil. What was appealing in the criticism of the authoritarians was that they also recognized that it was fundamental to face the problem of the formation of nationality in colonized countries. Their contributions on the issues of nation formation, the identity of the Brazilian people and a strong and hierarchically organized conception of the State were essential during the formation of movements that challenged the ongoing liberal order. The World War I further deepened these issues, with yet another decline in the worldwide coffee demand and the questioning of liberalism as a form of economic and social organization.

The Russian Revolution of 1917 and the organization of workers in Brazil also made up the framework of criticism of liberalism, however from the left. Since the end of the 19th century, there was a strong anarchist influence on the movements of Brazilian workers, marked by the migrations of European workers close to anarchism and communism. At the beginning of the 20th century, even before the Russian Revolution of 1917, we can see the influence of the *Ensaio Geral* of 1905 (the 1905 Russian Revolution) on the organization of workers in Brazil, as well as the conservative reaction to these movements. In 1907 and in 1913 deportation laws were passed for foreign agitators who were on Brazilian soil. The years 1917 to 1920 would also be emblematic in Brazil, because they would be marked by a series of manifestations and strikes.

The first general strike in the country began in June 1917 following the demands of a group of about 400 workers, mostly women, from a textile factory in São Paulo (Cotonifício Crespi, in the Mooca neighborhood). The agenda of that movement – such as reduced working hours, wage increases, among other specific issues such as the issue of sexual harassment in the factory – became widespread, with the participation of male and female workers from other categories, spreading throughout the capital of São Paulo, throughout cities in the interior of the state of São Paulo, reaching the states of Minas Gerais, Rio de Janeiro, Rio Grande do Sul, until mid-July of the same year. According to Konder (2003), this mobilization reached about 100 thousand people. Between 1917 and 1920 there were more than 200 strikes in Rio de Janeiro and São Paulo. In other parts of the country there were also actions influenced by the Russian revolutionary movement. For example, in Recife, the *Federação das Classes Trabalhadoras* (Federation of Working Classes) was created.

Marxism and socialism were sparse references among workers' organizations and intellectuals in Brazil until the founding of the *Partido Comunista do Brasil* (PCB) – Communist Party of Brazil – in 1922. In 1921, the *Grupo Comunista* (Communist Group) was formed with the objective of later founding the *Partido Comunista do Brasil* (PCB) – Communist Party of Brazil – and gathering the dispersed communist nuclei spread throughout Brazil. A dissent from the anarchist movement with representatives from São Paulo, Porto Alegre, Recife, Cruzeiro and Niterói would be responsible for the foundation, between March 25 and 27, 1922, of the PCB. There was a certain urgency in the creation and organization of the party, in view of the 4th Congress of the Communist International (Comintern) in Moscow that same year. As published in the *Movimento Comunista* (Communist Movement), a magazine edited by the party's founding group, the PCB's goal was to act as a political organization of the proletariat at the international level. The recognition of the PCB by the Comintern would only come in 1924, when it became the Brazilian section of the Communist International.

From the point of view of the left and the working class, two other movements that occurred in the 1920s were important, marking what became known as *Tenentismo* (derived from the word *tenente*, lieutenant in Portuguese). It was a time when the situation of the Army was very disheartening, with a lack of weapons, horses, medicines, instructions for the troops, with low salaries, with no indication of an increase on the part of the government, besides the slowness of the promotions of the career of the officers. Those primarily affected by these conditions were the lieutenants. In addition to being unhappy, the officers also disagreed with the appointment of a civilian, Pandiá Calógeras, to the War Ministry under the presidency of Epitácio Pessoa. Due to the situation described, several military uprisings broke out that aimed to overthrow the government, led, in its majority, by lieutenants, therefore, the name *Tenentismo*. The main *tenentista* (an adjective for *tenentismo*) movements were the *Movimento dos 18 do Forte de Copacabana* (movement of the 18 of the Copacabana Fort) in 1922 and the *Coluna Prestes* (Prestes Column) of 1924–1927.

The uprising of *Movimento dos 18 do Forte de Copacabana* (movement of the 18 of the Copacabana Fort) was triggered by the electoral dispute for the presidency of the Republic of 1921. The movement's list of criticisms was organized around the aforementioned *República do Café com Leite* (Coffee Milk Republic) and the officials' discontent on account of the work conditions. At first the uprisings would take place with several battalions in Rio de Janeiro. However, on July 5, 1922, only in Fort Copacabana and in the Military School there were uprisings, which were soon fought.

The *Coluna Prestes* (Prestes Column) was a popular uprising against the government led by Army captain Luís Carlos Prestes, who rebelled in October 1924. A group of about 1500 military personnel traveled around 25 thousand kilometers, crossing 13 Brazilian states. They demanded social legislation that covered all the country's needs and constitutional reform. They had a highly critical political program. The movement gained strong popular support wherever it went, also receiving strong opposition from the official political structure. The movement was harshly persecuted.

In this direction, Marxist interpretations of the Brazilian reality also emerged not only with the theoretical synthesis of the influence of intellectual formulations from abroad, but also through the confrontation of different theoretical-political formulations of organic intellectuals of the Brazilian working class whose purpose was to intervene politically in that Brazil in deep dispute. During that wave of historical events, the debate between Octavio Brandão, Mario Pedrosa and Lívio Xavier took place. Authors who sought to understand the sense of the Brazilian historical process to transform the country toward socialism. A theoretical itinerary that culminates in the elaboration of Marxist images of Brazil, fundamental to demarcate the origins of the controversy on the Brazilian revolution. The controversy between Octávio Brandão, Mario Pedrosa and Lívio Xavier will be presented in the *chapter Revisiting the origins of the controversy on the Brazilian revolution: a debate between Octavio Brandão, Mario Pedrosa and Lívio Xavier*, written by Filipe Leite Pinheiro.

It is central to note, however, that the 1929 crisis was crucial in giving space in the political arena to the movements that embodied the so-called "1930 revolution", a coup d'état that transformed into an authoritarian regime of fifteen years, especially after it called itself *"Estado Novo"* ("New State") in 1937, when it closed the congress and produced a new constitution. The crisis seemed to demonstrate the failure of capitalism and the liberal political regime. Thus, the "1930 revolution" wanted to be the answer to this problem, and it was a

movement led by the urban petty bourgeoisie, mainly lawyers, civil servants
and military officers and marked by authoritarian thought.

In these conditions, the Brazilian authoritarian dictatorship was born considered by its leaders as the regime best suited to the country's characteristics,
and not just an expedient dictated by circumstances. Despite this, in political
discourse and intellectual formulations, authoritarianism presented itself as
a true democracy, a regime that freed the Brazilian people and the State from
the paraphernalia of parties and elections, typical of liberal regimes. However,
Vargas' policy did not only have liberals as his enemies, in fact his declared enemies were communist organizations and militants, who were explicitly persecuted in this period, including with the enactment of the national security law.

The 1930s were a politically intense decade in Brazil. In addition to the
"revolução de 1930" ("1930 revolution"), other political movements shook
the national scene. As a reaction to Vargas' rise to power, the *"Revolução
Constitucionalista"* ("Constitutionalist revolution") of 1932 took place in São
Paulo. As we stated earlier, São Paulo was the main political center of the
Oligarchical Republic, so it was where the Vargas government encountered
the most resistance. Since Vargas came to power in 1930, tensions have marked
the relationship between state policy and the federal government. On July 9,
1932, the *"Revolução Constitucionalista"* ("Constitutionalist revolution") broke
out in the capital of São Paulo, led by General Isidoro Dias Lopes, the same man
responsible for the 1924 lieutenant uprising. The conflict lasted a few months,
until it was defeated on October 1, 1932, with the signing of the surrender that
ended the *"Revolução Constitucionalista"* ("Constitutionalist revolution"). Even
though they were defeated, there were political gains, with the strengthening
of the constitutional project. After all, Vargas reactivated the commission that
would be responsible for drafting the Constitution with the creation of new
parties to run for the elections to the National Constituent Assembly. However,
with the establishment of the "Estado Novo" ("New State") in 1937, the 1933
constituent movements were eventually suppressed, and their gains lost.

From the perspective of the left, in the 1930s were marked by the 1935 insur-
gencies, also known as *"Intentona Comunista"* ("Communist Uprising"). Still
in the spirit of the *Tenentista* revolts of the 1920s, the *"Intentona Comunista"*
("Communist Uprising") had the support of the PCB and was led by the Aliança
Nacional Libertadora (ANL) – National Liberation Alliance –, a political organization that had Luís Carlos Prestes as its honorary president. The organization
was led by communists, but which was broad, made up of diverse groups and
sectors disillusioned with the political processes of the Vargas government.
ANL's agenda revolved around nationalist proposals, particularly, the struggle for land reform. ANL was spread across several cities around the country,

counting thousands of supporters. Still in 1935, just a few months after its creation, the ANL was made illegal. Even when they were illegal, the ANL continued to organize rallies and to issue bulletins against the government. More specifically, starting in August 1935, they began to prepare an armed movement to overthrow Vargas. In November 1935 there were military uprisings associated with the ANL. The rebellion was not supported by the working class and was restricted to these cities, being quickly and violently suppressed. From then on, repression against communists and government opponents intensified, with thousands of arrests, including senators, federal representatives and even the then mayor of the Federal District.

The 1930s were also marked by the *levante integralista* (integralist uprising) in 1938. Founded by Plínio Salgado in 1932, *Ação Integralista Brasileira* (AIB) – Integralist Brazilian Action – was a movement of fascist inspiration organized in Brazil, with wide national capillarity, marking the authoritarian ideas of the Brazilian extreme right in that period. Plínio Salgado would run for president in 1938, if an election had taken place. However, with the 1937 coup and the establishment of the *"Estado Novo"* ("New State"), Plínio Salgado then goes to support Vargas against communism. Plínio Salgado and AIB had the expectation that the *"Estado Novo"* ("New State") would get closer to *integralismo* (integralism), having *integralismo* (integralism) as the regime's political reference and even being able to compose ministries such as the Ministry of Education. However, when Vargas decrees the *"Estado Novo"* ("New State") there is no mention of *integralismo* (integralism). And when the regime decrees the closure of political parties, AIB was included in the parties to be closed. When the *integralistas* (integralists) realized that there would be no space for participation in power, the *integralistas* (integralists) leaders linked to the armed forces began to organize a coup against the government in 1938. In March, the *integralistas* (integralists) started unrests in navy posts and an attempt to occupy Radio Mayrink Veiga, the leading radio station in Rio de Janeiro at the time. Other attacks in other parts of the city had been planned but failed due to the disorganization of the *integralistas* (integralists).

From an economic point of view, the country was experiencing something new. The world crisis of 1929 significantly altered the centrality that coffee exports had in the Brazilian economy, paving the way for an import substitution industrialization process. The exchange of imported industrial products for domestic production in the domestic market is what is conventionally called import substitution industrialization. The Vargas government gradually approached the industrial bourgeoisie, pursuing an expansionary fiscal policy and an exchange control policy that generates protection for national industry.

In a context of escalating international conflicts that would lead to the Second World War, Vargas plays both American and German interests, adopting a trade policy that favored the change in the profile of Brazilian exports, which were previously highly dependent on coffee. There was then greater diversification of exports and agricultural production for the domestic market. The US attempt to bring Brazil to their side in international politics was bargained by Vargas and the Brazilian industrial bourgeoisie, in exchange for financial and technical support from the USA for the implantation of the *Companhia Siderúrgica Nacional* (National Steel Company) in 1940, advancing industrialization for the heavy industry sector.

As a main consequence of this policy, we could say that the "*Estado Novo*" ("New State") was responsible for Brazil's first step towards industrial capitalism, with industry gaining centrality in the Brazilian economy. It left a mark on Brazilian history as one of the periods of success in terms of building "national interests" from a bourgeois point of view.

After the "*Estado Novo*" ("New State") coup, the industrial bourgeoisie embarks completely on Vargas' political project, and the country experienced a period of intense industrialization through authoritarianism. An industrial policy to protect the consumer goods industry and to support the importation of production goods marks the period, deepening import substitution. To organize the urban labor market and guarantee the supply of workers for industry, the government draws up the *Consolidação das Leis Trabalhistas* (CLT) – Consolidation of Labor Laws. Brazil is in full transition to an urban-industrial society, which would be consolidated in the 1960s. In this period of transition, a central controversy unfolds in Brazilian economic thought, analyzed in the chapter by Bruno Borja, *Controversy on Economic History of Brazil: Roberto Simonsen, Caio Prado Jr. and Celso Furtado.*

In 1945, another coup d'état was proposed, aiming to end the Getúlio Vargas dictatorship. After more than 10 years without presidential elections, an army officer and minister of war during the dictatorship of the "*Estado Novo*" ("New State"), General Dutra was elected. With the Allied victory in World War II and the consequent defeat of the nations that made up the Axis alliance, the most diverse social groups began to call for an urgent international re-democratization. Dutra realigned Brazil as a supposedly democratic country under the US area of influence. Despite the Stalinist Soviet Union participation in the victory of the war, the message that spread throughout the Americas was that liberalism and democracy should be supported by all governments. It was the period of the creation of the UN, the sign of the Declaration of Human Rights and the spread of decolonization movements.

In Brazil, even with the popularity of President Getúlio Vargas expressed in the *Queremista* movement ("we want Getúlio movement"), this protest for "freedom" materialized in the growth of criticisms of the *"Estado Novo"* ("New State"). Sectors of the military and the press led the opposition to Vargas' dictatorship. The military forces organized a coup that in October 1945 removed Vargas from the presidency and called for new presidential elections, in which Vargas had been forbidden to participate. Eurico Gaspar Dutra, one of the articulators of the coup, was supported by Vargas during his campaign and emerged victorious.

That is why we can say that Brazil's internal policies have not changed very deeply, but a new Constitution has been created. The constitutional text incorporated well-known liberal principles such as freedom of thought and expression, freedom of the press and party organization. However, the construction of the young Brazilian democracy was deeply shaken by the influence of the Cold War. Under Dutra administration, Brazil has aligned itself with the American guidelines, which motivated the breaking of diplomatic relations with the Soviet Union, in addition to the persecution of communist politicians. More exemplarily, the case of the *Partido Comunista do Brasil* (PCB) – Communist Party of Brazil –, which was legalized in 1945 and was made illegal again in 1947, having the mandates of its elected representatives revoked.

In 1951, Getúlio Vargas returned to the presidency, now democratically elected. In this government, known as *"segundo Vargas"*, (the second Vargas), he built a strong group of planners, forming the economic advisory to the Presidency of the Republic. It was during this government that the Joint Brazil-United States Commission for Economic Development, an effort by Brazilian and American planners, developed its work and delivered its report. One of the technical contributions of the Joint Commission was to form a team of Brazilian workers to develop economic development projects. This commission had both developmentalist, authoritarian and conservative thinkers. In 1952, it approved a total of 41 transport and energy projects to be financed by Eximbank (Export-Import Bank USA), the International Development Association (IDA-World Bank) and European capitals. However, in 1953, the Commission was extinguished, with the rise to power of Republican Eisenhower in the USA, ending the Commission works and delivering a final report.

Vargas once again commands a government with contradictory characteristics. In order to advance with the project of substitutive industrialization, the government introduced instruments such as Instruction 70 of the *Superintendência da Moeda e do Crédito (Sumoc)* – Superintendency of Money and Credit –, of October 1953, through which there was an exchange reform that devalued the currency of the time, the *cruzeiro*. With this instruction, the multiple exchange rate regime was introduced with hierarchization of foreign trade sectors according to an essentiality criterion that established currency auctions. The State began to appropriate non-budgetary revenue from the account of premiums and bonuses with the intention of having a source to counter inflation. By penalizing the entry of non-essential imports, this action deepened the import substitution process. In addition, the government conducted projects that have proved to be essential for Brazilian economic development, such as: the creation of the *Banco Nacional de Desenvolvimento* (*BNDE*) – National Development Bank –, in 1952 – later called the *Banco Nacional de Desenvolvimento Econômico e Social, BNDES* (National Economic and Social Development Bank) –; the creation of the *Grupo Misto Cepal-BNDE* –ECLAC-BNDE Joint Group –, with the Economic Commission for Latin America (ECLAC), in 1953; the inauguration of *Petrobrás* – *Petróleo Brasileiro* (Brazilian Petroleum Corporation) –, in 1953, maintaining the state monopoly on oil production; and the presentation, in 1954, of the project to create *Eletrobras* – *Centrais Elétricas Brasileiras* – (Brazilian Power Stations) which would only be inaugurated in 1962. The oil case oil was the target of an important public campaign called *"o petróleo é nosso"* ("oil is ours"). Vargas supported the campaign, but there was considerable political polarization.

In addition to joining the development debate, conservatives in the 1950s and 1960s had a strong anti-corruption discourse that led to an unsuccessful demand for Vargas's impeachment. In a troubled political environment, Vargas was accused of corruption and attempting to assassinate one of the opposition leaders, journalist and politician Carlos Lacerda. There was yet another coup attempt, this time, interrupted by Vargas' suicide in August 1954. Vargas' vice president, Café Filho, took office and adopted a more liberal economic policy, establishing Instruction 113 of the *Superintendência da Moeda e do Crédito* (*Sumoc*) – Superintendency of Money and Credit –, which liberalized the entry of foreign capital through import licenses without exchange hedging for industrial equipment. In practice, Instruction 113 consolidated the advantage to international capital started during the second Vargas administration and worked to the advantage of foreign investors, who could bring in resources at a lower exchange rate than the free exchange rate. The Brazilian investor, on the other hand, did not count on financing from abroad, and was therefore harmed. However, the end of Café Filho's government was turbulent. In the last three months of the government there were two substitutions of finance ministers.

The next elected president was Juscelino Kubitschek (JK), who would govern from 1956 to 1961. JK had João Goulart as vice president and they led a developmental government, relying on a large inflow of foreign capital, via instruction 113 from *Sumoc*. At the beginning of JK administration, the *Plano de Metas* (Targets Plan) was presented, based on studies by the Joint Brazil-United States Commission for Economic Development and the *Grupo Misto Cepal-BNDE* – ECLAC-BNDE Joint Group. *Plano de Metas* (Targets Plan) was also based on projects already developed, especially in the areas of energy and transport infrastructure. The focus of the plan, which had 31 objectives, was the development of energy, transport and the durable consumer goods industry, with the aim of intensifying import substitution. Furthermore, there was an opening to foreign capital, especially with the entry of the international automobile industry, which began to set up a large production park in Brazil, mostly concentrated in São Paulo.

At the same time, many engineering works were implemented for the construction of the new capital: Brasília. The city was being designed and built from scratch. With so many works in progress, the Brazilian domestic debt had increased, and inflation had risen significantly. There were also rumors of embezzlement, because, in order to speed up the construction of Brasilia, the president had rejected the use of the public bidding system. This economic instability also generated discontent, in addition discontent generated by the transfer of the capital (from Rio de Janeiro to Brasília). The next opposition candidate, Jânio Quadros, took advantage of the situation and promised to restore order by investigating, punishing, and administering the country with more honesty. Once again, it was the general anti-corruption agenda that elected the next Brazilian president, a fervent conservative with authoritarian tendencies.

Jânio Quadros did not spend much time in the presidency. He resigned within seven months, arguing strong pressure from the US government, and hoping that the Brazilian people would put him back in charge with an intense mobilization, which never happened. Because of the very characteristic organization of the Brazilian elections during that period, the president and vice president could be elected from different party lists, and that was the case. Vice President João Goulart was a member of the *Partido Trabalhista Brasileiro* (PTB) – Brazilian Labor Party – and was almost prevented from being president by a coup in parliament. The solution found, also of a coup nature, was to establish, for the only time in the history of the Brazilian Republic, a parliamentary regime. For an year and a half, João Goulart ruled shielded by a prime minister, which made full government impossible. In January 1963 there was a public plebiscite that restored presidentialism in Brazil.

João Goulart had Celso Furtado and several developmentalists on his team and presented a more nationalistic and independent economic agenda. Even though Celso Furtado was not a radical, some of his measures regarding control of the repatriation of profits from foreign capital and his plan for agrarian reform were not well received by the national and international bourgeoisie. Behind these decisions there was a strong history of popular movements organized in the city and in the countryside, fighting for these changes. It came as no surprise when allegations of corruption began to be published in the mainstream media, and on April 1, 1964, a coup d'état occurred.

In this context of great national transformations, communist organizations acted almost the entire time in a clandestine way. With less than two years of permition to act legally (1945–1947), the *Partido Comunista do Brasil* (PCB) – Communist Party of Brazil – was being organized as a space for formulations and actions against the grain. The escalation of the national and international conjunctures posed the question of the Brazilian revolution as a central one. Thus, it was among the third great turning point of the international communist movement, also in the context of the crisis of the leadership of the communist parties around the world, that the controversy on the Brazilian revolution was reopened.

The late 1940s and 1950s were a time of height of the cold war, with a great expansion of communism after the Chinese revolution of 1949, the Cuban revolution of 1959 and also with the Korean war (1950–1953). The Cuban revolution brought the feeling that the revolution was an urgent matter, since it had reached Latin America. The revolutionary flame had remained lit and the contention intensified in Brazil. Working class organizations were reinforced by the development of cities and the industrial growth of the country, in addition to the legalization of the union movement, the progressive implementation of laws that guaranteed workers' rights with the *Consolidação das Leis Trabalhistas* (CLT) – Consolidation of Labor Laws – and the development of social struggles.

Social tensions were increasing in the 1950s, especially during the second Vargas government (1951–1954). In the years that followed, under the governments of the *Partido Trabalhista Brasileiro* (PTB) – Brazilian Labor Party – and the *Partido Social Democrático* -PSD- (Social Democratic Party) – with a small interregnum of 7 months of a coalition led by conservative *União Democrática Nacional* -UDN- (National Democratic Union) –, but in all cases allied to international capital, the country has advanced in its industrialization under the aegis of national-developmentalism, with the tripod for financing: state investment – international capital – national capital. Despite this development of urbanization and modernization, especially in the center-south of the country, the dream of overcoming underdevelopment was not reachead.

The national-developmentalist project would influence even the positions of organized sectors of the communists. The PCB's famous *"Declaração de março de 1958"* ("March 1958 Declaration") indicated democratization as the trend for the country and the goal of action. The Declaration was based on a characterization of the Brazilian economic structure as backward, even with the greater pace of industrial development since the 1930s and with the increase in the number of industrial proletarians, that is, the development of the productive forces and of new capitalist relations of production. In the Declaration they characterize agriculture as still organized on the basis of pre-capitalist labor relations and on land monopoly, with agricultural production and export of primary products as the dynamic axis and dependency of the national economy in relation to the capitalist center, with strong presence of monopoly capital in the key posts of the economy. In other words, it emphasizes the characterization of capitalist development in Brazil as unequal, by combining capitalist methods with the monopoly of the land and semi-feudal relations of production. In the *"Declaração de março de 1958"* ("March 1958 Declaration") they also identified that this process of unequal development takes place within the framework of dependency and influence of imperialism.

The official position orientation for communist militancy became to integrate a nationalist and democratic front – composed of heterogeneous forces: proletariat, peasants, urban petty bourgeoisie, national bourgeoisie, landowners who have contradictions with imperialism, groups of the bourgeoisie to imperialist monopolies rivaling the US monopolies – with a program of emancipation of the nation, of modern economic development and of the implantation of the bourgeois-democratic revolution. The orientation of political practice was anti-feudal and anti-imperialist. Thus, the foundations were forged for what became known as the national democratic program.

In the early years of the 1960s, the advance of Brazilian capitalism brought with it a deepening of its contradictions. On the one hand, it established the strengthening of organized struggles of workers, able to represent themselves in a broad labor movement, but also with communist wings, pressuring governments for distributive changes, improvement in working conditions, control of profit remittance to abroad and agrarian reform. On the other hand, the Brazilian bourgeoisie did not identify in that movement the birth of allies for a national or anti-imperialist revolution, on the contrary, it articulated itself with the international bourgeoisie and with conservative sectors of the armed forces in a preventive counter-revolution, giving rise to the political coalition that delivered the coup d'État of 1964.

The civic-military regime needed to create a series of institutional reforms, in order to gain some legitimacy in the eyes of the population, given that its oppressive and repressive nature was clear from the beginning with the series of evocations of political rights promoted by the institutional acts and the strong repression of the working class. The option was to deepen dependency in order to promote economic growth through conservative modernization. The diagnosis of the obstacles to the Brazilian economy involved a peculiar perception of financing of investment. According to Roberto Campos and Octávio Bulhões, the economists who represented economic policy at the time the dictatorship was established, the system's inability to generate credit and terms compatible with the investments underway reinforced the dependency of the Brazilian economy's technical and financial structure on international funding. This also made explicit, for the regime, the need to create a new internal economic scheme.

At first, the funding issue was sustained, basically, via currency issuance and resources coming from the already existing Sumoc instructions: Instructions 70 (of 1953) and 113 (of 1955). With the economic and political instability of the early 1960s, these mechanisms became unsustainable, and the state was crucial in creating and managing compulsory savings funds and credit institutions. The absence of a sound private banking and financial system made the financial and tax reforms of the *Plano de Ação Econômica do Governo* (PAEG) – Government's Economic Action Plan – essential for sustaining development in a context of conservative modernization.

The creation of fiscal and parafiscal resources such as the *Programa de Integração Social/Programa de Amparo ao Servidor Público* (PIS/Pasep) – Social Integration Program / Support Program for Public Servants –, the *Fundo de Garantia por Tempo de Serviço* (FGTS)– Guarantee Fund for Time of Service – and the taxes created by the reform were added to the creation of key institutions for conducting macroeconomic policy. Among them are the *Banco Central do Brasil (Bacen)* – Central Bank of Brazil –, the *Conselho Monetário Nacional* (CMN) – National Monetary Council – and the Banco Nacional de Habitação (BNH) – National Housing Bank–, all from 1964. Furthermore, forms of financing were created, the Obrigações Reajustáveis do Tesouro Nacional (ORTN) – National Treasury Readjustable Bonds –, subject to monetary adjustment and mechanisms to attract capital via Resolution 63 of *Bacen*, of 1967, which complemented the raising of funds; finally, Law 4.131, of 1962, was modified, an instrument to control the remittance of profits and reinvestment. Based on these modifications, it allowed the reinvestment of profits not only in national currency, but also in foreign currency, and liberalized the remittance of profits.

Even though the 1964 coup resulted in violent persecution of left-wing organizations, thinking about the Brazilian revolution and the possibilities for a democratic and socialist future continued to happen, especially with the purpose of understanding the nature of the bourgeois revolution in Brazil and the possible steps of resistance and reaction of the Marxist domain. Among the debates about the future, the theme of revolution was resumed by the hands of exponents of Brazilian Marxism. Elements of this controversy are presented in this book in the chapter *Visions of the Brazilian Revolution: Nelson Werneck Sodré, Caio Prado Jr and Florestan Fernandes* written by Bruno Borja, Carla Curty and Jaime León.

Regarding economic development, authoritarian thought supported the idea, maintaining the hallmark of State centralism. This perspective was reflected in the specific content of the economic policies of the military governments in the 21 years after the 1964 coup. The authoritarian and dictatorial government was justified as necessary to ensure a good method of development and was presented to the population as a strive for democracy and against communism. However, the national aspect was put into perspective. The coup government's project largely allowed the entry of foreign capital both for financing structuring projects and for ownership control of large companies.

The question of the defense of democracy was also clearly a fantasy, since it was an experiment in dictatorial, openly authoritarian government, now at the height of the Cold War. The defense of the capitalist order was what was effectively the core of politics. The dominant ideas were those of the dominant classes of the hegemonic country in the world order and were imported by the dominant classes of the peripheral countries. No wonder that abstract values such as "hemispheric solidarity" or "defense of Western Christian civilization" were advocated, even to override the interests of each country. Contradictorily, with "freedom" as the central issue, democracy was put in the background.

The 1964 coup interrupted the national-democratic project, beginning 21 years of an autocratic civic-military government, leaving a strong centralized State, with an authoritarian structure of laws that the government wanted to make it look like a formal democracy. The country had a constitution, open Congress and elections taking place for most of the period. However, a series of institutional acts were passed that would change the shape of Brazilian "democracy", particularly *Ato Institucional número 5 (AI-5)* – Institutional Act number 5 –, of December 13, 1968. Among the measures of the various institutional acts, we can cite: the revocation of political rights of many citizens, the use of torture as a state practice, press censorship, the closing of Congress at critical political times, indirect elections for president, the end of the multiparty system, and the fact that governors and mayors of the capitals were appointed by the president, without any electoral process. In other words, a dictatorship trying to pass itself off as democracy.

In the late 1960s, the golden age of capitalism was showing signs of crisis. European reconstruction had been completed, the Cold War between the USSR and the US was escalating, the Vietnam War was moving hearts and minds in favor of pacifism and against colonialism. In the early 1970s, the Bretton-Woods system began to crumble. The dollar-gold monetary standard was questioned, the first oil shock raised prices worldwide and a decade of high inflation and speculation ensued. During this period, the growth rate in the central economies, which had been accelerating since the end of World War II, decreased considerably, in some cases even reaching economic stagnation. In the search for the causes of this instability, controls, expenses and corruption of the welfare state were pointed out as the culprits. This was the beginning of the era of neoliberalism.

In Brazil, the picture was a little different, as a dependent economy, the moment of crisis in the central economies can open important opportunities for development strategies. In the Brazilian case, the development process, according to Furtado (1981) opened doors for significant gains for transnational corporations, especially after the 1964 banking law and the 1965 capital market law, which "would expand the field of action of financial intermediaries which later on gained great autonomy in the creation of liquidity, in the management of financial resources and in attracting foreign savings" (Furtado, 1981, p.39). This movement was a major force behind the high growth rates (between 9.5 and 13.9% per year in the period 1968–1973) that led the country to the "economic miracle", in addition to choosing a growth based on income concentration. Such concentration was so significant that at the end of the "miracle" period, by any measure, income distribution had worsened. Despite this, growth rates did not resist the first oil shock in August 1973 and led the Geisel government to propose a plan to deal with the crisis that was already impending.

The strategy of the Geisel government was the *2º Plano Nacional de Desenvolvimento (II PND)* – 2nd National Development Plan. The starting point was the goal of "completing" the domestic production chain by developing the capital goods sector, but also integrating industry and national production through heavy investments in infrastructure and in the capital goods industry. It is worth remembering that the agricultural sector was not excluded from the process, which was later called "conservative modernization". The degree of indebtedness under which this project was implemented had undeniable consequences for the external dependency of the Brazilian economy, especially because it was based on a strategy of external loans at flexible interest rates in a regime of dollar high inflation. At the same time, some claim that without this plan, Brazil would not have completed its industrialization. This process would be marked by a new dynamic in the relationship between urban and rural areas, since most of the Brazilian population had been living in urban areas since the 1960s, and the demands on the food and export goods producing sectors grew with the expansion path chosen by the civic-military dictatorship.

This period was marked by many controversies, including the different interpretations of Brazil's economic history at the time. In his text *Underdevelopment and Dependency: An analysis of Celso Furtado's thought and its approach to Dependency Theory*, Wilson Vieira highlights the contribution that dependency theories have in the modifications in Furtado's thought regarding the analysis on the development dynamics of the Brazilian economy, as the "dependent modernization" advances. The chapter by Larissa Veiga and Maria Malta, *Seeds of Brazilian underdevelopment: a controversy on property, labor force and production*, also raises a very important debate, when the planning of the Brazilian economy put the focus back on the agricultural sector with the "bottleneck" to be overcome for the acceleration of production and the technical "innovations" of agriculture seemed to be the "salvation of the crop".

In the late 1970s, the international situation took an important turn, which, given the external exposure of the Brazilian economy, had profound consequences on the country's policy and economy. The second oil shock in 1979, international pressure on the US to reestablish a new parity of its currency (dollar) with gold, recognizing its devaluation, implied a US economic policy decision that had an impact on the entire international monetary system: the rise in the prime rate, the US interest rate, on which all loans from underdeveloped countries taken during the 1970s were anchored. A period of debt crisis erupted in Latin America.

From the point of view of thought, the impact of this shift on the conjuncture was, mainly, that stability became the central issue for economists, and in Brazil, an economy of very high inflation, it was no different. With the rise of neoliberalism, we can find a series of very acute transformations in the conservative and authoritarian Brazilian thought, that formed the profile of those who ran the country at that time. It is possible to observe a transformation of arguments that have put nationalism aside and started to justify adherence to the idea of receiving international capital to finance strategic actions. There was also a defense of less state participation in the direction of investments and direct actions on the economy.

It is worth to note that the idea of planning had began to be criticized and replaced by a free market perspective. Conservative and authoritarian thinkers began to fight for a state that would guarantee a market society, which is the change that will lead them to a neoliberal way of thinking. It is also very important to note that Delfim Netto, an influential economist and politician from the civic-military dictatorship, responsible for vital economic matters, who became Minister of Finance (1967–1974), Minister of Agriculture (1979) and Minister of Planning (1979–1985). Delfim Netto sent some of his pupils to study at the University of Chicago, a historic liberal cradle. And they returned to Brazil in the 1970s to implement the most up-to-date principles of neoliberal economics at home.

The importance of developing of the financial system, which had gained centrality since the early 1970s, opened the 1980s as a key issue to be addressed in order to guarantee, in the rhetoric, both economic growth and monetary stability, in a context of high inflation. Regarding this specific aspect, the transition between the civic-military dictatorship and the democratic period of the New Republic was strangely smooth.

During that period, projects for the development and transformation of the global and local financial market emerged, with the defense of the flexibilization of capital control by the State. At the same time, international capital was seen as very valuable for the monetary stabilization policy, insofar as it enters the Brazilian economy for short-term actions and for the purchase of assets of the Brazilian State. This is the beginning of a privatization program that would be the axis of the government's actions during the 1990s. A very important senator and soon to be a presidential candidate, Mário Covas said in the Senate session of June 28, 1989: "Brazil needs more than a fiscal shock. It also needs a shock of capitalism, a shock of free initiative, subject to risks and not only to rewards" (Covas, 1989). Covas' speech went down in history as a milestone in the process of change in political, economic, and ideological terms, a mark of social acceptance of the arrival of neoliberalism in the country.

In the transition from the civic-military dictatorship, a congress of representatives was convened to write a new Constitution, which enshrined the liberal formula of representation in presidentialism. The new Constitution sought to incorporate some social demands of the working class, but it did not change a single line in maintaining the private ownership of the means of production and its codes of registration and inheritance. Some important social rights have been left to be regulated in future governments by future legislation. Florestan Fernandes – a prominent interpreter of Brazil referred to in several of the controversies addressed in this book – who was a parliamentary representative in the construction of the new Constitution, observed that writing the text of that constitution had been an effort of patience and negotiation. Because the interests that had put an end to the dictatorship were the same ones that had put it in power in the first place.

At that point in Brazilian history, conservative and authoritarian thoughts converge with the liberal perspective, to replace political issues by issues supposedly of economic technique and of search for stability. To achieve this goal, in their perspective, "there is no alternative" other than to enter the international market. It is what Boffo, Saad-Filho and Fine (2019) called the authoritarian perspective of neoliberalism.

The 1988 constitution and the period of re-democratization represented a new period for the Brazilian republic, the *Nova República* (New Republic), marked by issues such as the "co-optation democracy". The beginning of that period of the Brazilian republic was analyzed by authors such as Carlos Nelson Coutinho and Florestan Fernandes, two important organic intellectuals. Shapping in the 1980s a controversy about democracy. It is worth mentioning that it was after the workers 'strikes in the ABC region of São Paulo in 1978, during a period of intense contestation by the regime, that there was a qualitative leap in workers' consciousness and organization nationwide. Not by coincidence, the *Partido dos Trabalhadores* (PT) – Workers' Party – was founded in 1980, with the direct participation of Florestan Fernandes and Carlos Nelson Coutinho. A popular democratic program was born, which revived discussions on the Brazilian revolution, although it did not succeed in overcoming the limitations of a bourgeois democratic program.

We define the *Nova República* (New Republic) as the period between the formalization of the democratic rule of law in 1988, with the *Constituição Cidadã* (Citizen Constitution), until today. In this period, co-optation would be taken to its maximum level by PT, as will be discussed in the book. We can identify the crisis of the New Republic with the 2013 movements, the crisis of the Dilma government, her impeachment in 2016 and its ramifications. These elements of the New Republic, the controversy around the question of democracy and its crisis, are presented in the chapter *Restricted democracy, mass democracy and the crisis of the New Republic*, authored by Jaime León and Maria Malta.

•••

From the perspective of Brazilian economic and social thought, the transformations in the world after the implementation of neoliberalism and the end of the Soviet Union were quite blunting. The main economic debates were restricted to short-term issues related to macroeconomic stability – inflation, monetary policy, exchange policy, fiscal policy – and more structural issues related to debates about the project of the nation and the disputes around them lost relevance. The issues of development, underdevelopment and dependency, for instance, were sidelined or simply left the agenda of the main formulations of Brazilian thinkers. The controversies in the history of Brazilian economic thought, in the sense explored here in this book have vanished.

Political and social debates also lost the broader and more structural horizon of reflection. The end of the Soviet Union and the loss of this reference for communist organizations in Brazil, as well as the hegemonic strength of neoliberalism, manifested themselves in hollowing out the debates about the Brazilian revolution and the possibilities of structural transformation of the country.

In the 2000s, the rise to power of the main party of reference to the left in the country Partido dos Trabalhadores (PT) – Workers' Party – also generated important and contradictory issues. The popular democratic project did not implement radical and transformative changes in the economic and social structure, but rather continued the neoliberal policies initiated in the 1990s, although punctuated by the implementation of focused social policies, not so far from the liberal prescriptions. This contradiction has generated questions for the organization of the left in the country, also hollowing out the discussions about more structural transformations traditionally on the historical agenda of the leftist movements. Issues such as land reform, housing distribution, urban mobility and labor and social security rights were not central to the government. On the contrary, there was even a pension reform right at the beginning of the PT government. At the same time, with some union leaders incorporated in the State structure and in the management of public funds, together with the development of focused policies, which partially contemplated some of the social movements' demands, generated a process of co-optation.

This hollowing out of the structural debates about the Brazilian economic and social formation and its possibilities for transformation is associated, in the scope of thought, with the movement of fragmentation of the areas of knowledge. Starting in the 1960s to the 1970s, the compartmentalization that has occurred since the process of implementing and consolidating postgraduate studies in the country, some of them adequate to an internationalized standard and producing "science through papers", made reflections in the scope of what we call "Interpretations of Brazil" rarer. With the reinforcement of the specialization of the areas of knowledge and the weight of academic productivism, the space for broader reflections is narrowed. We consider those types of refletions involve moviments in order to analyze in depth the Brazilian economic and social formation, identifying the issues related to the specificities of its capitalist development, which can help the analysis of the conjuncture on what is contemporary Brazil and its issues, aiming to build a proposal of a project for the country. Since the 1990s, few authors have proposed this type of analysis. We can highlight the works of Darcy Ribeiro, Carlos Nelson Coutinho, Francisco de Oliveira, Maria da Conceição Tavares, Virgínia Fontes, João Antônio de Paula, Silvio Almeida, Marcelo Paixão, José Luís Fiori,

Leda Paulani, Plínio de Arruda Sampaio Junior, Sueli Carneiro, Lilia Moritz Schwarcz and Marcelo Badaró, among others.

Bringing these recent interpretations to the center of the political debate can help to elucidate the possible ways of transforming the Brazilian economy and society. By tracing the History of Brazilian Economic Thought since the founding of the republic, through some of its most important controversies, this book seeks to contribute to the reformulation of current Brazilian economic and social thinking. In critical moments, moments of confusion and mystification of public debate, looking at the past can open a window to the future.

· · ·

Originally the research presented in this book was conducted from publications in Portuguese, after all, its object is Brazilian economic and social thought and the vast majority of works used as bibliographical references only have Brazilian editions. Hence, we have chosen to maintain all the bibliographic references of Brazilian editions. Throughout the book, we have presented free translations into English of quotations, expressions and titles of these references, but always keeping original terms and references in Portuguese, since many of the specific terms have no correspondence in English or are known by their original terms in Portuguese.

Bibliographic References

Boffo, Marco; Saad-Filho, Alfredo; Fine, Ben. Neoliberal Capitalism: the authoritarian turn. *In:* Socialist Register 2019, p. 247–270, 2019.

Covas, Mario. Choque do Capitalismo, Discurso pronunciado pelo Senador Mário Covas na Sessão do Senado a dia 28 de junho de 1989, Brasília: Senado Federal. Available at: https://tucano.org.br/choque-do-capitalismo/.

Furtado, Celso. O Brasil pós-"milagre". Rio de Janeiro: Paz e Terra, 1981.

Ianni, Octavio. Raízes da antidemocracia na América Latina. Lua Nova, São Paulo, n. 14, p. 17–22, Junho 1988.

Konder, Leandro. História das ideias socialistas no Brasil. São Paulo: Expressão Popular. 2003.

Malta, Maria Mello de. (coord.). Ecos do desenvolvimento: uma história do pensamento econômico brasileiro. Rio de Janeiro, IPEA/Centro Internacional Celso Furtado de Políticas para o Desenvolvimento, 2011.

Tavares, Maria da Conceição; Fiori, José Luís. (Des)ajuste global e modernização conservadora. São Paulo: Paz e Terra, 1993.

PART 1

*How to Tell the History – Method,
Thought and Versions in Dispute*

∴

CHAPTER 1

Methodological Elements for the Organization of the History of Brazilian Economic Thought

The Approach of Controversies

Carla Curty and Maria Malta

1 Introduction

The history of economic thought (HET) is a history of controversy. Virtually no author in the HET field would disagree with this statement, however, methodologically, there are several ways to approach it. It is possible to construct the history of economic thought from an evolutionary point of view, taking the movement of the history of thought as a linear movement, in which controversies are resolved by hegemonic absorption of winning ideas, ensuring that there are no disruptions in their development. The theory considered as the frontier of knowledge represents in this evolutionary view the most advanced developments in that field, reducing the history of economic thought to the history of a "victorious" way of thinking (Arida, 2003). But this is not the only way, nor the most useful, although it is the one most commonly found in books on history of economic theory.

Taking as an analytical reference the work of Karl Marx, in particular, Theories of surplus value ([1905] 1980) and the contributions of Isaak Rubin ([1929] 2014) and Maurice Dobb ([1973] 1977) to the approach of history of economic thought, methodologically, one can analyze the HET by valuing the influence that the real and concrete historical movement establishes on ideas, highlighting the debates that lead to movements of theoretical rupture and the processuality of the transformation of thought. With this process in focus it is possible to maintain vivid divergent approaches to economic issues, without generating a unique synthesis, even if creating hegemonic interpretations, establishing the notion of controversy.

Controversies are shaped by different analyzes that can be formulated on the same object evidenced by the historical movement and can be organized based on specific ideological, political, theoretical and social elements. These controversies make it possible to capture the historicity and processuality of thought, making it possible for the history of economic thought to be told as the history of controversies organized from different scientific contributions and marked by history and politics.

In this conception, theory and history cannot be dissociated. The knowledge construction process is marked by historical elements and the analysis of the history of economic thought involves the perception that the historically accumulated theoretical production influences the contemporary theoretical formulation, therefore, working in HET means not only referring to the knowledge elaborated in the past, but also to reflect on the relevance of the theoretical elements developed throughout history.

What is sought to be discussed in this chapter is precisely a method of analysis and presentation of HET that challenges that common view and reveals it as a history of controversies. At the same time, the systematization of this method to address the history of Brazilian economic thought is presented. Regarding this objective, this chapter is divided, in addition to this introduction and final considerations, into three sections: Controversy as a key to reading history of thought – it is subdivided into two subsections: Historical materialism and dialectics and The perception of history of thought as the object of the approach of controversies –; Controversy in history of Brazilian economic thought (HBET) ; and Incorporating the contribution of interpreters of Brazil to the history of Brazilian economic thought (HBET).

2   Controversy as a Key to Reading History of Thought

2.1   *Historical Materialism and Dialectics*

The use of the notion of controversy as a key to reading and systematizing the history of thought results from a method of analyzing HET in a critical and historicized way. And, therefore, referenced in Marxist theory, based on the materialist and historical perception of thought and organized from a dialectical perspective.

It starts with the notion that thought is a procedural movement, and that the different historical experiences, different theoretical developments and formations, the different political, social and ideological positions of the individual who formulates the thought establish a strong influence on his/her work – even though this is not necessarily a conscious movement of his/her part. In this sense, the individual formulates the thought influenced by the theoretical development elaborated until then – that is, by the trajectory of the history of thought that formed him/her and permeates the environment in which he/she circulates – and by the degree of development of the field of knowledge in which he/she intends to insert him/herself and, in this context, he/she positions him/herself in theoretical terms. Your theoretical choice, in turn, is highly influenced by your conception of the world and is conditioned to certain concrete historical contexts. The historical movement (thought and material reality) allows different interpretations and positions about yourself, which leads to the existence of different formulations, often highly conflicting with each other. From this conflict, controversies and debates arise, confronting different analyzes of the same situation.

In the famous *Preface to a contribution to the critique of political economy*, Marx ([1859] 2008, p. 45) claims to have concluded that "the anatomy of bourgeois society must be sought in Political Economy". For Marx, what we can call elements of the superstructure – legal relations, political relations, and forms of social consciousness – find their roots in the elements and "material conditions of human existence" – that is, in the economic structure of society. Marx characterizes the economic structure as follows:

> in the social production of their own existence, men enter determined, necessary relationships, independent of their will; these relations of production correspond to a determined degree of development of their material productive forces. The totality of these relations of production constitutes the economic structure of society, the real basis upon which a legal and political superstructure rises and to which certain social forms of conscience correspond.
>
> MARX, [1859] 2008, p. 45

It is important to analyze this structure-superstructure relationship carefully. Here Marx builds the connection in a dialectical way. The mode of material production of life presents itself with the problem (object) to be understood. From its analysis are found the dimensions of the social relations of production and the development of the productive forces, composing the structural dimension of the mode of production. At the same time, this same analysis reveals that this particular form of material production of life opens up in its political, legal and ideological dimensions, forming its superstructural aspects.

In this way, the elements of the structure and the superstructure[1] they are moments of the analysis of the concrete form of the material production of life that come together in a dialectical synthesis for the formation of the category

---

1 Györg Lukács, when dealing with the issue of democracy from a perspective inserted in Marxism (Lukács, [1968] 2008), reinforces this historical, materialistic and totalizing perception of the analysis of concrete phenomena, including in the so-called superstructural forms, such as politics or ideology, in its terms, a historical being-precisely-so.

mode of production as the concrete by way of thought concrete thought, synthesis of these multiple determinations. This process – analysis-synthesis – however is carried out continuously, at each moment when it is desired to understand new aspects of the way in which it produces material life in history.

ForMarx ([1859] 2008, p. 45), "the way of producing material life conditions the process of social, political and intellectual life. It is not the conscience of men that determines their being; on the contrary, it is their social being that determines their conscience". In these short sentences, Marx presents fundamental elements of his materialist perspective. It states that the material elements condition human existence in its multiple aspects and that the understanding of reality is conditioned by the concrete elements of this reality, and not only the result of human abstraction. Therefore, the formulation of thought carried out by human beings, including scientific production, has in its essence the materiality of historical experience.

In *The German ideology* Marx and Engels ([1846] 2007) say that the connection between the production of ideas and their movement is directly linked to material activity and social relations, stating that material reality is what conditions thought. Although this thought, after being externalized, may appear as a condition of reality.

Thought is, therefore, the result of reality and not the starting point for that reality.[2] This notion is central to historical materialism and to using this materialism to understand the history of economic thought.

According to José Paulo Netto, theoretical knowledge consists of "knowledge of the object – of its structure and dynamics – as it is in itself, in its real and effective existence, regardless of the researcher's wishes, aspirations and representations" (Netto, 2011, p. 20, italics by the author).

This origin of knowledge in the concrete existence of its object raises an important question, which often leads to confusion in the process of constructing theoretical abstraction.[3] The method used by a given theorist implies a certain perspective, and this position, this perspective, can be extremely relevant. After all, it is from this perspective that the observer analyzes reality and extracts from reality its multiple determinations (Netto, 2011, p. 53). The

---

2   For further reflections on this issue, see the Introduction (Fernandes, 1946) made by Florestan Fernandes to the 1946 Brazilian publication of Karl Marx's A Contribution to Critique of Political Economy ([1859], 2008).

3   "Now, it is not just as a critique of Hegelian metaphysics that Marx's thinking is erected. It is also in opposition to the classic method of production of knowledge that it asserts itself. It is, therefore, important to examine what Marxist dialectics is precisely opposed to"(Tolipan, 1982b, p. 2).

observer's position even influences their understanding of what is essential in the existence of the object to be analyzed.

It is important to note that the existence of the object determines its essence. It is essential that the observer is able to differentiate what the object looks like from what its essence consists of. The research method that Marx proposed is one that starts from the appearance of the object seeking its essence. As José Paulo Netto (2011, p. 22, original italics by the author) points out,

> [...] by reaching the essence of the object, that is: capturing its structure and dynamics, through analytical procedures and operating its synthesis, the researcher reproduces it in the plane of thought; through research, made possible by the method, the researcher reproduces, in the ideal level, the essence of the object he investigated.

This question of the distinction between appearance and essence is very important within the debate about the history of economic thought. For many authors, such as José Paulo Netto (2011) and Aloisio Teixeira (2000), in Marx's conception, one of the main errors of classical British political economy was not to differentiate what the essence and appearance of their analytical objects would be:

> Marx never tires of repeating that "all science would be superfluous if there were an immediate coincidence between the appearance and the essence of things" (Marx, 1894, p. 939). And, once again: "all sciences, except political economy, recognize that things appear opposite to their essence" (Marx, 1867, p. 620). Or: "the bourgeois economist whose limited brain does not know how to distinguish between the apparent form and what is hidden in it" (id., p.662).
>
> TEIXEIRA, 2000, p. 100

Understanding the elements of the essence and appearance of the phenomena allows a better understanding of the phenomena themselves. In the dialectic perspective, this means understanding the analyzed object as a whole, with all its contradictions, movements and procedures. And this would be the best way to analyze reality and its phenomena. Therefore, a better way to carry out theoretical analyzes, including in the field of economics.

As Malta and Castelo (2012, p. 90) state, dialectics seeks the proper movement of the object under analysis, and it is not possible to understand this object without understanding its movement. The object "was, is and tends to be", performing a continuous movement. This movement depends on the contradiction, and the contradiction is present in all objects, thus, each form is a "union of opposites", an "identity of opposites", which "makes the movement permanent, since each form brings in itself the germ of its overcoming, its contradiction". The movement, generated by the contradictions, leads to a breaking point in which "a leap in quality" occurs, thus emerging a new form, which surpasses the previous one, but also carries with it some of its elements. In addition, this new form is also part of the germ that will generate its overcoming, that is, its denial. In this logic, the concrete appears in thought as a synthesis, being the result and not only the starting point (although it is the starting point of intuition and the representation of the concrete), it is thus, the concrete-in-thought, "a reproduction of the concrete by way of thought" (Marx, [1857] 2008).[4]

In this method, the analysis and the synthesis are unified. Therefore, the abstract determinations lead to the reproduction of the concrete, now understood (through thought). In other words, the way the individual observes reality and learns from this observation the elements to be abstracted is a fundamental determinant of the process of understanding reality. In this regard, the differentiation of what is essential from what is accessory is relevant. Marx, unlike classical economists who built their analyzes in such a way that "full conceptions evaporated to yield abstract determinations" (Marx, [1857] 2008, p. 257). Marx departs from the reality, of the concrete, whose analysis of "abstract determinations a[that] lead to the reproduction of concrete through thought "(Marx, [1857] 2008, p. 257) through an understood reconstruction process. The concrete manifests itself in thought, therefore, as a result of the analysis and synthesis processes. The thought itself, when formulated, gains the feature of a real and concrete object to be understood as well and will, in turn, deserve an analysis of its multiple determinations so that it can be understood after synthetic reformulation as concrete by way of thought.

---

4   The complete quotation would be "The concrete is concrete because it is the concentration of many determinations, hence unity of the diverse. It appears in the process of thinking, therefore, as a process of concentration, as a result, not as a point of departure, even though it is the point of departure in reality and hence also the point of departure for observation [Anschauung] and conception. Along the first path the full conception was evaporated to yield an abstract determination; along the second, the abstract determinations lead towards a reproduction of the concrete by way of thought. In this way Hegel fell into the illusion of conceiving the real as the product of thought concentrating itself, probing its own depths, and unfolding itself out of itself, by itself, whereas the method of rising from the abstract to the concrete is only the way in which thought appropriates the concrete, reproduces it as the concrete in the mind. But this is by no means the process by which the concrete itself comes into being." (Marx, [1857] 2008, p. 257)

2.2   The Perception of the History of Thought as an Object of the Approach of Controversies

The study of the history of thought through historical materialism and dialectics opens space to perceive it as constructed by diverse controversies, raised from the concrete reality in different historical moments and constituted by different formulations of thought that aim to account to analyze and synthesize these concrete realities. From the point of view presented in this chapter, controversies are fundamental elements for the organization of debates in the field of the history of thought. And this perception of the organization of the history of economic thought has Marx as its main reference.

The dialectic of Marx's thought can lead to the interpretation that the determination to which Marx refers to is a conditioning of social, political and intellectual life based on the social relations of production and the degree of development of the productive forces. However, this conditioning occurs in a dialectical way, in permanent interaction, and not linear-unidirectional. From this, it can be said that the economic, political, social, cultural, intellectual and historical elements must be coordinated in the process of understanding the phenomenon observed and analyzed, always taking into account the dialectical articulation between the elements of the structure and the elements. superstructure. Aloisio Teixeira (2011) makes a relevant contribution in this regard: "economics, politics, anthropology, and above all history – of facts and ideas – are specific angles and organically constitutive parts of the critique of political economy, not mechanically juxtaposed instruments" (Teixeira, 2011, p. 331).Thus, it is understood here that the object of the economy transcends the purely economic elements – questioning even the possibility of the existence of these pure elements[5]– and also incorporates political, ideological, social and historical elements. As Dobb ([1973] 1977) points out, Marx, by emphasizing the importance of incorporating issues related to the social world view, issues, therefore, linked to the field of ideology, follows a different path than the path traditionally approached.

---

5   A broad debate on HPE and economic methodology is about the possible positivist dissociation between what John Neville Keynes (1891) called "positive science" and later Milton Friedman (1953) called "pure economy" – that is, the positive elements, considered as purely theoretical and analytical and without the influence of factors considered to be outside the economy, such as political, social and ideological – the elements that Keynes called "political economy" and Friedman called "normative economy" – which could be understood as the instance in which the political and ideological elements would have space and influence in the field of economics and would address issues related to the duty to be of the economy and society, such as the orientation of economic policies, and which, therefore,it would not have the same degree of scientificity as the so-called "positive economy" or "pure science".

It is yet important to point out an observation on the issue of ideology and the conscience of the individuals who formulate the thought. Although the object has an objective existence, verifiable in the process of social and historical practice, which is independent of the observer's conscience, the process of theoretical knowledge cannot be understood in isolation from the observer's reality, nor in the observer's real existence – which is contextualized. historically. Their analysis will be rife with their experiences, worldviews, as well as praxis and politics, even if this influence is not clear.

It is possible to perceive, throughout Marx's theoretical production, and also in the construction of his method of study, many of the main elements of his analysis in the history of economic thought. The process of constructing and formulating Marx's ideas is an inseparable process from his study of the thinkers of his time and their predecessors. *Theories of surplus value* would be "par excellence, a critical history of economic thought" (Sant'anna, 1980, p. 9) and can therefore be considered the main work that reveals Marx's approach to HET.

Working the history of thought from a dialectical perspective implies the perception of criticism as a reading key. As highlighted by Paula and Cerqueira (2014, p. 15), Marx, following the path opened by Hegel, treats criticism not as what is normally understood by criticism. That is, as a comment on an object apprehended in an external and superficial way, but rather addresses criticism as "an operation of appropriation, of suprasumption,[6] in which the emancipatory contents are preserved from the object, while discarding what, in the object, is perfectly dead".

Paula and Cerqueira (2014, p. 15–6) also point out that, for the elaboration of the critique of political economy, Marx highlighted the importance of differentiating between the research method and the presentation method, with the research method prior to the presentention method, in a movement in which Marx combines the elements of dialectics and historical materialism. As an investigation method, it comprises the process of apprehending the concept, revealing (unveiling) its functioning, structure and dynamics of the real. That is, understanding the object to be analyzed in its essence and its appearance, as a whole. With this research process carried out, the presentation consists of

---

6   Suprasumption, from the German noun *aufhebung*. This term appears in the original German as the verb *aufheben*, which can have a direct translation such as supersuming, abolishing or overcoming, "which refers to the notions of raising, sustaining, erecting, canceling, abolishing, destroying, revoking, canceling, suspending, conserving, saving, preserve" (Wood apud Paula, 2014, p. 302). Suprasumption refers at the same time to the notions of elimination and conservation.

the ordering of concepts, the sequencing of the necessary forms of appearance of the object, which must occur in a dialectical and materialistic way, that is, "passage from the simple to the complex, from the simple totality to the complex totality, from the abstract to the concrete, a movement that 'is nothing but the way thought proceeds to appropriate the concrete, to reproduce it as concrete in the mind' (Marx, [1857-1859]2011, p. 123)" (Paula; Cerqueira, 2014, p. 15). Paula and Cerqueira conclude that, for Marx, the presentation is "the totalization of the concept apprehended and reproduced by the thought that opens the way for a second fundamental operation – the critical appropriation of the set of thought on the object in question, political economy" (Paula; Cerqueira, 2014, pp. 15–6). Criticism is, therefore, for Marx, a fundamental step in the presentation of his argument and with regard to the history of economic thought, a fundamental part of his understanding of the object of political economy.

Marx's approach in the field of the history of economic thought can be understood at the critical level, differing strongly from what is understood in the traditional view of HET.

Traditionally, when dealing with the history of economic thought, the popular notion that permeates imagination of economists has an idea of the history of thought linked to the view that Schumpeter presents in his book *History of Economic Analysis* ([1954] 1964), in which the author separates the history of ideas in the field of economics at three levels. The *history of economic thought*, which would be what is generally referred to as common sense, namely, everything that is said about economics in a given historical context, in a given society, that is, all opinions and affirmations associated with economic themes, given by any individual of this determined community, fitting in this bulge the opinions represented in the media, in the daily discussions, in the most varied spaces, for example. On another level, would be the so-called *history of political economy systems*, which would express the sets of economic policies, in the words of the author, "broad set of economic policies that the authors maintain based on certain unifying (normative) principles, such as the principles of economic liberalism, socialism, etc." (Schumpeter, [1954] 1964, p. 64). And, finally, the supposedly most theoretically relevant level in the history of economic ideas, the so-called *history of economic analysis*, which would express what, in Schumpeter's conception, would be the most relevant of economic ideas, the evolution of analytical instruments – where one could read, economic models – as reference for economic theory.

There are some questions to be questioned about this traditional view of the history of thought, such as the positivist separation[7] between science and

---

7 In a reasoning very close to that made by Milton Friedman in the previous year of Schumpeter's publication, when Friedamn advocates the separation between positive

theory, history and ideology,[8] the notion that the theory is "a definitive product, free from metaphysical interventions, normative concerns or value judgments" (Silva, 2013, p. 52).

According to Ricardo Tolipan (1982a), the traditional view of HET sees it as "curiosity of scholars", a conclusive account of "past mistakes", being considered even "an uncomfortable appendix that needs to be neutralized":

> academic dissemination of the History of Economic Thought is, when not simply avoided, reduced to the posthumous celebration of genius, that is, to the eclectic and punctuating description of the circumstances that accompany and "explain" the emergence of ideas; its historical account. This has a curious practical consequence: the encyclopedic account of the origin of ideas requires, as a fundamental quality of those who practice it, erudition. Now, this is also the result of a process that "takes time", hence the old economist, the ideal teacher for this chair. He had time for learning, nothing more natural than to "specialize" in the past. Furthermore, its erudition is an essential "something more" that can now be used as such. The young economist does not have this right, because active intellectual life must be dedicated not to the rumination of the past, but to the animated preparation of some future detail on the secure basis of the present specializations. It is only at the end (retrospective myth) of a productive life that the right to "historical reporting" is gained.
>
> TOLIPAN, 1988, p. 22

Tolipan (1988) also highlights that the traditional view of HET ends up relegating it to a secondary position in the theoretical field, being even considered an exclusive task of "historical reporting" by older teachers (and theorists). Thus, making it impossible to make original and expressive formulations in this field, which would be another big mistake in the traditional view.

This more traditional perception of HET treats it as "an irrepressible element of curiosity about the past, (which) could be completely detached from economic theory" (Arida, 2003, p. 16). As Arida (2003) points out, it is possible to associate this perspective of HET with the notion – taken from the so-called exact sciences – of the frontier of knowledge, in which the history of thought

---

economy and normative economy (Friedman, 1953). This reasoning is widespread in the perception of what economics is, being present in a significant portion of textbooks around the world.

8   In the same sense that Schumpeter had already stated in a previous article on ideology and science (Schumpeter, 1949).

has no importance for the formation of knowledge in the theoretical field in question, whereas that the relevant theoretical contributions made in the past are already incorporated into the contemporary state-of-the-art of knowledge, and the others, which have not been incorporated, are considered obsolete.

As highlighted by Malta et al. (2011, p. 32), this traditional view addresses HET from the notion that there is a continuous and unique theoretical line in economics that has its greatest evolutionary degree in contemporary times, in which there is a progressive accumulation of knowledge, which marks the strong evolutionary character in this perception. Joseph Schumpeter can be considered the greatest exponent of this evolutionary perception of the history of economic thought, as can be seen in this passage of his greatest work on the history of thought:

> the work of the present generation, from what I think, preserves from what was done by the previous generation everything that is still susceptible to use. Concept, methods and results that do not remain in this way, presumably will not be of great interest.
>
> SCHUMPETER, [1954] 1964, p. 24

The analysis of HET from a critical point of view considers that "the study of the History of Thought would be an analysis of how a science produces its future – of how its frontier evolves – instead of a description of its past" (Tolipan, 1988, p. 4).

As Malta & Castelo (2012, p. 98) conclude in their article *Marx and the history of economic thought: a debate about method and ideology*:

> in this sense, Marx's proposal to read the history of economic thought is an essential part of his critical construction. Studying the way of apprehending the capitalist reality expressed by the social scientists of his time was the way to access the historical understanding of the problems of his time. Without giving up being a man of his time, Marx introduces the contradiction in the dominant thought with which he was confronted and builds a unique synthesis that is expressed in his way of interpreting current social relations.

Marx's approach to the history of economic thought can be considered an exemplary movement in this critical analysis. Since he formulates his conclusions and interpretations about the economy and capitalist society based on his study of HET developed until then, seeking to go beyond the simple understanding of the formulation of the analysis of the other theorists starting only from their internal logic, but also seeking to understand the process of formulating these theories, in order to identify their limits – making, later, the criticism. And taking into account the specific social environments in which they were formulated, the context that led their authors to develop them. That is, considering the social world view[9] originated from the authors to formulate their interpretations of capitalist society and its phenomena.

The HET method developed and used by Marx understands the history of thought as a process in which the formulation of the history of thought implies the theoretical formulation and vice versa. As stated previously, the process of criticism in Marx is a process of appropriation, of suprasumption of the object in question, in which there is preservation of some of the elements of the object and simultaneous disposal of other elements, thus building a new analysis of the object, in which there is preservation and innovation. When working on the history of economic thought, Marx does it in a way that, based on this analysis, critically incorporates some elements of political economy, overcoming them, presenting his criticism to them and formulating his theoretical view of the object of political economy.

In this sense, Isaak Rubin, an author strongly influenced by the perception of the history of economic thought presented by Marx and developed by him in a work by HET in this perspective, states that the study of the development of HET is a mean of understanding theoretical political economy (Rubin, [1929] 2014).

The critical view of the history of economic thought systematizes it from the confrontation of these different formulations that may come to be formed from the elements that are manifested in reality, thus constituting controversies. Raised from a concrete problem in their particular historical context, controversies, in their development, allow to capture the historicity and the processuality of a given thought. That is, it is considered the historical process of formation of thought expressed in the author's work, with its sources, its inflections and its own syntheses over time, without taking it as something closed and finished, impervious to change. From our point of view, controversies are fundamental elements for the organization of debates in the field of the history of thought.

---

9 There is a wide and controversial debate around the question of ideology, especially within the Marxist field. In order not to escape the scope of this chapter, the term social world view will be used to address issues related to the field of ideology. As a social world view, the definition of Michael Löwy (1985, p. 13) follows, which understands it as "all those structured sets of values, representations, ideas and cognitive orientations. These sets are unified by a determined perspective, from a social point of view, of determined social classes".

This approach has as its fundamental issue the understanding of economic thought as an object in which the analysis of historical reality and the world view on which this analysis is made are inseparable. After all, economic theory is permeated with ideological elements.

> From a historical point of view, economic doctrines and ideas can be included among the most important and influential forms of ideology. As in other forms of ideology, the evolution of economic ideas depends directly on the evolution of economic forms and the class struggle. Economic ideas are not born in a vacuum. Often, they arise directly from the agitation of social conflicts, from the battlefield between different social classes. In these circumstances, economists acted as squires of these classes, providing them with the ideological weapons necessary to defend the interests of particular social groups – often failing to worry about the development of their own work and giving it a deeper theoretical foundation.
>
> RUBIN, [1929] 2014, p. 29

Treating HET from this perspective allows us to understand the theoretical and methodological contradictions, disputes and disruptions that are at the heart of the history of thought. Giving space for the perception of the existence of ideological, historical and political elements in the theoretical formulation allows to understand the whole theory. And, with this, the method allows to perceive ruptures and dispute movements that exist in the trajectory of the history of thought. The traditional view of HET, by placing it as a one-way avenue of formulating thought, invisibilizes these elements that are constituents of thought and its trajectory.

From a critical perspective, it is understood that the construction of HET would, therefore, be a process of understanding the ways of apprehending the structured economic reality in each specific historical time, substantially influenced and determined by social values of this specific time. Therefore, the presence of historical, social, political and ideological elements cannot be ignored in the process of theoretical formulation in economics.

To conduct studies in the history of economic thought means to understand the various economic interpretations and formulations according to their historical time, their ideological elements and their values.

And this a complex task, since the object of the history of economic thought is a complex object in which the theoretical and historical elements are continuously merged, and the historical reality in which the thought is formulated is marked by contradictions.

What makes treatment of the history of economic thought particularly difficult is this dual nature of our task: the need to provide the reader, at the same time, with an exposition, both of the historical conditions from which the different economic doctrines emerged, and they developed, as much of their theoretical meaning, that is, of the internal logical connection between ideas.

RUBIN, [1929] 2014, p. 30

[...]

The readers will only be able to understand this process correctly if their own thinking moves in parallel with the historical exposition, proceeding to a critical analysis and overcoming the problems and contradictions that confronted economists in the course of history. To successfully conduct this critical analysis, there is no other option but to turn to the theoretical political economy.

RUBIN, [1929] 2014, p. 33

Critical approaches to HET, such as that carried out based on controversies, have as a central element the notion of theoretical rupture (Malta et al., 2011; Malta, 2005). After all, the history of thought is constituted by different theoretical formulations with different methodological devices:

This notion raises the fact that economic thought develops under the dispute of different world views, which are revealed in different analytical conceptions about the functioning of the economy. In HET there are brutal ruptures between the methods of theoretical analysis that occur over time. Such breaks do not imply any overcoming in logical terms. In addition to identifying the rupture in the development of economic theory, the contribution of critical HET is, fundamentally, to demystify the idea that the history of thought would be essentially a one-way avenue, starting from primitive concepts to arrive at more sophisticated concepts. On the contrary, what is established is that HET would be a history of controversies under which scientific contributions marked by history and politics flourish.

MALTA ET AL., 2011, pp. 32–33

Addressing the history of economic thought from the controversies allows us to explain the multiplicity and heterogeneity of theoretical and methodological conceptions that exist in the field of knowledge of economics. So that the analyzes formulated from this approach highlight the procedural and historical elements of knowledge, emphasizing the inseparability between theory, social context and history.

3   Controversy in History of Brazilian Economic Thought (HBET)

It is possible to question the consequences of the dominant view of HET, based on Schumpeter (1954), to the history of Brazilian economic thought (HBET). Some authors even claim that there would be no significant HBET, as there is no significant development of theories or economic models in Brazil. Amadeo (1989), commenting on the treatment and space given in Brazil to the theoretical formulations of authors of great importance for economic theory, "like Ricardo, Marx, Marshall, Keynes, Kalecki and Steindl" (Amadeo, 1989, p. 8), claims that production in the field of economic theory in Brazil is not rich, being underdeveloped and not a priority object of the economists' research agenda, for reasons such as difficulties in financing and prioritization of cyclical debates on the Brazilian economy.

In this same direction, Bielschowsky (1988), when presenting the objectives and methodology for his work on the history of Brazilian economic thought between the years 1930 and 1964, affirms that in this period, with the exception of the ECLAC contribution, there was no relevant analytical production in field of economics, with no room for systematizing the history of economic analysis in Brazil in the period, within the framework of what had been suggested by Schumpeter:

> in the case of the period covered, there is little point in making a history of Brazilian analytical production in the field of economic science. This production, in addition to being scarce, was, in essence, a simple development of the only significant Latin American analytical production of the period, that is, the work of ECLAC, already widely evaluated.
>
> BIELSCHOWSKY, [1988] 2000, p. 6

In other words, from this perspective, there would be no legitimate "history of Brazilian economic analysis", in the sense of Schumpeter, and, thus, it would not be relevant to discuss, in the context of the history of general economic thought, the history of Brazilian economic thought.

This conclusion, from the perspective claimed in this chapter, is problematic. First, by treating the history of economic ideas based on this separation between different levels that make up economic formulations, in a positivist movement that tries to build the theoretical formulation as something neutral, emptied of its historical character and the world view from which is formulated, as problematized by Dobb in the following excerpt:

> to be brief, we will say that the distinction that Schumpeter tried to establish between economics as a pure analysis and as a view of the economic process, into which ideological trends and nuances inevitably enter, cannot be sustained, unless the first is limited to the formal structure, solely of economic statement, not economic theory as a substantial statement about the real relations of economic society; since in the formulation of the latter, and in the very act of judging its degree of realism, historical intuition, perspective and social vision cannot fail to be considered.
>
> DOBB, [1973] 1977, p. 52

Another problematic issue with Schumpeter's reasoning is its Eurocentric character. Revealing a position that places what is theoretically developed in Brazil subsumed to the thinking of the great economic centers, assuming that there are no great innovations or contributions to economic thought coming from peripheral and dependent spaces – such as Brazilian society – places where only the knowledge and analytical tools of the center would be reproduced, and the creativity of the formulations developed here would be restricted to the scope of conjunctural analysis and formulations – the Schumpeter's so-called history of economic thought – and to the scope of normative analyzes and formulations of economic policies – Schumpeter's history of political economy systems. That is, merely adapting the theoretical models formulated at the center to the specific issues of Brazilian society.

Although it is possible to argue for the existence of a process of organizing and disseminating training and research spaces in economics in Brazil, most notably research institutes and universities – universities as institutions, in general, were spread in Brazil from the 1920s and 1930s, undergraduate courses in economics started to gain greater dimension in the southeast and south regions from the 1940s onwards and postgraduate courses in economics were instituted from the 1960s and 1970s (Loureiro, 1997) – this does not mean that debates on economic issues, including theoretical ones, of analytical instruments, were not developed.

The formulations relevant to the history of Brazilian economic thought were (and are) elaborated by indivuduals from the most varied areas of education and performance, not being restricted to academic environments. There are specificities that permeate theoretical formulations made in Brazil that are different from the specificities that permeate theoretical formulations in England, for example, although both are inserted in capitalist contexts, both referring to the general object of political economy. It is necessary to analyze the different degrees of abstraction and generality of theoretical formulations, being careful, however, not to dissociate them from the concrete reality that originates them.

More precisely, based on the notion of national styles of political economy presented by Paula, Cerqueira and Albuquerque (2007), it is possible to state that HET needs to be understood as being the result of the historical process of certain specific societies: "that is, that the political economy, in spite of its specificities regarding objects-concepts-methods, is a tributary of culture, of the political and cultural physiognomy of an era and of a region". The historical and cultural circumstances in which the theories are formulated are relevant elements for the understanding of these theories:

> [...] it is assumed here that economic thought, despite certain discursive autonomy and certain methodological-conceptual requirements, reflects its time and place, expressing itself according to styles, metaphors, references, interests that transcend the specificity of economic analysis. It is, therefore, about understanding economic thought, as, to some extent, reflecting the national context, the historical circumstances that gave rise to it. In such a way that this is what would explain the existence of styles, of certain defining habits specific of the various national schools of economic thought, which concern both the form and the content of their respective theoretical elaborations.
>
> PAULA; CERQUEIRA; ALBUQUERQUE, 2007, p. 358

Although there are general features that can characterize capitalist economies, different economies have different processes of capitalist development, and the theoretical formulation carried out in these spaces carries a strong influence of these local specificities. It is possible to approach the history of economic thought from the theoretical formulations developed in different national spaces, that is, from different national styles of political economy.

In this sense, there is a history of Brazilian economic thought. There are theoretical formulations at the most different levels of analysis and abstraction that undertake to understand and to explain economic processes. Not only that. It is necessary to emphasize that not only are there formulations of theoretical and analytical content that originate a history of thought, but there are also systematic formulations of this history of thought.

There are three reference works for the systematization of the history of Brazilian economic thought: Ricardo Bielschowsky's doctoral thesis, which was published as a book in 1988 – *Pensamento Econômico Brasileiro*: *o ciclo ideológico do desenvolvimentismo* (Brazilian Economic Thought: the ideological cycle of developmentism) –; Guido Mantega's doctoral thesis, which was published as a book in 1984 – *A economia política brasileira* (The Brazilian Political Economy) –; and more recently the book *Ecos do Desenvolvimento: uma História do Pensamento Econômico Brasileiro* (Echoes of Development: A History of Brazilian Economic Thought,2011), the result of a collective research effort by the – Laboratório de Estudos Marxistas (LEMA) (Laboratory of Marxist Studies) – under the coordination of Maria Malta. The first two works address Brazilian economic thought until the 1960s. The third work aims to analyze Brazilian economic thought between the years 1964 and 1989.

The collective work carried out by LEMA researchers in the book *Ecos do Desenvolvimento* (Echoes of Development, 2011) is part of a critical dialogue with the two other main works of broader and more articulated systematization in the history of Brazilian economic thought. Works that even sought to affirm the same hypothesis that is developed here: that there is, in fact, a history of Brazilian economic thought and that this is an object of analysis of great importance, "configuring a project for the recovery of national economic thought" (Malta et al., 2011, p. 23):

> [...] in these works, the HBET systematization project appears for the first time as an object treated in depth, using theoretically grounded analytical cuts. Unlike the specific thematic works, the referred authors prepare their research to unveil the structure of HBET and find the question of development at its core. Although starting from different theoretical matrices, Bielschowsky and Mantega build their histories of Brazilian economic thought converging on a main point: to identify development and underdevelopment as organizers of economic thought and economic debate in the country.
>
> MALTA ET AL., 2011, p. 26

Guido Mantega (1984, p. 22) analyzes Brazilian economic thought in the 1950s and 1960s, highlighting three main currents of thought, which, according to the author, allowed the construction of three analytical models that are structural axes of his so-called "family tree of the Brazilian political economy". Namely, the import substitution model; the bourgeois-democratic model; and the capitalist underdevelopment model. All these models, for Mantega, were organized around proposals for development projects for Brazil and would gather the works of the main authors in the field of economics at the time. For Mantega, from the publication of *Formação Econômica do Brasil*, by

Celso Furtado (1959), it is possible to speak about a Brazilian Political Economy. That was a moment in which the "Brazilian economic thought starts to have a more meaningful production, when the works become more comprehensive, systematic and profound, as can be seen from the 1950s on" (Mantega, 1984, p. 19).

The Brazilian Political Economy "would be the result of an ideological clash between two main fronts that defended antagonistic political and economic interests from the point of view of projects for our economy" (Malta et al., 2011, p. 30). Considered by Mantega outside the field of political economy, there were authors associated with the *status quo* of that time. Those authors had neoclassical and liberal theoretical roots, but due to the peculiarity of the Brazilian underdeveloped economy, they inserted elements in their analysis for pro-intervention by the State, thus generating what Mantega called the Brazilian development model.

Mantega's systematization of the history of Brazilian economic thought was based on Marxist contributions and was carried out, according to the author, based on the following mechanisms:

> [...] thus, in this work, I intend to analyze the consolidation of Brazilian economic thought, characterizing the formation of the first Brazilian analytical models, their theoretical origins, their main sources of inspiration and, above all, their basic hypotheses and fundamental propositions. Each model received a critical appraisal, first, from the point of view of its internal coherence; second, regarding its explanatory power and its correspondence to the facts; and, finally, from the angle of an alternative view of the capitalist development process, which is not totally explicit, but only implied and disseminated throughout the work, so as not to divert the analysis of its main objective of faithfully reproducing Brazilian economic thought of the time.
>
> [...]
>
> In order to interpret the Brazilian economy, analysts have resorted to various conceptions about the articulation of economic systems, about their dynamics of operation, or about their fundamental laws and possibilities for transformation, resulting in different, if not conflicting, diagnoses about the same reality. It was our task here to make explicity these conceptions embedded in concrete analyzes, to organize them in theoretical systems and group them according to their proximity and complementarity, in order to form the analytical models and currents of thought in question.
>
> MANTEGA, 1984, pp. 18–19

Although it has its merits, this first major systematization of the history of Brazilian economic thought, organized from a single theoretical framework, presents important limits:

(a)   Mantega does not present more in-depth considerations on the methodological issue, Mantega does not explain in more detail than those mentioned here as a basis for the models, nor for the systematization of the family tree of the Brazilian political economy;

(b)   Mantega also does not discuss much about the criteria behind his periodization and the selection of authors he addresses, limiting himself to state that only after the Celso Furtado's work, in the late 1950s (1959), it is possible to identify the beginning of a Brazilian political economy, which would be the result of the ideological confrontation between agrarian liberals and industrial developmentists, as well as the influence of the Marxist tradition, especially the one organized by the Partido Comunista do Brasil (PCB) – Brazilian Communist Party –, and the ECLAC developmentists. This combination (industrialist, Marxist and ECLAC developmentalists) would result in the Brazilian Political Economy (the non-neoclassical side of the debate on developmentalism in Brazil in the 1950s and 1960s), that would give rise in the 1960s to the three models of Brazilian development thought: import substitution model; democratic-bourgeois model and capitalist underdevelopment model. Outside the Brazilian Political Economy, from the liberal (neoclassical) matrix, the Brazilian development model would develop. And, isolated, without being properly placed in the categories of family tree of the Brazilian political economy, Mantega puts the theory of dependency.

In summary, Mantega does not present a clear methodological framework for his work, he only lists the steps he took to construct his analysis. In addition, it is important to highlight that Mantega does not present a clear criterion for the choice of the approached authors, there existing arbitrariness in this choice, an element that he himself admits: "before beginning the analysis, it is convenient to draw the reader's attention to the arbitrary character involved in the choice of authors and the ordering of their theses into models of interpretation". (Mantega, 1984, p. 21).

On the other hand, Ricardo Bielschowsky (1988) analyzes the period between 1930 and 1964, justifying this periodization as it was the time of establishment of the industrial system in the country, and takes *desenvolvimentismo* (developmentalism)[10] as a key concept to organize and give unity to Brazilian

---

10   "By developmentalism, in this work, we understand the ideology of transformation of the Brazilian society defined by the economic project which is composed of the following

economic thought. Bielschowsky's systematization of Brazilian economic thought is carried out around this conceptual framework and is based on five main currents of thought in the period: neoliberalism; developmentalism of the private sector; the developmentalism of the "non-nationalist" public sector; the developmentalism of the "nationalist" public sector; and the socialist school of thought. Bielschowsky also analyzes the work of Ignácio Rangel, but Bielschowsky does so in an isolated manner, because he conisders that it would not be possible to fit Rangel into any of these currents. In addition, Bielschowsky on the basis of the notion of *"ciclo ideológico do desenvolvimentismo"* (ideological cycle of developmentalism), proposes a periodization for his systematization, based on the real movement of the Brazilian economy. The periods are: 1930–1945 – the origins of developmentalism; 1945–1955 – the maturation of developmentalism (subdivided into three subperiods: 1945–1947, 1948–1952 and 1953–1955); and 1956–1964 – the height and crisis of developmentalism (also subdivided: 1956–1960 and 1961–1964).

It is important to highlight that, unlike Mantega, Bielschoswky explicitly states his methodological framework. Bielschowsky claims to refer to Schumpeter's formulation for the history of economic thought. As previously presented, Schumpeter ([1954] 1964) separates the history of economic analysis, the history of economic thought and the history of political economy systems. Starting from the notion that developmentalism is a unifying normative principle that organizes Brazilian economic thought and considering that Brazilian economic thought in the analyzed period did not happen in academic circles, but in discussions in the political sphere about the Brazilian industrialization process, Bielschowsky states that the best way to organize Brazilian economic thought in the period is based on what Schumpeter called the history of political economy systems. With the proviso that part of his analysis also involves organizing the history of economic thought – in the sense that Schumpeter gives to the term –, since a significant part of the formulations of the period does not take place in academic terms and that there is an analytical dimension in economic reflections analyzed in the period., However, Bielschowsky points out that this is not the focus of his analysis.

---

fundamental points: a) integral industrialization as the path to overcome poverty and Brazilian underdevelopment; b) there is no way to achieve efficient and rational industrialization in Brazil through the spontaneous forces of market; therefore, it is necessary for the State to plan industrialization; c) planning should define the desired expansion of the economic sectors and the instruments for promoting this expansion; and d) the State also should organize the execution of the expansion, raising and guiding financial resources, and promoting direct investments in those sectors where private initiative is insufficient "(Bielschowsky, [1988] 2000, p.7).

It is possible to make a critical caveat about the methodology claimed by Bielschowsky. Even though Schumpeter (1954) is a reference, it is possible to see that Bielschowsky does not follow exactly what Schumpeter proposes. According to the analysis proposed by Borja (2013), Bielschoswky, despite denying the existence of a history of economic analysis in Brazil in that period, accomplishes a combination of what Schumpeter called the history of the systems of political economy and the history of economic thought. And Bielschowsky in making this junction, "ends up abandoning the Schumpeterian criteria, stating that it is impossible to think about the history of economic thought or political economy systems without analytical reference systems" (Borja, 2013, p. 30).

Finally, the work done by Malta et al. (2011) proposes to continue the work of Mantega (1984) and Bielschoswky (1988), by approaching the subsequent period (1964–1989) in a critical way, from another theoretical proposal. That is controversies as a systematizing element of the history of Brazilian economic thought.

This theoretical proposal has as reference the work of Karl Marx, in particular, *Theories of surplus value* ([1905] 1980) and the contributions of Rubin ([1929] 2014) and Dobb ([1973] 1977). That is, it is organized from the concepts of historical and dialectical materialism that were previously presented in this chapter. Starting from the opposite notion to Schumpeter's – which separates theoretical analysis from ideology – the authors claim that it is not possible to make such a separation. The proposal of systematization of HBET made by the authors is that the systematization should be done "at a theoretical-analytical, historical and political level in an integrated manner" (Malta et al., 2011, p. 35).

From this perspective, it is impossible to dissociate ideology, politics, history, economics and theoretical analysis; "because they are umbilically connected, they need to be articulated simultaneously in the definition of the concepts and the periodization necessary to build the study outline of the history of economic thought" (Malta et al., 2011, p. 51). The fundamental relevance of historical processes for the development of thought and, in this sense, the social context, the authors' world view, their theoretical references, make the formulation of thought impregnated with elements that cannot be embedded in what Schumpeter wanted to identify it as pure economic theory. Analyzing HET means discussing these elements – ideology, politics, history, economics and theoretical analysis – in an indissociable, totalizing way:

> [...] in our view, the most effective method to research the history of economic thought combines the study of the historical period of reference with a study of economic theory elaborated until then, in order to

understand the intellectual production resulting from these influences. This perspective, borrowed from Rubin ([1929] 1989), is based on historical materialism, in contrast to the Hegelian idealism under which it would be possible to have ideas from an "absolute spirit", without the need for a material basis that originate the ideas. The ideas of an era are the intellectual expression of prevailing social relations with all the contradictions and influences inherited from history, whose dynamics are fundamentally given by the class struggle.

MALTA ET AL., 2011, p. 34

This is also the general meaning of the proposed method for the history of economic thought presented here. Controversies, in this method, are central to the organization of economic thought as they allow to capture the movement and historicity of thought. Controversies are raised by issues of material reality and because of these different ideological, theoretical, social and political issues, material reality can be analyzed in different ways, with the systematization of HET being marked by ruptures, discontinuities and theoretical disputes.

In the specific case of the cited book, the proposal to systematize the history of Brazilian economic thought in the period 1964–1989 presents the issue of development as a central axis for the controversies of that period; "The development issue inhabited the thought of the vast majority of economists in Brazil and most of the debates of the period under study had as a fundamental reference a development project for the country" (Malta et al., 2011, p. 35). The different development projects in dispute, with their different theoretical orientations and theoretical formulations, different analytical framework and different political projects are the scenario in which the controversies are established. It is around this issue that the main economic controversies listed in the book were organized.Namely, the debate on the tendency to stagnation; the controversy on income distribution; the controversy on the Brazilian revolution; the controversy on the causes of inflation, among others.

This work is revisited not so much because of the details of the controversies analyzed in the book, or because of the specificities of the analyzed period (1964–1989). This proposal is revisited because it is considered that this approach of controversies for the history of Brazilian economic thought can be used more widely in other periods of the HBET.

Due to the strong mark of historicity and processuality in this approach, it is possible to think of the systematization of Brazilian economic thought based on the controversies in different periods. For example, one can analyze the unfolding of the debates on development by industrialization or by commodity production between Eugênio Gudin and Roberto Simonsen in the 1940s;

the discussions about the characterization of the mode of production in Brazil that spanned several decades of the 20th century; the issues surrounding the revival of development in the first decade of the 21st century; the controversy on Brazilian inflation in the 1980s, among others. Anyway, the point is that due to the issues of material reality in different historical periods, controversies arise. Controversies that are organized based on different analyzes of reality, and it is possible to trace a history of economic thought from the ruptures and disputes that these controversies indicate.

In this sense, exploring the debates that permeate the reality of Brazil's socio-economic formation, highlighting the elements in which they out-line an interpretation of the functioning of the economic structure and the country's legal, political and ideological superstructure, broadens our object of systematization, when talking about the history of Brazilian economic thought. Authors who would be excluded from the field of economic thought, if we used the methodology indicated by Schumpeter (1954), Mantega (1984) or Bielschowsky (1988), become part of the object of analysis of the history of Brazilian economic thought. Among them, those who have been known as interpreters of Brazil stand out.

4 Incorporating the Contribution of Interpreters of Brazil to the History of Brazilian Economic Thought (HBET)

What is understood as interpretations of Brazil – a significant group of con-tributions designed to systematize the Brazilian historical reality, especially in the late 19th century and from the 1930s onwards – is generally discussed in the field of Brazilian social thought, but hardly ever in the field of the history of Brazilian economic thought (HBET).

The field that became known as interpretations of Brazil appeared, as pointed out by Ricupero (2008, p. 21), in the period initiated with the aboli-tionist and republican debate, at the end of the 19th century, unfolding with the establishment and broader development of the university in Brazil, in the 1920s and 1930s. It is possible to identify in these authors the theme of the formation of Brazil as a fundamental issue of their work.That is, they were concerned with the debate on the establishment of a more autonomous national social framework that would contrast with the colonial origin of Brazil, marked by several types of dominance, such as cultural, political and economic.

Generally, their works deal with the three historical moments, the present, the past and the future. That is, they begin with a great historical review– focus on the past –, they analyze how the elements of this historical review and the formation process contributed to the construction of the Brazil – the present – and they close their analysis with a political program on how to overcome Brazil's problems – the future. These are formulations that, even when dealing with the past, always aim to investigate the "present as history" (Hobsbawm, 1993).

The idea here is that interpreters of Brazil have an intellectual mission with him, as they seek, through historical research, to understand the contemporary reality of the country. The interpretations of Brazil are presented as the first properly Brazilian thought that is autonomous in relation to the theories of the main world centers, paving the way for a specific type of analysis that will highlight, albeit in different ways, the productive structure, in an attempt to understand Brazil and its formation.

The concern with the establishment of an autonomous social framework, which would oppose to the situation of colonial subordination, is the core of a thought that places at its main dynamic center what occurs internally in the country. The interpretations of Brazil are marked by the analysis of the structural forms of the social production of material life, which express themselves in certain necessary social relations and independent of their will and to which correspond production relations referring to a determined phase of the development of the material productive forces. At the same time, an interpreter cannot fail to realize that upon this structure rises a legal, political superstructure and corresponding forms of social consciousness that necessarily make up his object. Thus, attempts to interpret Brazil will not be able to escape the tricks of their object and will end up giving way, here and there, to dialectics, radicalism and criticism.

In order to understand the nation that was formed in Brazil or that could come to be formed in Brazil it was necessary to be willing to unveil the Brazilian reality and propose an explanation for the economic and social formation that was presented within the borders of the National State. Even though they do not explicitly address the economy – the exceptions being Caio Prado Junior and Celso Furtado. The so-called interpreters of Brazil have relevant elements of their analysis in the economic (structural) issues. After all, to approach the process of socio-economic formation, one must treat the formation process in a totalizing way, exposing its social, political, cultural, and also economic characteristics, that is, the analysis of the formation process and the analysis of the constitution of its productive and social structures. It is therefore possible to understand the work of the interpreters of Brazil as part of the history of Brazilian economic thought and insert the contribution of these interpreters in the different controversies that make up HBET.

Taking the perception of economic thought advocated here, the analyzes focused on socio-economic economic-social formation can serve as a guide for Brazilian economic thought. After all, to think about the elements of the economic structure, of the social relations of production and of the productive forces cannot be done in a way dissociated from the political, social and cultural elements. However, as previously stated, throughout the 20th century there was a strengthening of the process of specialization and fragmentation of knowledge.[11]

Aloísio Teixeira (2002) affirms that, in the scope of economic thought, as well as in the fields of teaching and practice of economics, this process have been even more accentuated since the analytical horizons of the mainstream theory in the field of economics focus on the issues of the appearance of reality. This mainstream theory is "dominated by a pseudo-scientific view, whose analytical horizons do not go beyond the abstract notions of market and competitiveness, on the assumption that the economist is always faced with economic systems in pure form" (Teixeira, 2002, p. 57). In thisregard, Teixeira highlights the need to resume this broader, more comprehensive view, resuming studies, analyzes and debates on the historical formation of Brazilian society.

Following what was previously stated regarding political economy as a key to think about a way to interpret Brazil, authors such as the already mentioned Celso Furtado and Caio Prado Jr., but also Nelson Werneck Sodré, Ignácio Rangel, Florestan Fernandes, Octavio Ianni, Ruy Mauro Marini, Vânia Bambirra, Maria da Conceição Tavares, Francisco de Oliveira, João Manuel Cardoso de Mello, among others, produced analyzes that can be seen as interpretations of Brazil, as they deal with the structural elements of the social production of material life and its conditioning relation with the elements linked to the political, legal and ideological superstructure.

Therefore, there is a dynamic relation between the contribution of interpreters of Brazil in the history of Brazilian economic thought and the contribution of authors recognized as economists in formulations considered to be interpretations of Brazil, significantly expanding the possibility of writing a wide HBET through the approach of controversies.

---

11   Here it is worth stating that it is not denied that this process of development of the university and later of postgraduate studies in Brazil has not fostered significant advances in the production and dissemination of knowledge. However, it is considered necessary to expose the limitation of that process and their consequences.

5   Final Considerations

This chapter sought to present the methodological elements that make it possible to systematize based on controversies the history of economic thought, in general, and the history of Brazilian economic thought, in particular. As presented in the chapter, the methodological framework for this approach to the history of economic thought is based on dialectics and historical materialism and as the reference authors Karl Marx, Isaak Rubin ([1929], 2014), Maurice Dobb ([1973], 1977) and for the case of the history of Brazilian economic thought, Malta et al. (2011).

Starting from an understanding of economic thought as a theoretical formulation that is an expression of historical reality, in which the world view on which this analysis is made and the historical context in which it is inserted are inseparable elements of thought, the construction of history of economic thought can be understood as the systematization of the different forms of apprehension of the economic reality structured in each specific historical time, substantially influenced and determined by the social values of that specific time. Therefore, the historical, social, political and ideological elements are part of the theoretical formulation process in economics. To make history of economic thought means, therefore, to understand the various economic interpretations and formulations according to their historical time, their ideological elements, and their values. These formulations and interpretations can be systematized on the basis of the controversies.

In the case of the history of Brazilian economic thought, for the construction of the approach of controversies for its systematization, we add the contribution of the so-called interpretations of Brazil as important analytical formulations on the process of Brazilian socio-economic formation. These formulations compose different controversies that are part of the history of thought and that can contribute to the systematization of the history of Brazilian economic thought.

The debate around the different approaches in the history of economic thought is not over. After all, it is a debate continually increased by the historical movement and the methodological questions it raises. In addition, there are other ways of systematizing the history of economic thought that were not covered in this chapter.

The idea of this chapter is to bring the theme of the history of Brazilian economic into focus so that, based on these elements, it is possible to make collective considerations on how to systematize knowledge in the economic field. It is considered that the approach of controversies is a fruitful method to make this systematization that expands the object of the history of Brazilian economic thought in order to include the contribution of the interpretations of Brazil, and reveals a richer HBET than that identified by the methodology used so far.

Bibliographic References

Amadeo, Edward. Introdução: Vertentes da economia política moderna. *In*: Amadeo, Edward. (org.) Ensaios sobre Economia Política Moderna: teoria e história do pensamento econômico. São Paulo: Editora Marco Zero, 1989.

Arida, Pérsio. A história do pensamento econômico como teoria e retórica. *In*: Rego, José Marcio (org.) A história do pensamento econômico como teoria e retórica. São Paulo: Editora 34, 2003.

Bielschowsky, Ricardo. Pensamento Econômico Brasileiro: o ciclo ideológico do desenvolvimentismo. 4ª ed. Rio de Janeiro: Contraponto, [1988] 2000.

Blaug, Marc. Economic history and the history of economics. Brighton: Wheatsheaf, 1986.

Borja, Bruno. A formação da teoria do subdesenvolvimento de Celso Furtado. 2013. Tese (Doutorado em Economia Política Internacional) – Rio de Janeiro: Universidade Federal do Rio de Janeiro, 2013.

Dobb, Maurice. Teorias do valor e da distribuição desde Adam Smith. Lisboa: Ed. Martins Fontes, [1973] 1977.

Fernandes, Florestan. Introdução. *In:* Marx, Karl. Contribuição à crítica da economia política. 2ª ed. São Paulo: Editora Expressão Popular, [1946] 2008.

Friedman, Milton. A metodologia da economia positiva. Edições Multiplic, v. 1, n. 3, fev, [1953] 1981.

Furtado, Celso. Formação Econômica do Brasil. São Paulo: Companhia das Letras, [1959] 2006.

Hobsbawm, Eric. O presente como história. Novos Estudos CEBRAP nº43, [1993] nov/ 1995, p. 103–112.

Loureiro, Maria Rita (org.). 50 anos de ciência econômica no Brasil: pensamento, instituições, depoimentos. Petrópolis: Editora Vozes, 1997.

Löwy, Michael. *Ideologias e ciência social: elementos para uma análise marxista.* 18ª ed. São Paulo: Cortez, 1985.

Lukács, Györg. O processo de democratização. *In:* Socialismo e democratização: escritos políticos 1956–1971. Rio de Janeiro: Editora UFRJ, [1968] 2008.

Malta, Maria Mello de. Controvérsia sobre a teoria da acumulação de James Steuart. Tese (Doutorado em Economia) – Faculdade de Economia, Universidade Federal Fluminense, Niterói, 2005.

Malta, Maria Mello de et al. A história do pensamento econômico brasileiro entre 1964 e 1989: um método para discussão. *In:* Malta, Maria Mello de. (coord.).

Ecos do desenvolvimento: uma história do pensamento econômico brasileiro. Rio de Janeiro: IPEA/Centro Internacional Celso Furtado de Políticas para o Desenvolvimento, 2011, p. 23–52.

Malta, Maria Mello de; Castelo, Rodrigo. Marx e a história do pensamento econômico: um debate sobre método e ideologia. In: Ganem, Angela; Freitas, Fábio; Malta, Maria Mello de (orgs.) Economia e filosofia: controvérsias e tendências recentes. Rio de Janeiro: Editora UFRJ, 2012, p. 85–100.

Mantega, Guido. A economia política brasileira. São Paulo: Polis; Petrópolis: Vozes, 1984.

Marx, Karl (1867). O Capital (Livro 1), Rio de Janeiro: Bertrand Brasil, 1989, 12ª ed.

Marx, Karl. Introdução à Contribuição à crítica da economia política. In: Contribuição à crítica da economia política. 2ª ed. São Paulo: Editora Expressão Popular, [1857] 2008.

Marx, Karl. Contribuição à crítica da economia política. 2ª ed. São Paulo, Editora Expressão Popular, [1859] 2008.

Marx, Karl. Teorias da mais-valia: história crítica do pensamento econômico. v. 1–3. Rio de Janeiro, Civilização Brasileira, [1905-1910] 1980.

Marx, Karl. Grundrisse: manuscritos econômicos 1857-1859. São Paulo: Boitempo; Rio de Janeiro: Editora UFRJ, [1857–1859] 2011.

Marx, Karl; Engels, Friedrich. A ideologia alemã. São Paulo: Boitempo Editorial, [1846] 2007.

Netto, José Paulo. Introdução ao estudo do método de Marx. São Paulo: Editora Expressão Popular, 2011.

Paula, João. Antonio de. Crítica e emancipação humana – ensaios marxistas. Belo Horizonte: Editora Autêntica, 2014.

Paula, João Antonio; Cerqueira, Hugo. E. A. da Gama; Albuquerque, Eduardo da Motta. Nações e estilos de economia política, Revista de Economia Política, v. 27, n. 3 (107), jul/set. 2007.

Paula, João Antonio; Cerqueira, Hugo E. A. Gama Apresentação – Sobre Isaak Rubin e sua História do pensamento econômico. In: Rubin, Isaak Ilich. História do Pensamento Econômico. Rio de Janeiro: Editora UFRJ, 2014, p. 11–24.

Ricupero, Bernardo. Sete lições sobre as interpretações do Brasil. São Paulo: Alameda, 2008.

Rubin, Isaak Ilich. História do pensamento econômico. Rio de Janeiro: Ed. UFRJ, [1929] 2014.

Sant'anna, Reginaldo. Nota do tradutor In: Marx, Karl. Teorias da mais-valia: história crítica do pensamento econômico. v. 1–3. Rio de Janeiro, Civilização Brasileira, 1980, p. 9–12.

Schumpeter, Joseph. Science and Ideology, The American Economic Review, v.39, n.2, mar. 1949.

Schumpeter, Joseph. História da Análise Econômica. Rio de Janeiro: USAID, [1954] 1964.

Silva, Juliana Nascimento. Distintas leituras da história do pensamento econômico. 2013. Dissertação (Mestrado em Economia) – Faculdade de Economia, Universidade Federal, Rio de Janeiro, 2013.

Teixeira, Aloisio. Marx e a economia política: a crítica como conceito, Revista Econômica, v. 2, n. 4, dez., 2000.

Teixeira, Aloisio. Raízes do Brasil: o lado oposto e os outros lados, Revista Tempo Brasileiro, n. 149, Repensando o Brasil com Sérgio Buarque de Holanda, Rio de Janeiro: Edições Tempo Brasileiro, 2002, p. 55–73.

Teixeira, Aloisio. Posfácio: Uma agenda para a (re)descoberta do Brasil. *In:* Malta, Maria Mello de. (coord.). Ecos do desenvolvimento: uma história do pensamento econômico brasileiro. Rio de Janeiro. IPEA/Centro Internacional Celso Furtado de Políticas para o Desenvolvimento, 2011, p. 329–352.

Tolipan, Ricardo. A necessidade da história do pensamento econômico, Texto para discussão, n. 3, IE/UFRJ, 1982a.

Tolipan, Ricardo. A questão do método em economia política, Texto para discussão, n. 5, IE/UFRJ, 1982b.

Tolipan, Ricardo. A ironia na História do Pensamento Econômico. Tese (Professor Titular) – Rio de Janeiro: Universidade Federal do Rio de Janeiro, jul. 1988.

CHAPTER 2

Interpreters of Brazil

Influences on the Origin of Brazilian Economic Thought

Maria Malta, Carla Curty and Bruno Borja

> The publication of a book cannot be approached as an event, but as
> the result of a historical process.
>
> TAMAS SZMRECSÁNYI (1999)

∴

1   Introduction

It is possible to indicate two historical foundational moments referring to concrete problems that place Brazilian society in a critical position in relation to
its own reality and provoke a Brazilian thought developed from the reflection
on its social condition and historical formation process. These moments are, at
the end of the 19th century, the abolition of slavery, undermining the foundations of the Empire's political form and, at the beginning of the 20th century,
Brazil's historic transition from an agrarian-exporting country to an urban-
industrial country, reference to the 1930s.

In both cases, these are times when the process of productive transformation had definitive implications for the structuring of Brazilian society. In the
first case, the abolition of slavery meant, from the point of view of capital, a
gigantic expropriation of wealth and, from the point of view of the worker,
the need to establish a new framework of political-legal relations on labor in
the country. The workers won their personal freedom, formally started to have
the right to speak, to attend schools, to formulate and present proposals for
social change, but they still lacked to effectively obtain all these rights. That
is why the struggle for their rights, on the path to effective liberation, had to
continue.[1]

---

[1] A good reference on the history of the struggles of Brazilian workers since the beginning of
the 20th century is in Mattos (2009).

In the second case, the ongoing social transformation had its origin in the transmutation of agrarian capital into industrial capital, which implied a reorganization of the traditional Brazilian rural society, progressively becoming an urban society, questioning all the prevailing social relations and spreading within the communities, Brazilian borders the industrial pattern of capitalist social relations, including in what concerns struggles for workers' rights.

In addition, the movement that is taking place in Brazil concerns the perception of the limits of the liberal State accompanied by the institution of the self-regulating market, which had guided the action of the Brazilian State since independence. The perception of these limits led Brazilian thought to the controversy of the foundation of a State that was effectively based on Brazilian society. It is in this core that the necessary debate about the process of economic and social formation in Brazil takes place.

Thus, our objective in this chapter is to recover in the thoughts of some of Brazil's interpreters the elements of the configuration of Brazilian economic and social structures that gain centrality in their views on Brazil and influence the origin of Brazilian economic thought.

2   The Notion of Interpreter of Brazil

Coutinho ([1988] 2011) identifies the "malaise" of the late 19th and early 20th centuries in Brazil, affirming something that is valid for all radical thinking[2] this time. The author states that even when dealing with the past, that thought always aims to investigate the present as history, which implies for him a dialectical analysis of the genesis and perspectives of this present. Although few authors of the time can claim dialectics as logic, in many cases using self-declared methods as positivists, it is not difficult to identify it, as an invasion of the logic of real history, object of the work of these authors, in their thinking and formulation.

---

2 Antonio Candido, in his article "Radicalismos" of 1986, establishes a categorization of thinkers in Brazil as belonging to three categories according to their social-political position. For Candido (1986), thinkers could be conservative, revolutionary or radical. Radical thinking would be a progressive way of reacting to the stimulation of pressing social problems, a thought generated in the petty bourgeoisie and in enlightened sectors of the ruling classes that is identified, in part with the interests of the working classes, but which opposes their class only to a certain extent. The radical would think of problems and solutions on the scale of the nation as a whole, overcoming antagonism between classes. Even so, Candido affirms that the radical often had a transforming role in Brazilian thought, as it was able to really advance, or serve as a transforming ferment in some contexts.

The first generation of these interpreters is concerned with the pregnancy of republican Brazil from the belly of the slavery empire, as a formation that needed to finally account for its non-colonial national identity. This is the generation of Joaquim Nabuco, André Rebouças, Castro Alves, Euclides da Cunha, Manoel Bomfim and Machado de Assis. In Nabuco and Euclides there is an important questioning of the status quo, identified by modernists as a monkey[3] of European thought or the Federative Republic of the United States of America. This generation brought to light the inadequacy of Brazilian institutions to their social reality, the result of a totally copyist formulating thought (as described by Euclides when referring to coastal populations),[4] or decadent and dependent, as Nabuco (1884) classified it.

The generation of the 1920s/30s has as main anxiety, in its different theoretical-political orientations, the attempt to understand the socioeconomic formation of Brazil in the context of the beginning of the transition from an agrarian-exporting society to an urban-industrial society. This generation formed by modernist authors, in literature, found intersections with thinkers of social structures, as in the case of Sérgio Buarque de Holanda. This group also included more conservative authors, such as Gilberto Freyre, but whose stance of revealing the pattern of social formation made it radical. It is also worth mentioning the presence of Caio Prado Júnior, who is identified by several authors[5] as the author who devised one of the first successful attempts to apply Marx's method to the analysis of Brazil, a milestone in Brazilian Marxism.[6] All these thinkers, from both generations, denounced the disconnection of the institutional forms in force in Brazil in relation to the society that effectively produced its social relations in Brazilian territory.

The field that became known as interpretations of Brazil appeared, as highlighted by Ricupero (2008), exactly in this period started with the abolitionist and republican debate, at the end of the 19th century, unfolding with

---

3 Sérgio Buarque de Holanda popularizes this terminology for reference to the thinking of the Brazilian elite in his article Ariel [1920] 1989.

4 See Cunha ([1902] 2000, section II, item V). For an analysis of the implications of the term, see Lima (2009).

5 Among the commentators who support this opinion, the following stand out: Francisco Iglésias, 1982; Carlos Nelson Coutinho, [1988] 2011; and Bernardo Ricupero, 2008.

6 In 1926, Octávio Brandão had published *Agrarismo e industrialismo: ensaio marxista-leninista sobre a revolta de São Paulo e a guerra de classes no Brasil* (Agrarianism and Industrialism: a Marxist-Leninist essay on the São Paulo revolt and the class war in Brazil), which can be considered a first Marxist interpretation of Brazil (see Pinheiro, 2021 in this book). However, there are controversies about the work, the author himself in the 1950s recognizes the limits of his work due to the mechanical application of a Stalinist view of Marxism.

the establishment and broader development of the university in Brazil in the 1920s/30s. It is possible to identify in these authors the question of the formation of Brazil as a fundamental issue of their work, that is, they were concerned with the debate on the establishment of a more autonomous national social framework that would contrast with the colonial origin of Brazil, marked by several domain types, such as cultural, political and economic. Seeking to understand the Brazil of his time, his works generally deal with the three historical moments, present, past and future, that is, they start with a great historical review – focus on the past –, analyze how the elements of this historical review and the formation process contributed to the construction of Brazil – the present – and end with a political program on how to overcome the problems of the country – the future.

Our point is that an interpreter of Brazil has an intellectual mission with him, as he seeks, through historical research, to understand the present reality of the country. Thus, it is not intended to state that at the end of the 19th century or in the 1920s/30s, the first properly Brazilian thought was presented, autonomous in relation to the theories of the main world centers. What is intended is to identify a type of interpretation that will highlight, albeit in different ways, the productive structure to try to analyze and understand Brazil and its formation. Or even, we wish to affirm that the authors of these studies must be understood as interpreters of Brazil, for placing the formation of the nation in a historical perspective. And in the process, these authors build an interpretation of Brazil.

It is also worth proposing another hypothesis: if the core of the interpretive movement of these authors is the production and the structural and superstructural social relations related to it, we could identify this moment as the foundation of Brazilian economic thought[7].

We take the method presented by Curty and Malta (2021, in this book) for understanding and systematizing the history of Brazilian economic thought. More specifically, the processuality of thought, in which different historical, theoretical and political, social and ideological experiences configure strong influences on the configuration of thought. We understand that the theoretical, historical and ideological spheres cannot be dissociated and that the history of economic thought must be told and systematized based on controversies. We also approach economic thought more broadly than the economicist and positivist views of compartmentalization in the field of economics

---

7   There is a controversy regarding the ideia if the is of the is not a orininal Brazilian economic and policial tought. To understand that debate see Faoro (1994), Santos (1978), Schwarz (1977), Ricupero (2008) e Botelho (2009).

suggest. The understanding of the object of economic thought worked on here is constituted by questions related to the structural elements of production: work, technology, the availability of natural resources, associated with the organization of class society. We understand the authors analyzed here as part of the history of Brazilian economic thought, being able to include them in their original movement.

If we borrow from Ricupero (2008) the idea that formation is a recurring theme in a country with a colonial past and a persistent situation of dependency, and if we add the notion that the intellectual mission of an interpreter of Brazil is to understand the formation of nation in historical perspective, we encounter a typical challenge for a social scientist in general, and a Marxist economist in particular: to understand reality in order to transform it.

It is true that in the Brazilian case, this intellectual mission was not taken, and not even in its majority, by Marxist authors. However, the works developed by interpreters of Brazil still have their radical or critical bias, as far as the questions they propose to answer. Even so, to take Brazilian economic thought as an object and affirm the method of historical-dialectical materialism as a reference is to seek a form of analysis of Brazilian thought that is seldom used, especially in the field of political economy.

On the other hand, the concern with the establishment of an autonomous social framework, which is opposed to the situation of colonial subordination is the key to a thought that places what happens internally in the country at its main dynamic center. For this reason, the interpretations of Brazil are marked by the analysis of the structural forms of social production of material life, which are expressed in certain social relations necessary and independent of their will and to which correspond production relations referring to a determined phase of the development of the material productive forces. At the same time, an interpreter cannot fail to realize that a legal, political superstructure and corresponding forms of social conscience are raised on this structure (Marx, [1859] 2008) that necessarily compose your object. Thus, attempts to interpret Brazil will not be able to escape the tricks of its object and will eventually give way, here and there, to dialectics, radicalism and criticism.

As already mentioned, Candido's (1986) cut presents Brazilian radicalism as a set of ideas and attitudes forming a counterweight to the conservative movement that has always prevailed in Brazil. This Brazilian version of radicalism includes the definition of a progressive way of reacting to the stimulation of pressing social problems as opposed to the conservative one.

The radicalism contained in the interpretations of Brazil is revealed in the concern of these authors with the formation of the nation. To understand the nation that was formed here or that could come to be formed it was necessary to be willing to unveil the Brazilian reality and propose an explanation for the economic and social formation that was presented within the borders of the National State. The reality, the material basis, had to be the starting point of these authors and it was.

In this perspective, we chose representative authors from the two generations mentioned to highlight how their thinking can be seen as a carrier of founding elements of Brazilian economic thought.

3   The First Generation of Interpreters: Abolitionists and Workers

Joaquim Nabuco was the most mentioned abolitionist of his time, despite having been part of a much broader movement that had more extreme and more moderate facets than the position he assumed. Born in 1849 in Pernambuco, the following year and site of the Praieira Revolution, the last of the provincial revolts of a liberal character, he was the son of a wealthy family, owner of lands and slaves, and frequented the halls of the court. He was a young man of his time, trained in law within the liberal and Americanist doctrine that attended the debates of his generation. At the Faculty of Law in São Paulo, he was a classmate and debate with Castro Alves, Rui Barbosa, Rodrigues Alves and Afonso Pena. However, he ended up transferring to the Recife Faculty of Law to finish his studies and scandalized the local elite, for defending, in a jury, a black enslaved person who had murdered his master.

Even though he was a darling of the empire's salons, this attitude created great opposition from the local elite to his work and his thinking, only getting a job in 1876, when he was appointed to a diplomatic post through his mother. However, the Brazilian reality movement put him at the center of action in later years when he was elected deputy by the Liberal Party and installed the Brazilian Society Against Slavery in his residence. Thus, he deepened the disagreements with his party and made his reelection impossible. Without a mandate, he spent a season in London, where he wrote *O Abolicionismo* (The Abolitionism) and prepared himself in 1885 to be elected for a new mandate as an abolitionist and federalist monarchist, taking the English liberal model as a political reference.

In *O Abolicionismo*, Nabuco denounces the common sense about slavery in Brazil in the 19th century. He stated that it was found in the newspapers and in the whole society "repeated declarations that slavery among us is a very mild and gentle state for the slave, of a better fact for him than for the master, so happy with the description, that it is assumed that slaves, if consulted, would prefer captivity to freedom; (...)" (Nabuco, [1884] 2012, p. 97) and acidly concluded "(...) which all proves, only, that the newspapers are not written by slaves, nor by people who exist mentally placed, for a second, in their position. " (Nabuco, [1884] 2012, p. 97).

This is the starting point for a reflection that will contribute decisively to the understanding of what a Brazilian nation was and could be marked by the sign of slavery. For Nabuco, a country whose main producers of wealth and the majority of the population was formed by "a class without any right: that of slaves"[8] (Nabuco, [1884] 2012, p. 98) would be doomed to decay.

Their question is that slaves constitute the largest forming group of the Brazilian people and their condition of submission to terror and the lack of any kind of right is as harmful and destructive for themselves as for the formation of the nation. From his point of view, the first "revenge of the victims" of slavery is that the main inhabitants, the future of the Brazilian people, would be composed mostly of descendants of enslaved people,[9] class subjected to brutality. Furthermore, according to Nabuco, slavery was not only harmful to the slave, but also to the masters, who were degraded by the brutalization of their customs in relation to the slaves. In the author's words: the consequence for the formation of the people was "(...) the crossing of the characters of the black race with those of the white race, such as they appear in slavery; the mixture of the servile degradation of one, with the brutal imperiousness of the other" (Nabuco, [1884] 2012, p. 107).

Still, he warned of the fact that the enslaved person was the great supporter of production in Brazil, and not only on farms. It was the enslaved person who took care of the master's family, who taught his children, who transmitted a relevant part of morals and customs to the captives and the free.

The territory also suffered from the slave organization of production, since in this regime the soil was divided into a number of large rural properties.

---

8   Nabuco ([1884] 2012) informs us that there is no mention of enslaved people in any of the nation's codes, whether in the Constitution of 1824 or elsewhere in the legislation. There was not even a slave code. According to Martins (2017), while it is true that there was no slave code that dealt with the administration and treatment of the living conditions of the enslaved population, in Portugal there was ample legislation on this human traffic, including two slave codes linked to this issue, one in the 17th century, and the other in the 19th century. This legal order that aimed to regulate the work under the slave regime in the colony included laws, letters of law, licenses, regiments, statutes, regal letters, decrees, provisions, notices, resolutions, and other pieces about the administration and slave economy of Portugal in the colony.

9   Brazilian interpreters covered in this chapter always use the word slave to refer to an enslaved person. We are in agreement with the current understanding of the condition of enslaved people, not slaves. However, this is not the position of these interpreters, which creates a significant difficulty in expression. Thus, we chose to maintain, in most cases, the reference to slaves, in order to express the position of the interpreters.

These rural properties were characterized as true penal colonies, resistant to progress, stately spaces in which only the will of the landlord prevailed. The problem with this social construction identified by Nabuco is that this structure is maintained by dependence and that is why it cannot seek to progress or benefit the free population that lives in it at the risk of destroying its social base. Thus, the territory tends to create isolated and self-sufficient formations at a very basic subsistence level, with local decentralized power and refractory to the functioning and norms of the National State. In this way, a nation is created which lacks local centers and cities, with a dullness of commerce and liberal professions and with no room for the middle classes.

Joining these factors in his analysis, the abolitionist points to a synthesis about the economy of a slave country, stating that "(...) the end result of that [slave system] is the country's poverty and misery. Nor is it any wonder that soil cultivation by a class with no interest in the work that is extorted gives these results" (Nabuco, [1884] 2012, p. 116).

Thus, we can affirm that Nabuco contributes and influences Brazilian economic thought insofar as he identifies in the form of the organization of work the source of the problems and the possibilities for improving the social and economic formation of Brazil.

Euclides da Cunha represents a second phase of this first generation: the republican phase. If Nabuco was concerned with modifying the bases of the monarchy he defended, Euclides sought to build the arguments for support of the new republican order of the nation.

Euclides is a character full of contrasts and contradictions, but undoubtedly an authentic republican. He was born in 1866, in the Province of Rio de Janeiro and was orphaned at the age of 3, having been raised by his aunts. He studied at S. Fidelis, then in Bahia and finally in Rio de Janeiro until in 1886 he took exams at the Escola Politécnica, but he abandoned the course a year later, moving to the Military School. The Military School was, at the time, a radiating pole of republican ideas, marking the influence of Benjamin Constant, positivist and who would become one of the leaders of the Proclamation of the Republic, in his thought. His adherence to republican and anti-slavery ideas led him to star in an episode that ended up marking his life and giving him fame. To prevent the cadets from participating in a demonstration of support for Lopes Trovão, notorious republican returning from Europe, an inspection of the troops was scheduled by the Minister of War, Tomás Coelho. During the inspection, Euclides went out of shape, tried to break the marlin and threw it at the Minister's feet, disrespecting him. An attempt was made to cover up what had happened, but Euclid was dismissed from the army in December 1888, on the grounds of physical disability. However, famous for the marlin episode, he was invited by Júlio de Mesquita, still in 1888, to write in O Estado de São Paulo (at the time – The Province of São Paulo) where he started to openly defend republican ideas. With the proclamation of the Republic, he was amnestied, reinstated to the Military School (in his class) and formed an officer in 1896, he definitively left the Army and went to work as a civil engineer in São Paulo when the Canudos War broke out, which changed his life again, as he left for Bahia the following year, as special envoy of the newspaper O Estado de S. Paulo.

His view was strongly influenced by the science of his day, but it carried a contradiction. The science he knew was highly justifying, ultimately, the colonial enterprise and the exploitation of the peoples of the periphery, presented the concepts of climate and race to affirm the superiority of the countries of the capitalist center over the rest of the world and affirmed that the climate of the tropics would never allow modern forms of social, economic or political organization. On the other hand, his personal and historical experience made him not accept these ideas entirely, even though he did not have the instruments to criticize or overcome them. Nelson Werneck Sodré even observes on this theme that "there is a singular dualism in Euclides" (Sodré, 1961, p. 142), which distances his testimony from his reflection.

It is possible to perceive this dualism in the lines of Os Sertões. If his work is organized within the framework of Von Martius' theory of history (race, environment and historical moment as determinants of the movement of history), his solution for overcoming the problems he identifies in contemporary Brazil is linked to a view that the Brazilian mestizo conceived in the climate of the sertão is the national hero.

The sertanejo of Euclides represents the sector of the working class that finds no place in the central production of its time. His mode of social production of life appears as a form of resistance to the limits of the climate and society that put him in a situation of permanent expropriation. His description of the current society in Canudos mixes horror with the barbaric form of sociability with an admiration for its potential to create life from hostile conditions. Canudos-type social organizations would be forms of resistance to the purge of the central production sector.

Contradictions aside, Euclides ends up directing his analysis to affirm that a nation effectively Brazilian and capable of carrying out an autonomous national project would have to originate in the backcountry population. From his point of view, social organizations of the type found on the coast were limited to copying European forms, with the country destined for permanent submission.

Unlike Nabuco, with its liberal vision of society and progress, the nation of Euclides could not come from outside, or from copyist sectors located on the coast, it would have to organize itself based on the resistance production of the sertanejo.

4 The Second Generation (1920s/30s): Demiurges and the Centrality of Social Relations of Production

The next generation will discuss republican Brazil, which, influenced by the recent First World War and the crisis of 1929, begins to organize small manufactures of workers' goods production around the cities of the Republic, such as textiles, processed foods and potteries. The discussion of interpreters of this period already gains the dynamics of what Francisco de Oliveira and Antonio Candido ended up calling demiurges of Brazil (Candido, 1967). The idea of demiurges considers that these authors would be discussing a new Brazil, which intended to be on the route of becoming a mostly urban and industrial country.

The triad traditionally chosen to represent the interpreters of this generation is Gilberto Freyre ([1933] 2000), Sérgio Buarque de Holanda ([1936] 2011) and Caio Prado Júnior ([1933] 2007; [1942] 2000). These authors have in common the choice of a starting point to seek to understand Brazil: Portuguese colonization. None of them will look for the origins of Brazil in the original peoples existing in the territory when the Portuguese arrived. This option reveals a specific understanding of what should be considered as the origin of Brazil: Portuguese occupation in the tropics, be it "cordial", as Sérgio Buarque wants, be it exploratory as Caio Prado points out.

The present is described by each of these interpreters as a moment of crisis, already quite different from Brazil at the time of Portuguese colonization. Gilberto Freyre ([1933] 2000) speaks of a patriarchal nation threatened because of a "re-Europeanization" of the country, an attempt to import the social and political forms prevailing in Europe at the beginning of the 20th century and which did not correspond to the historical process experienced by Brazil. Sérgio Buarque ([1936] 2011) describes a country in crisis because it is in contradiction between what it is and what needs to be. The Brazil of Buarque de Holanda is a territory of exile from the European that is constituted here as a cordial man and is organized by personalism, patriarchalism and authoritarianism, but that needs to become a democracy. Caio Prado also says something different about the crisis that he also identifies in the present of the country.

He indicates a disagreement between the economic system bequeathed by the colony and the new need for a free and politically emancipated nation, a real contradiction between the degree of development of the productive forces and the social relations of production.

Even more interesting is the future imagined by these authors as the true Brazilian nation. Gilberto Freyre ([1933] 2000) points out that the revelation of the true Brazil is in place. It would be patriarchal society to be recovered from our colonial origins, already adapted by the time of relationship between the various races in the form of social production of life in Brazil. Such a process, according to Freyre, would occur in an original way and different from the European one. Sérgio Buarque de Holanda looks at the past in a very similar way to Freyre. His cordial man has several points of contact with the lord of the Big House (Casa Grande) of Freyre. However, he affirms that there is no burden in losing Brazil's roots so that this country can constitute itself as a truly national democratic space. Because, in his conception, the space of the nation's creative democratic policy would be urban and public, which do not derive from the roots identified by him. Caio Prado, in turn, radicalizes the idea that there is no nation in Brazil. His point is that the country's future needs to be democratic and national, and it is necessary to make a Brazilian revolution to constitute the nation, which would not exist because we organized all the country's organic life turned outwards.

From our point of view, this generation contributes to the Brazilian economic thought insofar as it gives centrality to the history and social relations that were established in the midst of the country's productive organization for its understanding.

Casa Grande e Senzala: formação da família brasileira sob regime da economia patriarcal (*Casa Grande and Senzala: formation of the Brazilian family under the patriarchal economy*) carries in its title the cut that we have mentioned. The social spaces indicated in the title are the living spaces of the private in the class structure established by the form of production developed in Brazil. Despite a greater interest in detailing the relationships developed within the family, Freyre's work opens a new path in Brazilian historiography. Because until then the history of most peoples was limited to grandiose episodes: it was a chronological record of wars and coronations, acts of heroism and rebellion, illustrated with monuments, equestrian statues and decorations. This new path places the people as the actor of history and sets history in motion from the usual way of producing and reproducing material life.

Freyre was part of an intellectual movement that, based on the work of Franz Boas, vehemently criticized biological and geographical determinisms, in addition to the belief in cultural evolutionism. Boas pointed out that each culture is an integrated unit, the result of a peculiar historical development. He emphasized the independence of cultural phenomena in relation to geographical conditions and biological determinants, stating that the dynamics of culture are in the interaction between individuals and society. Freyre, then, proposes to replace the concept of race with the concept of culture. However, it ends up falling into a neolamarkianism[10] in which the races change when adapting to the environment (especially the climate), which put it in the field of tropicology for some time.

Another very interesting point in Freyre's project that begins with *Casa Grande & Senzala* (Freyre, [1933] 2000) is the use of antagonistic pairs to understand Brazilian dynamics. Big house and slave quarters; European culture and indigenous culture; European culture and African culture; the Jesuit and the farmer; agrarian and pastoral economics; the master and the slave are examples of the antagonistic pairs that give the dynamics of their argument. However, its synthetic presentation is not exactly a unit of opposites, but a balance established between these opposites, a synthesis in docility accompanied by command. These would be "two fraternizing halves that have been mutually enriching each other from different values and experiences", albeit through descriptions of sadism, sexual violence and submission. It is in this context that miscegenation appears as a solution for the harmonious integration of opposites in Brazil, as an intercultural encounter in the tropics. It is the encounter between the Portuguese, seen as a plastic and accommodating, a person without absolute ideas or uncompromising prejudices, and the enslaved African people. This encounter made possible by what Freyre imagines to be the specificity of Brazilian slavery, which, despite being violent, would admit proximity and reciprocal influence. However, this is a meeting between dominant and dominated, full of perversion and sadism, in which equality is never present.

It is from this process of balance through domination that Freyre removes what he considers to be the singularity of Brazilian social formation: the patriarchal family. The main reference of the Brazilian social organization, as described by Freyre ([1933] 2000), is the productive unit of the farm, a great producer of social wealth. Thus, the patriarchal family and their farm form the social cell of Brazil. From his point of view, there is an extraordinary influence of the family in the Brazilian social organization, since it brought together all dimensions of society, given the distance from the Portuguese State. At the

---

10   Neolamarkian notion of race: characters acquired by beings when adapting to the environment define their race.

same time, it indicates that there is a permanent Brazilian cultural "ambiguity" due to the clash between patriarchal tradition (16th, 17th and 18th centuries) and the process of westernization influenced by "bourgeois" Europe (19th century).

Sérgio Buarque de Holanda has a different contribution. As we have already said, in the 1930s he was already a critical modernist. So critical that he had been dismissed even by modernists since the publication of his text *O lado oposto e os outros lados (The opposite side and the other sides)*, in 1926. In the 1930s he went to Berlin where he got in touch with the sociology taught and discussed in Germany at the time – Max Weber, Georg Simmel, Wilhelm Dilthey, Karl Mannheim, György Lukács, Croce, Vico, Krakauer, Sombart, among others. It is in Germany that he writes the texts that would be published as *Raízes do Brasil* in 1936. For Antonio Candido, Sérgio Buarque has:

> The only explanation of Brazil at that time composed in function of the present. (...) the reference to the present was guided by an acute perception of Latin American dialectic in general, Brazilian in particular, of insubordination and submission, the political consequence of which is the game of authoritarianism and a libertarian outbreak.
>
> CANDIDO, 2008, p. 35

Teixeira (2002) points out that the work of interpreting Brazil by Sérgio Buarque in the 1930s can be seen as "half German", as it is nourished by a diffuse Hegelianism and a strong influence of the German historical school. The authors of this tradition were critical of English liberalism; they fought for social reform, although, theoretically, they were averse to recipes (typical of the liberalism they criticize); they rejected broad generalizations, peculiar to all philosophies of history: "the very idea of a simple theory of historical evolution seemed to them to be erroneous and unscientific" (Teixeira, 2002, p. 65); they criticized insulating analyzes of economic phenomena, believing that their essence was lost when we isolated them.

The roots of *Raízes do Brasil* are to assess the difficulties and possibilities of establishing democracy in Brazil. As already noted, Buarque de Holanda ([1936] 2011) starts with Portuguese colonization, however, he does not shy away from characterizing Portuguese as a socially plastic man and Portugal as a nation between Europe and Africa. He points out that the success of Portuguese colonization in the tropics is related to its neglect, the willingness to be confused with the landscape lines, at the same time that it does not aim to create anything here, just to explore it commercially. Colonization is still characterized as being based on the culture of personality, in which aristocratic ethics of little value to work created the difficulty of making associations and solidarity avenge, determining a prevalence of private space over the public. Such hypertrophy of the domestic environment would imply a rural legacy in an authoritarian political form. This political form would have in its origin the "nature" of the Brazilian people: cordiality. The sense of this cordiality is normative, it implies that Brazilians obey the imperative of the heart and not abstract impersonal norms, making democracy in Brazil "a misunderstanding" (Holanda, [1936] 2011, p. 113), since the fundamental liberal principle that everyone is equal before the law is subordinated to personal ties of private origin.

Thus, the author's interpretation appears as a counterpoint to the conservative views of Oliveira Vianna ([1920] 2000) and Gilberto Freyre ([1933] 2000), whose valorization of the Iberian heritage is notorious. For Sérgio Buarque ([1936] 2011), our revolution, which would be ongoing and would be slow and gradual, was the liberation of Iberian roots: opening space for democratic social organizations with new content, different from European ones.

The interpreter's great formulation is that Brazil is not his roots. Brazil is a place of exile: a project for the future with no past or present, with a people in eternal movement indicating that our identity is projected in a future that we still do not know what it is.

However, Teixeira (2002) makes us realize that exactly what gives strength to the interpretation of Holanda to renew the trajectory of his activity is also the origin of its limits.

> Its method will always be that of the composition of totalizing panels, in which the singularity of the contemplated phenomena does not allow the generalization of the laws of motion; his vision of the present will never be presented clearly and his proposal for the future will never take concrete forms, since it supposes an abstract and virtual state seen as the realization of freedom; its dialectic will never cease to be the dialectic of reason."
>
> TEIXEIRA, 2002, p. 68

We can now say that Sérgio Buarque de Holanda influences Brazilian economic thought as it opens space for the perception of Brazil as a new social formation, not identifiable with the European one, despite being heir and submitted to it. It affirms our social relations of production as specific and the need to constitute them as a delimited object and to be analyzed with its own method. Such stance has a strong reverberation in the understanding, for example, of Brazil as an underdeveloped structure, dependent on central capitalism, but with its own history and formation in this context and not as a simple reflection of the European economy and social formations.

However, the deepest influences of interpreters of Brazil on Brazilian economic thought need to be recovered in Caio Prado Junior's thought. *Evolução Política do Brasil (Political Evolution of Brazil)* (1933), his first intervention text in the debate, in the 1930s, already contained the elements that developed in the dominant historical interpretation of Brazilian colonization.

Caio Prado Júnior (1907–1990) was the son of the São Paulo coffee bourgeoisie, the Silva Prado, receiving all the creation and education of his social class at the time. However, his political and intellectual trajectory comes from Marxism and militancy in the Brazilian Communist Party (PCB), to which he joined in 1931 and remains linked to the party throughout almost his entire life, although in a good part of his trajectory in the party was a dissonant voice of the hegemonic line. Strongly influenced by the political, intellectual and cultural effervescence of the 1920s and 1930s, he studied law at the traditional Faculty of Largo do São Francisco, between 1924 and 1928, when he began his direct political activities.

In 1928 he joined the Democratic Party (PD), a liberal-oriented party. The PD and Caio Prado Júnior opposed Júlio Prestes and supported the candidacy of Getúlio Vargas in the presidential elections of 1930. There was a suspicion that the elections had been rigged, in order to put Júlio Prestes as victor, Caio Prado Junior supports[11]the armed movement to challenge the results of the 1930 elections that brought Vargas to power. But soon he became disillusioned with the direction of the movement and the government, he started to adopt a more critical and radical posture, when he joined the PCB.

Throughout the 1930s, after the publication of *Evolução Política do Brasil*, approaches history and geography, participating in classes in these areas at the University of São Paulo (USP), at the time, recently founded. These areas that will strongly mark your reflections on Brazil. At this time, he also assumed the position of vice president of the São Paulo section of the Aliança Nacional Libertadora (ANL) and participated in the organization in an intense manner, being one of the main articulators of the ANL in the State of São Paulo. Soon the ANL is made illegal and undone, its main activists, including Caio Prado Júnior, are arrested. Caio Prado remains in prison for two years and after his release, he went into exile in France between 1937 and 1939, where he began to write his most emblematic work regarding his interpretation of Brazil,

---

11   In this period, Caio Prado Júnior is arrested for the first time. Throughout his life, because of his political activism, he will be arrested many more times. See Pericás (2016).

Formação do Brasil Contemporâneo: colônia (Formation of Contemporary Brazil: colony) (1942). Studying at the Sorbonne, approaches the French Communist Party and participates in anti-fascist movements in the context of the Spanish Civil War. Upon his return to Brazil, he published the book in 1942 and in the same year, he founded Editora Brasiliense, which will be of great importance to the left and to critical intellectuals, especially Marxists and Communists. In this return to Brazil, he also returned to political militancy, in a delicate context, since the PCB was illegal during the dictatorship of the Estado Novo.

Many of Caio Prado Júnior's theses are so widespread that almost nobody else knows that he was the author. It is rare to find someone who is still researching the economic history of Brazil and thinks that there was a feudal past in the country. At the same time, everyone perceives Brazilian colonization not as something particular, but in the context of European maritime expansion. However, few know that both notions were formulated by Caio Prado Júnior.

In his day, these theses were warmly received: within his party, the Brazilian Communist Party, there were those who claimed that "to deny feudal remains without proving ... is a clear manifestation of what can be called foreign ideology to the proletariat infiltrated in the party" (Martins, 1947). However, the question in Caio Prado was methodological. He did not see historical materialism as a set of formulas with supposed universal value and he did not accept the theses of the 3rd International for the "colonial, semi-colonial and dependent countries" transmitted from Moscow to the South American Bureau of the Communist International (located in Montevideo) and radiated from there as a single model, recommending to everyone the creation of the conditions for the realization of a bourgeois revolution. However, he was never a relativist or theoretical adaptationist, "Because if your Marxism were able to absorb any form referring to the most varied societies, it would no longer be Marxism, not even theory, but just an almost unmediated expression of reality" (Ricupero, 2009, p.230). Thus, Caio Prado Júnior does not fail to affirm Marxism as a method for the interpretation of different historical experiences. It carries out the Brazilianization of Marxism, the translation of this theory to the conditions of the Brazilian reality.

It is from this interpretation of Brazil, under the baton of Marxism, that Prado Júnior places the centrality of his research in the relationship between colony and nation. Thus, one of its main axes of discussion is the transition between the colonial situation and the national situation. For that, it was necessary to diagnose the colonial situation. Caio Prado sees Brazil Colony formed in the context of the European overseas expansion, being an exploration colony. Such colonies would feature the monoculture production of high-value goods on the foreign market, productive organization in large units (large properties) and the predominant use of slave labor. The meaning of Brazilian colonization would be large-scale production of tropical genera for the world market, as presented in *Formação do Brasil Contemporâneo*.

This economic structure would have strong consequences for Brazil, since society and the economy were organized based on this external objective and were unaware of the needs of the population. The men and the few women who came here from the metropolis would be moved only by mercantile considerations, they would not think of creating society here. They would be those who wanted, above all, to be leaders and not "mere" workers.

It is from this assessment of the Brazilian historical reality that Caio Prado proposes that the exploration colonies were reduced to a "vast commercial enterprise", with an almost total absence of superstructure: slavery was based on relations of power. Recalling Joaquim Nabuco's study, Caio Prado states that in fact there was no law that spoke of slaves. There was simply no reference by the State to the existence of slaves. There was not even a slave code that dealt with the administration and treatment of the living conditions of the population in conditions of slavery. However, according to Martins (2017), there was a broad legal system in Portugal that aimed to regulate the work of the slave regime in the colony and economic issues, especially fiscal, linked to the exploitation of slavery.

Thus, the organic life of the colony was linked to the great exploitation that produced the goods demanded by the foreign market. As the needs of the population were ignored for this purpose, the consumption of this population was met by the inorganic sector. The inorganic sector was one that did not belong to the great exploration and it had a subordinate role.

The colonial social structure reflected this division of the colony's organic sector: rural masters and slaves. However, over time, the number of those whose marshy social situation is increasing, the "disqualified", those who have no place in this social division. It is in this growing social group that Caio Prado places his hopes for transformation. For him it is this social group that points to the orientation that the Brazilian nation must follow in the future.

As we have already stated, the concept of nation is central to the research of the São Paulo historian. In its conception, the nation to exist must attend to the internal needs of the population. However, he realized that Brazil had enormous difficulties in establishing itself as a nation because even after independence, the main orientation of Brazilian life continued to be turned outward. Even so, it highlights the fact that the formation of the National State marks a new phase in Brazilian history.

In Caio Prado's formulation, the transformation movement would come from the fundamental contradiction present in Brazil of his time: a disagreement between the economic system bequeathed by the colony and the new needs of a free and politically emancipated nation. It was the contradiction between the economic structure and the political-legal organization copied from the liberal States of the capitalist center.

From our point of view, Caio Prado's interpretation of Brazil leaves, in addition to a whole new perspective on economic history, two great legacies for Brazilian economic thought. The first refers to his view on the continuity with the past, present in Brazilian agrarian structures and in the slaveholdings in social relations of production. On the other hand, it revealed the need to think of Brazil as part of a global system and not be in search of the country's idiosyncrasies and individualities, a predominant movement of Brazil's interpretations until then.

5   Conclusion

The purpose of this text was to highlight the thought of interpreters of Brazil, from the two generations analyzed (late 19th century and 1920s/30s), the most important elements that had influenced the origin of Brazilian economic thought.

In this sense, we sought to emphasize how some of the authors of these two generations emphasized the issues of the productive structure, that is, the issues of production and the structural and super-structural social relations related to it. In this way, such interpretations deal with themes from the field of economics, and, in particular, from political economy, even before there is a formalization of knowledge in this area in Brazil. The ways in which these interpretations were constructed varied in the different historical moments in which the authors carried out their analyzes, as well as they varied from a theoretical point of view, but all put their interpretations from a historical perspective and from the Brazilian economic-social structure.

The authors of the first generation built their analysis against the backdrop of the process of transition from the structure of the slavery empire to republican Brazil, in which there would be changes in the forms of work organization and the social relations of production. Joaquim Nabuco organized his

interpretation based on issues related to the work process and the constitution of the Brazilian people, based on the notion that slaves constituted the
largest class that formed the people in Brazil and that the problems related
to their conditions of submission and absence rights would be problematic
issues not only for enslaved people, but for the formation of the nation as
a whole. Thus, in his analysis, any possibility of changes in the process of
economic and social formation in Brazil would have to undergo profound
changes in the form of work organization, as well as in the superstructural elements of this nation, which are linked to the economic structure. Euclides, on
the other hand, went further, stating that it was not enough to overcome the
slave form, but it was necessary to define a form of production and sociability
that effectively corresponded to the Brazilian reality, which, as in Canudos,
was characterized by being a form of resistance. In his work he highlights the
sertanejo as the historical character capable of carrying the formation of the
autonomous nation.

The second generation analyzed in the text starts from the attempt to
understand the Brazilian economic and social formation from the process,
which started in that period, of transition from an agrarian-exporting society
to an urban-industrial society. In the three authors considered emblematic,
three different ways of analyzing this process can be highlighted, both from
the theoretical, political and ideological points of view. But there are common
elements in their interpretations: in the three there is the centrality of the
analysis in the pattern of Brazilian social formation, as well as the diagnosis of
detachment, in that period, between the productive structure actually existing
in Brazil and the institutional forms in force here.

It is possible to highlight, synthetically, from the interpretations of these
authors some elements that have articulation with the Brazilian economic
thought: Gilberto Freyre organizes his interpretation around the analysis of
the articulation between the organization of private spaces (the patriarchal
family, which is the basis of his characterization of Brazil) with the class structure established from the existing form of production in Brazil. Sérgio Buarque
de Holanda, in turn, contributes with the perception that Brazil is constituted
as a new social formation, even if submitted to the European one, stating that
the social relations of production that exist here are specific and that they
must be analyzed based on own method. Lastly, Caio Prado Júnior is one of
the first authors to use the Marxist analytical framework to analyze the situation in Brazil. In addition, it has a wide influence on the construction of
Brazilian economic thought, with some of its formulations considered pillars
of the analysis of the historical process of the Brazilian economy. We highlight

as main contributions his notion about the continuity in the contemporaneity of the past existing in agrarian structures in Brazil and the perception of the importance of analyzing Brazil as an integral part of a world system, to the detriment of the previously prevalent notion of analysis of the formation process only from its internal movement.

In short, our research sought to find in these authors the discussions of the Brazilian economic and social structures that gain centrality in their views on Brazil and that give rise to the field of reflection that will be taken over by Brazilian economic thought.

As stated by Lapa (1980), to analyze the Brazilian economic thought engendered by this debate, we need to go through several elements,

> [...] the fierce discussions about the land structure, land rent and agricultural profit, the role of the State, the nature of production relations, the performance of productive forces, the expropriation of direct producers, the form of ownership (the landowner and the capitalist), the elusive accumulation processes, the origin and/or destination of surpluses, the character and dynamics of capital, the extent of its domination, the process and conditions of the organization of work, and so on aside, if we want to stay at the economic-social level, they have taken us to more refined theoretical exercises to adjust them to our conceptual conceptions and/or to empirical investigations – macro or microeconomic – aiming to surprise concrete data that lead us to the reworking of those conceptions."
>
> LAPA, 1980, p. 20

We therefore propose that to continue this research and to understand the work of interpreters of Brazil, seeking to access the economic elements of their thinking, it would be a good method to delve into their texts, under the inspiration of Candido (1986), seeking to find:

a)   Their view on population;
b)   The way they look at work;
c)   The way they describe the oligarchy;
d)   Their way of evaluating imperialism;
e)   The way they think about production;
f)   And his conception of the structure of society

We imagine that these would be good keys to access the Brazilian economic thought contained in the interpretations of Brazil and we intend to explore them.

Bibliographic References

Botelho, André. Prefácio: Intérpretes do Brasil, nossos antepassados? *In*: Ricupero, Bernardo. Sete lições sobre as interpretações do Brasil. São Paulo: Alameda, 2008, p. 7–18.

Buarque De Holanda, Sérgio. Raízes do Brasil. 26ª edição, 36ª reimpressão. São Paulo: Companhia das Letras, [1936] 2011.

Buarque De Holanda, Sérgio. Ariel. *In:* Revista do Brasil, n°53, São Paulo, 1920. (Mais recentemente republicado em BARBOSA, Francisco de Assis (org.). Raízes de Sérgio Buarque de Holanda. Rio de Janeiro: Rocco, 1989).

Buarque De Holanda, Sérgio. O lado oposto e os outros lados. *In:* Revista do Brasil, Rio de Janeiro, 1926. (Mais recentemente republicado em BARBOSA, Francisco de Assis (org.). Raízes de Sérgio Buarque de Holanda, Rio de Janeiro: Rocco, 1989).

Candido, Antonio. O significado de raízes do Brasil. *In* Buarque De Holanda, Sérgio. Raízes do Brasil. São Paulo: Companhia das Letras, [1967] 2011.

Candido, Antonio Radicalismos. *In:* Estudos Avançados 4 (8), 1986, p. 4–18.

Candido, Antonio. "A visão política de Sérgio Buarque de Holanda". In: Monteiro, Pedro M. & Eugênio, João Kennedy (orgs.). Sérgio Buarque de Holanda: perspectivas. Campinas, SP: Editora da Unicamp; Rio de Janeiro, RJ: EdUERJ, 2008.

Coutinho, Carlos Nelson. "A imagem do Brasil na obra de Caio Prado Júnior". In: Coutinho, Carlos Nelson. Cultura e Sociedade no Brasil – ensaios sobre ideias e formas. 4ª edição. São Paulo: Expressão Popular, [1988] 2011, p. 219–241.

Cunha, Euclides. Os Sertões, Coleção Intérpretes do Brasil, Rio de Janeiro: Nova Aguillar, [1902] 2000.

Curty, Carla; Malta, Maria. Methodological elements for the organization of the history of Brazilian economic thought: the approach of controversies. In: Malta, Maria; León, Jaime; Curty, Carla; Borja, Bruno (eds.). Controversies on history, development and revolution in Brazil: economic thought in critical interpretation. In this book, 2021.

Faoro, Raymundo. Existe um pensamento político Brasileiro? São Paulo: Editora Ática, 1994.

Fernandes, Florestan. A revolução burguesa no Brasil: Ensaio de Interpretação sociológica. 5ª edição, São Paulo: Globo, [1975] 2005.

Freyre, Gilberto. Casa Grande & Senzala. Coleção Intérpretes do Brasil, Rio de Janeiro: Nova Aguillar, [1933] 2000.

Furtado, Celso. Formação Econômica do Brasil. São Paulo: Companhia das Letras, [1959] 2006.

Hobsbawm, Eric. O presente como história: escrever a história do seu próprio tempo. Novos Estudos Cebrap n° 43, 1995.

Iglésias, Francisco. Celso Furtado, pensamento e ação. *In*: Iglésias, Francisco. História e Ideologia. São Paulo: Perspectiva, 1982.

Lapa, José Roberto do Amaral. Introdução ao redimensionamento do debate. *In*: Lapa, José Roberto do Amaral (org.) Modos de produção e realidade brasileira. Petrópolis: Vozes, 1980, p. 9–42.

Lima, Nisia Trindade. Euclides da Cunha: O Brasil como sertão. *In*: Botelho, André; Schwarcz, Lilia. Um enigma chamado Brasil: 29 intérpretes e um país, São Paulo: Companhia das Letras, 2009, p. 104–117.

Martins, Ivan. Sobre o camarada Caio Prado Júnior. *In*: A classe operária, 4/5/1947, p.3.

Martins, Roberto Borges. A obsessão com o tráfico, a legislação escravista e os códigos negreiros portugueses. *In*: Anais do XII Congresso Brasileiro de História Econômica & 13ª Conferência Internacional de História de Empresas. Niterói: UFF/ABPHE, 2017.

Marx, Karl. Contribuição à crítica da economia política. São Paulo: Editora Expressão Popular, [1859] 2008.

Mattos, Marcelo Badaró. Trabalhadores e sindicatos no Brasil. São Paulo: Expressão Popular, 2009.

Nabuco, Joaquim. O Abolicionismo. Petrópolis: Vozes, [1884] 2012.

Pericás, Luiz Bernardo. Caio Prado Júnior: uma biografia política. São Paulo: Boitempo Editorial, 2016.

Pinheiro, Filipe Leite. Revisiting the origins of the controversy on the Brazilian revolution: a debate between Octavio Brandão, Mario Pedrosa and Lívio Xavier. In: Malta, Maria; León, Jaime; Curty, Carla; Borja, Bruno (eds.). Controversies on history, development and revolution in Brazil: economic thought in critical interpretation. In this book, 2021.

Prado Júnior, Caio. Evolução Política do Brasil. São Paulo: Brasiliense, [1933] 2007.

Prado Júnior, Caio. Formação do Brasil Contemporâneo, Coleção Intérpretes do Brasil, Rio de Janeiro: Nova Aguillar, [1942] 2000.

Ricupero, Bernardo. Celso Furtado e o Pensamento Social Brasileiro. Estudos Avançados 19 (53), 2005, 371–377.

Ricupero, Bernardo. Sete lições sobre as interpretações do Brasil. São Paulo: Alameda, 2008.

Ricupero, Bernardo. Caio Prado Júnior e o lugar o Brasil no mundo. *In*: Botelho, André; Schwarcz, Lilia. Um enigma chamado Brasil: 29 interpretações e um país. São Paulo: Companhia das Letras, 2009, p. 226–239.

Santos, Wanderley Guilherme. Ordem burguesa e liberalismo político, São Paulo: Livraria Duas Cidades, 1978.

Schwarz, Roberto. Ao vencedor as batatas. São Paulo: Livraria Duas Cidades, 1977.

Sodré, Nelson Werneck. A Ideologia do Colonialismo. Rio de Janeiro: ISEB, 1961.

Szmrecsányi, Tamaz. Sobre a Formação da *Formação Econômica do Brasil* de C. Furtado. Estudos Avançados 13 (37), 1999, 207–214.

Teixeira, Aloisio. Raízes do Brasil: o lado oposto e os outros lados, Revista Tempo Brasileiro, n. 149, Repensando o Brasil com Sérgio Buarque de Holanda, Rio de Janeiro: Edições Tempo Brasileiro, 2002, p. 55–73.

Vianna, Oliveira. Populações Meridionais do Brasil, Coleção Intérpretes do Brasil, Rio de Janeiro: Nova Aguillar, (1920) 2000.

CHAPTER 3

Controversy on the Economic History of Brazil

Roberto Simonsen, Caio Prado Jr. and Celso Furtado

Bruno Borja

1 Introduction

Brazilian thought has a fundamental milestone in the historical transition from an agrarian-exporting to an urban-industrial country throughout the first half of the 20th century, having the 1930s as a point of reference. The social studies of this time express this transition of society and are bearers of this particularity, being influenced by the theories widespread in the world. The authors of these studies can be understood as interpreters of Brazil, placing the formation of the nation in a historical perspective. By capturing the sense of formation of the past, analyzing the present situation and presenting a political program for the future, they construct an interpretation of Brazil.

In these studies, it is worth highlighting research on the economic history of Brazil, or its economic formation. These are works that form the basis of Brazilian economic historiography, dictating the direction of research in the area (Freitas Filho, 1988; Szmrecsányi, 2004; Saes, 2009). Between 1930 and 1960, this economic thought was formed, with emphasis on three exponents: Roberto Simonsen, Caio Prado Jr and Celso Furtado. To present this pioneering debate in terms of the controversy of economic history, means to emphasize that each of the authors has their own theoretical perspective, with different worldviews.

Simonsen adopts an interpretation based on the analysis of production cycles, supported by the worldview of the rising industrial bourgeoisie. Caio Prado adheres to historical materialism, to make a Marxist interpretation of Brazilian history, from a world view attentive to the issues of the working class. Furtado inaugurated Latin American structuralism in the country, building an interpretation of Brazil based on the historical-structural method, with a petty-bourgeois worldview and social insertion in state bureaucracy and international institutions.

These authors will present different answers to common questions at the time, among which perhaps the main one is: why did Brazil and the United

States take such different courses? If both had a common historical origin in European colonization, what would be the reason for the USA to establish itself as the main industrial nation of the 20th century, while Brazil was a backward, underdeveloped and dependent area? How could that be changed? To understand these issues, interpretations of Brazil of the period are produced, consolidating Brazilian economic historiography.

2 Roberto Simonsen: Interpretation of Production Cycles

Roberto Cochrane Simonsen (1889–1948) is recognized as one of the largest Brazilian industrialists. In general, accredited as a "nationalist and progressive industrialist" and "great ideologue of developmentalism" (Bielschowsky, 2000). However, it is not with the industry that its professional and political trajectory begins. Born in an influential family of English origin, with an active participation in the business and politics of the empire and the first republic, Simonsen started his business with coffee production for export.

After graduating as an engineer at the Polytechnic School of São Paulo, he worked at the Southern Brazil Railway and, in 1911, he served as the general director of works for the Santos City Hall. Leaving the city hall, the following year, he founded the *Companhia Construtora de Santos* and the *Companhia Santista de Habitações Econômicas*, companies designed to carry out the urbanization of the then largest Brazilian port area, the exit point for more than half of the coffee exported by the country.

The 1920s would be a landmark of its industrial activities, founding several companies, but without losing connection with the export, associating with the Commissioner Murray Simonsen Co. and the English bank Lazard Brothers, financiers of the Coffee Institute (Carone, 1973). In 1928, already recognized as an industrial leader, he participates in the spin-off of the São Paulo Commercial Association that gave rise to the São Paulo State Center for Industries (Ciesp), being its vice-president. This does not prevent him from trying to reconcile industrial and agro-export interests, seeking support from coffee growers, who dominated the policy of the first republic.

The New York stock market crash in October 1929 and the 1930 movement would represent an inflection in Brazilian history, and Simonsen took a stand. At first, he joined forces with the São Paulo ruling classes against Getúlio Vargas, including being arrested after the fall of Washington Luís. Persecuted by the provisional government, he was an active part of the industrial mobilization in the so-called Constitutionalist Revolution of 1932.[1] Elected deputy by the Constitutionalist Party of São Paulo to the National Constituent Assembly in 1933, he never left political life.

Also in 1933, he participated in the founding of the Free School of Sociology and Politics, a class project for the formation of the ruling elites of São Paulo. In 1935 he assumed the presidency of the Industrial Confederation of Brazil (future National Confederation of Industry – cni). And, having defined Vargas' industrialist stance, he approaches the government, supporting the coup that would institute the dictatorship in 1937. He was president of the Federation of Industries of the State of São Paulo (Fiesp) throughout the Estado Novo, creating the National Service of Industrial Apprenticeship (Senai) and the Social Service of Industry (Sesi). It takes part in various organs of centralization of national policy created by Vargas, such as the National Council for Industrial and Commercial Policy, linked to the Ministry of Labor, Industry and Commerce. In this context, he engaged with Eugênio Gudin in the precursor debate of economic planning in Brazil in 1944 and 1945 (Teixeira; Gentil, 2010).

It was at the School of Sociology and Politics of São Paulo that he developed his most important intellectual work: *História Econômica do Brasil* (Economic History of Brazil), published in 1937. The school was a pioneer in Brazil by including this subject in its curriculum and Simonsen was the full professor. An interpretation of the colonial economy, approached from the perspective of the production cycles, contextualizing the different international moments and comparing the Brazilian trajectory with the other colonies of America.

Simonsen shared the political desires and aspirations of the nascent São Paulo industrial bourgeoisie, and his work at school sought to create and legitimize this ideology. Intention made explicit by the author in the first paragraph of the introduction:

> At the beginning of 1933, in a troubled phase of São Paulo life, a considerable number of intellectuals launched, in this city, a manifesto, which will become memorable with the passage of time. In that document, they demonstrated that having not been able to see their point of view triumphant by force of arms, they understood, more than ever, the profound disharmony between our aspirations and the country's political-economic-social reality. They preached the urgent need to create schools for the formation of "elites", in which the notions of politics, sociology

---

1   Uprising in arms that occurred in the State of São Paulo against the provisional government of Getúlio Vargas.

and economics were disseminated, awakening and creating a national conscience, capable of guiding public administration, according to the reality of our environment, thus contributing to put an end, within Brazil, to the reigning misunderstanding that São Paulo was, and is, the main victim.

SIMONSEN, [1937] 1978, P.19

Clearly, a work of legitimizing the industrial bourgeoisie of São Paulo in the "national conscience", forming its ruling elite to command the direction of the country. This ambition guides the research on the formation of Brazil, to understand the historical significance of the transformations observed in the 1930s. Which leads the author to make comparative history, highlighting the condition of "backwardness" in which the Brazilian economy was facing the other capitalist countries, especially the USA.

The dominant motivation in the exploration of America would have been, for him, of an economic order, aiming at commercial profit. However, even starting from a common objective, European countries would establish their colonies in America under conditions and with very different results. Spanish domains had their colonization based on the exploitation of precious metals and indigenous servile work. In the United States, colonization would only begin in the 17th century, when religious disputes in Europe motivated a large migratory flow to the north of the American continent, in conditions of climate, production and natural wealth similar to those of Europe.

Simonsen is convinced about the capitalist character of hereditary captaincies in Brazil, denying their feudal trait. In other words, it was a question of adopting "characteristically capitalist processes" for the occupation of Brazil, since the concessions of land and special political rights to grantees would have served as an incentive to invest in this high-risk and uncertain profit business. Therefore, it attributes to colonization the character of a capitalist enterprise with the commercial concern of profit. He argues that European feudalism was unstructured by the great Mediterranean trade and that maritime expansion would be a factor in the consolidation of national States and economies, with the "discovery" of Brazil coinciding with the commercial revolution.

Regarding the conception of production cycles, the author does not develop any formulation of his own. He follows the perspective of João Lúcio de Azevedo, in *Épocas de Portugal Econômico* (Times of Economic Portugal, 1929), when describing Portugal's economic cycles. Large-scale sugar production in Brazil would be, from the middle of the 16th century, the great business of the Portuguese empire, serving as an economic foundation for the occupation of the territory and being the first great cycle of the Brazilian economy.

However, Simonsen does not restrict the analysis to the economic cycles of the Portuguese empire, including those that were important for the formation of Brazil. Cycles that served as an economic base for the occupation of the interior: the cattle cycle, the indigenous hunting cycle, the gold cycle, and the spice cycle of the Amazon rainforest.

The research was completed in other publications, where the author expands the interpretation of Brazilian economic history through the production cycles, spanning the 19th and 20th centuries. *Aspectos da História Econômica do Café* (Aspects of the Economic History of Coffee) was presented as a thesis at the III Congress of National History of the Brazilian Historical and Geographical Institute in 1938 (Carone, 1973). According to Simonsen, coffee began to be exported in the first decades of the 19th century and in 1830 the country would reach the top of world production. Coinciding with large-scale coffee consumption in the industrial era, the rise of Brazilian production allowed the economic recovery of the center-south after the mining crisis, reversing the accumulated capital for coffee production.

Coffee, therefore, constituted the economic basis for the formation of the empire and the independent nation. Its production in the *Paraíba* Valley, taking advantage of the resources accumulated in mining and livestock, has greatly increased the world supply of the product, causing the international price to drop. Exhaustion of land is presented as a decisive factor in the decline of coffee production, with the modification of the producing regions, migrating to Minas Gerais and the west of São Paulo.

From 1870, the great expansion of São Paulo began, although the domain remained with the production of Rio de Janeiro until 1890. A transition period, with the construction of railroads and the progressive introduction of free work by immigrants in the plantations of São Paulo. For the author, the abolition of slavery in 1888 represented a blow to the economy of Rio de Janeiro, already threatened by competition from coffee plantations in São Paulo. The proclamation of the republic coincides with the hegemony of São Paulo in coffee growing.

Some points are listed for the great growth of production in São Paulo: ideal conditions of climate and soil; climate favorable to the European settler; credit facilities; the remuneration system for settlers; transport facilities with the railways; concentration of activities in coffee monoculture; and the great price increase verified between 1886 and 1896. From 1897, while the production multiplied, there was a drop in the international price, leading the country to a crisis of overproduction.

In 1902, the State of São Paulo instituted a tax on new coffee plantations, and in 1906, it organized in the Taubaté Agreement[2]the first intervention in the market. In the author's evaluation, the successive coffee valorization operations were successful, maintaining the product price and giving positive returns. But this stance allowed other producing countries to enter the international market, while, internally, São Paulo saw its political hegemony decline in the federation

Closing his interpretation of Brazil, Simonsen presents an analysis of the situation to lay the foundations of his political program. *Evolução Industrial do Brasil* (Industrial Evolution of Brazil), published in 1939, was written at the invitation of the Federal Council for Foreign Trade, for a US university mission visiting the country (Carone, 1973). At this time, Simonsen was president of Fiesp and professor of economic history of Brazil at the Free School of Sociology and Politics of São Paulo. The text intends to attract US capitals to assist heavy industrialization, in addition to the comparative perspective between the history of the two countries. He says that, from the point of view of economic production, Brazil was already much larger than the United States in the past, especially in terms of agricultural production for export in the colonial period. Thus, understanding industry as a higher stage of development of agriculture, asks:

> Why, then, has the economic evolution that has been taking place in the two countries over the past 150 years so diverse, in which industrial activities play such an important role? [...] And why is North American industrial production today more than 100 times higher than Brazilian, which nevertheless occupies the first place in South American industrial production?
>
> SIMONSEN, [1939] 1973, p. 6

This question, common to Interpreters of Brazil, guides Simonsen's work, and his first answer points to the "geological and geographic determinisms". In addition to the "determinisms", it also indicates the industrial protectionist policy as an element of differentiation between the two countries. If, in the colonial era, Brazil was unable to develop manufactures, after independence, for reasons of international politics, free trade was in force until 1844. The commercial treaties imposed on the Portuguese crown by the English in 1810

---

2 Agreement made in the city of Taubaté between the governors of the states of São Paulo, Minas Gerais and Rio de Janeiro, then the largest coffee producers in Brazil. It aimed to intervene in the coffee market, raising the sale prices of the product through supply control.

increased imports, making the industrial evolution and creating deficits in the trade balance.

Only in 1860 did the country experience positive trade surpluses, with the increase in import tariffs and coffee exports. In this second half of the century, according to Simonsen, tariff policy oscillated between liberalism and protectionism. With the end of slavery, the immigration of Europeans and the growth of coffee production, an internal market was formed for industrial production. And, in the beginning of the 20th century, after the overproduction of coffee, with a decrease in foreign currency for imports and a fall in the exchange rate, an incentive to industrial development was observed.

The author identifies the first Brazilian industrial boom between 1885 and 1895, the period of the largest coffee exports, allowing the formation of capital. This industrial growth was concentrated in Rio de Janeiro, given the economic leadership exercised by the coffee economy of *Paraíba* Valley. In the first years of the century there was a new industrial outbreak, the first in São Paulo, which had a well-developed rail network in the state and the introduction of electricity, replacing steam as the main driving energy. From 1910 onwards, São Paulo would be the largest industrial center in the country.

Unlike the USA, in these decades of more intense industrial development, there was no protectionist policy of an industrializing nature in Brazil. Tariff protection would have been much less decisive than the exchange rate devaluation and the rapid increase in the domestic market determined by population growth. The industry emerged from consumer needs not met by imports, forming an industrial park focused on consumer goods, without developing the basic industry. This would depend on government action and support from foreign capital.

> I sincerely enlist among those who have hopes that the United States will be able to really maintain with us, in the economic and industrial field, cooperation and approximation, in harmony with the political connections, which we all aspire to.
>
> SIMONSEN, [1939] 1973, p. 49

Considered, in general, as the greatest exponent of the national bourgeoisie, Simonsen, in fact, expresses the particular interest of the industrial bourgeoisie of São Paulo in the attempt of national affirmation. To this end, it does not refuse to demand the assistance of foreign capital. In this case, there was a clear exchange of favors with the USA, combining political alignment and economic aid at the time when the Second World War was starting. The intention to join foreign capital is registered. This political stance is in line with

Simonsen's interpretation of Brazilian economic history, based on production cycles, under the worldview of the owning class.

Bielschowsky (2000) considers that Simonsen was a "private sector developmentalist", who defended the integral industrialization planned by the State, but combined with the maintenance of private profit. Among his theoretical-political convictions, he highlights the need for protectionism, State intervention and the support of foreign capital for the formation of national industry, whenever possible prioritizing the performance of local private capital. As a legitimate organic intellectual of the bourgeoisie, he also criticized any type of taxation on production or a permanent increase in wages and labor charges.

In 1945, elected deputy and, in 1946, senator for the Social Democratic Party, he supports in 1947 the impeachment of the Brazilian Communist Party.[3] Also, that year he strongly criticized the Marshall Plan as a Brazilian representative on the Inter-American Council on Trade and Production, arguing for the need for a similar United States aid plan for Latin America.

3   Caio Prado Jr: Marxist Interpretation of Brazil

Born in the coffee bourgeoisie of São Paulo, Caio Prado Jr. (1907–1990) ended up becoming one of the most important communist intellectuals in Brazil. Immersed in the environment of the 1920s and 1930s, his formation was influenced by the rise of the proletariat on the political scene, by the modernist movement in culture and by new social studies with the organization of universities. He has been a member of the Brazilian Communist Party (PCB) for decades, although he is placed outside the party's hegemonic line.

He attended the Law School of Largo de São Francisco, between 1924 and 1928. His family was a coffee exporter, with a large participation in the first republic, and his initiation in political life occurs in the Democratic Party, of liberal orientation, founded in 1926 by dissident fraction of the oligarchy and middle classes in São Paulo (Iglésias, 1982; Ricupero, 2008). The party opposed Júlio Prestes, supporting Getúlio Vargas's candidacy in the 1930 presidential elections.[4] Caio supported the 1930 movement, but soon became disillusioned with its directions. He adopted a more critical and radical stance, joining

---

3 Throughout the 20th century, the PCB fluctuated between periods of legality and illegality. With the end of the Estado Novo in 1945, it conquered legality for a brief period until 1947, when the cold war began.

4 Dating back to the 1930 election campaign Caio Prado's first arrest, would be several throughout his life. (Pericás & Wider, 2014)

the PCB in 1931. Unlike his original social group, he did not participate in the "Constitutionalist Revolution" of 1932.

In 1933, he writes *Evolução Política do Brasil: ensaio de interpretação materialista da história brasileira* (Political Evolution of Brazil: essay of materialist interpretation of Brazilian history), considered by many to be one of the first successful attempts to apply the Marx method in Brazil, a milestone in Brazilian Marxism (Coutinho, [1988] 2011; Ricupero, 2008; Pericás & Wider, 2014).[5] It is a synthesis analysis, in which it seeks to challenge the "official history" of the ruling classes, as indicated in the preface to the first edition. Despite being a study focused on the political issue, the materialist perspective directs Caio Prado to research the economic structure of society, pointing out the direction his work would take.

For economic history, what seems most significant in this book is the understanding of the historical process in terms of the dialectic between economic structure and political superstructure. That is, starting from the analysis of production, understanding the social structure and its expression in terms of political disputes between social classes. This procedure is particularly well designed for the colonial period, extracting from there the internal contradictions that led to the country's independence.

It starts by disagreeing with the thesis, dominant until then, that there would be feudalism in Brazil, as experienced by Europe. Notes that the Portuguese maritime expansion was the result of the commercial bourgeoisie's ambition for profit and that the beginning of colonization, founded on the private exploitation of the territory with the hereditary captaincies, kept feudal characteristics in the land ownership regime, but that would not be marked in the Brazilian formation. Especially since the captaincy system was not successful and was reversed with the institution of the general government in 1549. The determining factor of Brazilian colonization would not be the ownership of the land itself, but also the availability of capital to undertake profitable production. Thus, the colonial enterprise in Brazil differed from European feudalism, as it depended on the accumulation of capital needed for large-scale production for trade.

Therefore, the economic base of the colony is defined, founded on the large rural exploitation for export, with slave labor. Hence the social structure derives, that is, in colonial society there would be two fundamental classes, the great landowners and the mass of slaves. For a poorly diversified colonial

---

5   Marxist interpretations were developed before in Brazil in the 1920s and 1930s, with emphasis on *Agrarismo e Industrialismo* (1926), by Octavio Brandão. See Pinheiro (2021, in this book)

economy, it points to low social stratification and the incipient political super-structure. Until the middle of the 17th century, the colonial State was reduced to the domain of the great owner, with power concentrated in the city councils. The author points out that there was a communion of interests between the large landowners and the metropolis, both aimed at the productive occupation of the territory and the expansion of export trade.

The inflection in Portuguese colonial policy would come after the Dutch wars. With the Iberian Union (1580–1640),[6] Portugal had its colonial empire dismantled, and the American colony grew in importance, establishing itself as the economic core of the empire. Portugal became a trading post and took all measures to strengthen trade, restricting the freedom of the colony. The kingdom was in decline and a migratory flow to Brazil is beginning. In terms of social structure, the main change was the formation of a new social class in the colony: the Portuguese mercantile bourgeoisie, which began to dispute power with landowners.

According to Caio Prado, from the middle of the 17th century onwards there is a continuous concentration of power in the metropolitan authority, to the detriment of the city councils. The colony's political balance was broken, and the differentiation of interests was made explicit: the colonial regime began to oppose the interests of producers and to favor Portuguese traders. This contradiction between class interests will generate social tensions that will intensify during the 18th century, due to the strict metropolitan control over the production of gold and diamonds in the colony. (Pericás & Wider, 2014)

The arrival of the royal family in 1808 indicates the centrality of Brazil in the Portuguese colonial system. By transforming Rio de Janeiro into the capital of the empire and breaking the colonial statute by opening ports, the government creates links in Brazil and getting closer to local interests, leaving Portuguese traders dissatisfied. For Caio Prado, this divergence of interests motivated the Constitutionalist Revolution of Porto in 1820,[7] explaining the polarization of forces that would lead to Brazil's independence.

Evidencing his Marxist interpretation, the author identifies the dispute between large Brazilian owners and Portuguese traders as the focal point of

---

6   Political union of the kingdoms of Portugal and Spain between 1580 and 1640. After conflicts in the succession of the kingdom of Portugal, the Habsburg dynasty, which reigned in Spain, conquers the unification of the kingdoms and Portugal temporarily loses its political autonomy.

7   Liberal movement that ended the absolutist monarchy in Portugal and established its first constitution. On the other hand, the Porto Revolution demanded restoration of the colonial pact between Portugal and Brazil, a fact that led to Brazil's declaration of independence.

the class struggle and states that the "political superstructure of Brazil-Colony, which no longer corresponds to the stage of the productive forces and the economic infrastructure of the country, is broken [...]" (Prado Jr., [1933] 2007, pp. 51–52). It concludes that the new national State established is the result of a "political arrangement" between the Portuguese court and the great owners of the colony, determining the conservative character of independence.

After the publication of *Evolução Política do Brasil*, Caio Prado travels to the Soviet Union. Then he went on to study History and Geography at the newly founded University of São Paulo, where he got in touch with important European intellectuals on a mission to Brazil, especially the French. He works with prominence in the Aliança Nacional Libertadora (ANL, National Liberation Alliance) of 1935, when he assumed the position of vice president of the São Paulo section. He is one of the main leaders of the ANL in São Paulo, touring the state to hold rallies and lectures, publishing articles and being the editor of party press (Ricupero, 2008). Placed in illegality, the ANL is dissolved and its leaders are arrested. Caio remains in prison for two years, leaving in 1937 for exile in France. Together with the French Communist Party he collaborates with the anti-fascist struggle, in support of Republicans in the Spanish civil war. (Iglésias, 1982)

Abroad, he began to write his most recognized historical work: *Formação do Brasil Contemporâneo – colônia* (Formation of Contemporary Brazil – colony). Book launched in 1942, the same year in which he founded Editora Brasiliense, of great importance in the dissemination of critical intellectual production. Caio had returned to Brazil in 1939, on the eve of the second world war, and, with the PCB in illegality, dedicated himself to the research and organization of the publishing house.

Formação do Brasil Contemporâneo seeks, through historical research, to understand the present reality of Brazil. Although he planned to continue the work in other volumes, Caio Prado is restricted to the colonial period, adopting as a historical point of view the turning point between the 18th and 19th centuries, taken as a moment of synthesis of Portugal's colonizing work. For the author, this historical period, which ends with the arrival of the royal family in 1808, constitutes the fundamental milestone of the formation of nationality, combining the elements that would spread throughout the 19th century to determine the essentials of the 20th century. In his evaluation, Brazil of the 1940s had not yet completed the transition between the colonial economy and the national economy.

The line of interpretation closely follows Marx's method to construct the category *sense of colonization*: abstracting what is considered accidental, there is the essential that gives intelligibility to a given historical formation. This would be the "sense" that would be interwoven and would direct all the most relevant facts in the history of Brazilian colonization, which would encompass different moments and particular aspects within a unitary whole.[8] In these terms, Caio Prado will build his fundamental category of analysis, the sense of colonization.

Part of the European maritime expansion, understood as a development of trade, moved from the land route to the sea route that skirts the continent through the Mediterranean. From this revolution in navigation and commerce derives the impulse that would launch Europeans in the search for new maritime trade routes to Africa and Asia, and that would finally give rise to the "discovery" of America. This determines the spirit of commercial enterprise with which they colonize the new territories reached.

Portugal, which had a pioneering role in this endeavor, tries to reproduce in America the type of trading post already employed in Africa and Asia, but without success, apart from the small trade in brazilwood. According to Caio Prado, no European country was in a position, in the 16th century, to undertake an effective colonization of America, as its population was decimated by the bubonic plague in the 14th century. The initiative to colonize emerged as a contingency, a need to make the commercial enterprise viable. Portugal reproduces in large scale in Brazil the experience that it had already developed on the islands of São Tomé and Príncipe, based on captaincies focused on the production of tropical products, in this case sugar.[9]

Caio Prado adopts the distinction made by the French Leroy-Beaulieu, to determine the characteristics of the colonization of America. In addition to the Spanish colonization founded on the exploration of precious metals, it distinguishes two specific areas: settlement colonies in temperate regions and exploitation colonies in tropical regions.

The temperate zone of North America would have been of little economic interest, subsisting on the extractive activities of timber, furs, and fishing. It would only be occupied in the 17th century, serving as a drain for the population repelled by political-religious struggles in Europe and by the enclosure of fields in England. They would be settlement colonies, with no direct link to the

---

8 Ricupero (2008) associates the *sense* of Caio Prado with the *totality* of Marx.

9 Here, an inflection in the interpretation: in *Evolução Política do Brasil* the determinant for the colonization is the defense of the territory against the French threats, in the expectation of a future commercial gain; in *Formação do Brasil Contemporâneo*, from the beginning, mercantile motivation was imposed as a priority for colonization, making commercial business viable in the tropics. This seems to be the general movement of his thought, moving towards the economic determination of historical events.

commercial objective, simply reproducing European society in similar physical conditions, with the political objective of occupying the territory.

Tropical colonization was quite different, permeated from the beginning by the commercial motivation of profit. If the physical environment presented itself as hostile to Europeans, on the other hand, it opened up new possibilities for the production of tropical products of high commercial value. Entrepreneurs of a great profitable business will be attracted to the tropics, taking on the character of large-scale production based on slave labor run by Europeans. On this basis of a colony of exploitation, a new society will emerge, unheard of in the world until then, but whose sense will be the production of tropical products for the market.

> As a whole, and seen on a world and international level, the colonization of the tropics takes the aspect of a vast commercial enterprise, more complete than the old trading post, but always with the same character as it, destined to exploit the natural resources of a virgin territory for the benefit of European commerce. This is the true sense of tropical colonization, of which Brazil is one of the results; and it will explain the fundamental elements, both economic and social, of the formation and historical evolution of the American tropics.
>
> PRADO JR., [1942] 1995, p. 31

All economic activities would carry the mark of the sense of colonization, and would present a social organization of production founded on the large monocultural property worked by slaves. These are the three central characteristics pointed out: large property, monoculture, and slave labor. These three elements are combined in a typical production system, the large rural exploitation. This will be the fundamental unit of the Brazilian economy, the basis on which the social and political structure rests. Caio Prado makes a significant distinction between large property and large exploitation: large property could be exploited on a parcelled basis, as in feudalism; large exploitation, on the other hand, combines large property with single direction of large-scale production.

From this system of production organization derives the extreme concentration of wealth and the slow development of the internal market. In addition, the sense of colonization also implies dependence on the foreign market and the cyclical evolution of the economy. Founded on large-scale production for export, the Brazilian colonial economy was organized according to objectives completely alien to the population, without even managing to provide the resources necessary for their subsistence.

Consolidating his interpretation of Brazil, in 1945, Caio Prado published *História Econômica do Brasil* (Economic History of Brazil). This book offers, in an unprecedented way until then, an analysis of the economic history from the conquest to the most intense industrialization process of the 1930s. He presents the argument about the dependency situation of the Brazilian economy on the international market and finance. From this perspective, he draws a line of continuity between the colonial past and contemporary dependency, emphasizing the conservative character of changes. The incomplete transition between colonial economy and national economy is taken up as a key to interpretation. Both the independence in 1822 and the Republic in 1889 would have been moments of perpetuation of the colonial system by other means, first by free-trade liberalism and then by the direct action of imperialism.

Caio Prado highlights the contradictions that maintained the sense of colonization in the Brazilian economic structure after independence. Free-trade opened up new possibilities of consumption for the population, increasing imports and rapidly leading to a trade imbalance, with currency devaluation and instability of the monetary system. Public finances were affected by the low tariffs: with the import tax as the main revenue of the State, there was a fiscal crisis. In a State in formation, the expansion of public spending, including frontier wars and internal revolts, was not covered by tax revenues. The commercial and fiscal deficit was covered by English loans, making the Brazilian economy dependent on its capitals.

Furthermore, competition from English industrial products made any industrialization project unfeasible. The productive specialization in tropical products for export was reinforced, dependent on the external market for the realization of production and for the import of the goods necessary for the subsistence of the population. England consolidated its commercial and financial domain: it controlled Brazilian foreign trade and provided the stabilization loans of the economy.

> The colonial economic system to which we have already referred was thus prolonged and worsened, although due to other circumstances. Brazil, already having so many difficulties in leaving this system that had bequeathed to it three centuries of colonial formation, and on the basis of which it had organized its life, was now witnessing its reinforcement: instead of the restrictions of the colony regime, it now operated commercial freedom in order to safeguard and ensure an economic organization willing only to produce a few export commodities.
>
> PRADO JR., [1945] 1970, pp. 134–135

The position of exporter of tropical goods is reaffirmed in the Empire. First, by restoring sugar and cotton production in the northeast, and then with the emergence of a new product: coffee. The turning point is the prohibition of the slave trade. Despite being the world's leading slave trader, England began a campaign against the trade in slaves in 1807. The class of landowners, dominant in Empire's politics and interested in maintaining slavery, opposed the English policy, initiating a series of diplomatic battles, which would only end in 1850 with the effective prohibition of the traffic.

The transformation of the work regime accelerated in the 1870s, when there was a change in the immigration system to Brazil. The new system was something unprecedented in Brazilian history: a policy of mass immigration of European workers for large-scale farming. This system of subsidized immigration, in which the State paid the immigrant's transportation costs, was based on free labor, and encouraged the abolition of slavery. The international situation has favored: the United States is beginning to restrict the entry of foreigners and the Italian unification process opens up a new source of workers.

From 1870 on, coffee expanded in the west of São Paulo, where wage work was introduced. Manufacturing and commerce develop in tandem with exports. Along with private capital, Caio Prado highlights the role of the State and foreign capital in industrial and urban enterprises, which lead the country to modern capitalism. It was the height of the system of large-scale production of tropical products for export. Once the labor force problem was solved and counting on the massive influx of foreign capital, the country embarks on the wave of liberalism and growth of international trade. It obtains the largest trade balances in history, however at the expense of productive specialization and dependence on the foreign market.

As a rising political force, the coffee-growing class from São Paulo will have an important role in the abolition of slavery and in the foundation of the Republic, processes that are, in fact, closely related. In 1889, the Republic would be the superstructural change corresponding to the development of the productive forces. However, the crisis would not take long to come, affecting coffee exports in the last years of the century. In the mid-1890s, international markets shrank and the country faced a crisis of overproduction, accumulating stocks.

In 1906, there was the first intervention in the coffee market. The producers, gathered in the Taubaté Agreement, take the initiative to store part of the production using external loans. Caio Prado points out that this is a time for the mass entry of international finance into the Brazilian economy, controlling its main productive activity. They finance the valorization operation and manage commercial speculation with the retained stocks, so that the financial interests are the big beneficiaries of the valorization policy, more than the Brazilian producers. The domain would be held by Lazard Brothers, of London, through the Coffee Institute. The support of prices encourages the entry of competitors and, with the crisis of 1929, another export cycle of tropical products in the Brazilian economic history declines.

Caio Prado points out the difficulties for the emergence of industry in a country without a manufacturing tradition, stuck by colonial restrictions and post-independence free trade. He considers that this industrialization was fragile, since it was based on a restricted domestic market and a weak capitalist accumulation. Thus, he believes that the fate of Brazilian industry would be associated with the conjuncture of international trade and finance, in the event of an improvement in exports and slack in the import capacity, there would be a colonial reversal. Only an industrial sector would have a more solid base: the subsidiaries of big foreign companies, which are installed in the country to circumvent import tariffs and exploit the labor force.

This will be the form of imperialist action in Brazil from the end of the 19th century on, first by controlling coffee production and speculating, then by penetrating with industrial and public service companies. For the author, the investment of foreign capital in industry leads to the internationalization of the Brazilian economy, transforming national capital into a smaller partner in its initiatives. In this way, the nation loses potential for accumulation and becomes hostage to the objectives of imperialism.

> The situation of dependency and organic and functional subordination of the Brazilian economy in relation to the international community in which it participates, is a fact linked to the roots of the country's formation [...]. Export economy, constituted to supply tropical foodstuffs and raw materials to the countries and populations of the temperate regions of Europe and later also of America, it will organize and function in intimate connection and close dependency on overseas trade on the basis of which it was formed and developed. It will essentially be a colonial economy, in the most precise sense, in opposition to what we call "national" economy, which would be the organization of production according to the needs of the population that participates in it. This is the main circumstance that will make Brazil so vulnerable to the penetration of international finance capital when capitalism reaches this stage of its development.
>
> PRADO JR., [1945] 1970, p. 270

The Brazilian economy would, therefore, be conditioned by the role of imperialism and the possibilities of international trade. However, the 1929 crisis shook the foundations of the economic system that perpetuated for more than four centuries. In the 1930s, the flight of foreign capital and the retraction of the foreign market placed the country in a situation of strong restriction in its capacity to import, favoring the national import substitution industry. This process was consolidated with the increase of the urban population, developing the internal market, and the Brazilian economy, which traditionally produced for export, started to produce for own consumption. However, the author would never fail to remember the potential colonial reversal in a dependent country, after centuries of colonization.

At the time of book's publication, Caio Prado participates in the campaign for re-democratization. He was elected state deputy for the PCB in 1947, but with the start of the Cold War the PCB was again made illegal in 1948. Caio has his mandate revoked and is arrested again. From then on, he articulates a group of intellectuals and founded the Revista Brasiliense in 1955. Through the journal, he published important contributions to the debate on the agrarian question, at a decisive moment in the struggle for agrarian reform and the articulation of rural workers in the Ligas Camponesas (Peasant Leagues).

The 1964 coup closes the journal. Still in the aftermath of the coup, Caio Prado writes his most impacting book: *A Revolução Brasileira* (The Brazilian Revolution, 1966), which would lead him to prison again. An outstanding contribution, where he maintains the arguments developed since the 1930s about the capitalist characteristic of the Brazilian economy, criticizing the feudal thesis of the PCB and its strategy of alliance with a supposed "national bourgeoisie" interested in the country's autonomy from imperialism.[10]

4 Celso Furtado: Structuralist Interpretation of Brazil[11]

The trajectory of Celso Furtado until the publication of *Formação Econômica do Brasil* (Economic Formation of Brazil, FEB), in 1959, has its starting point in the doctoral thesis defended at the University of Paris – Sorbonne, in 1948, goes through almost a decade of services in the Economic Commission for Latin America (ECLAC) and ends in Cambridge, where he wrote his famous book.

---

10   This interpretation of the feudal thesis and the revolutionary strategy of the PCB, especially from the perspective of Nelson Werneck Sodré, as well as Caio Prado's critical position, are analyzed in detail in this book. See Borja; Curty; León (2021).

11   For a more detailed analysis, see Borja (2013).

FEB is the synthesis of more than ten years of research on Brazilian economic history. As Szmrecsányi (1999) points out, the publication of a book cannot be approached as an event, but as the result of a historical process.

In the early 1940s, at the Faculty of Law of Rio de Janeiro the author made contact with historians of the capitalist economy, particularly the Belgian Henri Pirenne and the Portuguese António Sérgio. He also deepens the study of sociology, especially Max Weber and Karl Mannheim (Furtado, [1972] 1997). Upon joining the *Departamento Administrativo do Serviço Público* (Public Service Administrative Department, DASP) in 1943, Furtado directed his research to the field of organization and planning theory. These influences of history and planning finally lead him to the study of economics.

After serving in the Brazilian Expeditionary Force in the World War II, he endeavored to return to Europe to see the reconstruction of the continent. Through Maurice Byé, his future advisor, then a member of the French mission at the University of Brazil, he entered the doctorate at the Faculty of Law and Economic Sciences at the University of Paris. In France, he also enrolled at the Institute of Political Sciences, studying the work of Marx and Engels with Professor Auguste Cornu.

The first thing to be analyzed in Furtado's thesis is the title: *Economia Colonial no Brasil nos séculos XVI e XVII: elementos de história econômica aplicados à análise de problemas econômicos e sociais* (Colonial Economy in Brazil in the 16th and 17th centuries: elements of economic history applied to the analysis of economic and social problems). There, he explains his adherence to the concept of colonial economy, developed by Caio Prado, and in the subtitle it reveals the intention of the historical approach: searching in economic history for elements to understand contemporary Brazil – central concern of the interpreters of Brazil. In the thesis there is a section with the sources. The notable omission of the sources in FEB gives great importance to this section, where the author exposes his influences. In addition to Pirenne, a central figure in Furtado's thought, Portuguese historians António Sérgio and Jaime Cortesão, as well as Gilberto Freyre, stand out. As to the more direct influences of Simonsen and Caio Prado, Furtado is explicit:

> One of the dominant ideas of this work – the absence of feudalism in Brazil – is indicated in the *História Econômica do Brasil*, by Roberto Simonsen, São Paulo, 1937. Having this indication, we seek to develop a body of ideas consistent with the modern economic definition of feudal institutions and faithful to the social and economic reality of colonial Brazil. The idea, also dominant in the present work, that monoculture, the foundation of the Brazilian colonial economic organization, was an

imperative of the tropical environment is developed in the work of Caio
Prado Jr., *Formação do Brasil Contemporâneo (Colônia)*.

FURTADO, [1948] 2001, p. 19

In the section entitled the sense of colonization – Caio Prado's concept – he
argues that the concession of captaincies represented an incentive to private
initiative, with the objective of investing in the production of sugar for the
foreign market. Thus, the captaincies would be capitalist enterprises for trade,
albeit in feudal legal guise. Like Caio Prado, Furtado recovers Leroy-Beaulieu's
conception of the types of colonization in America and presents Brazil as a colony of exploitation. He argues that the sugar economy was the economic basis
of colonization: large-scale production for the market was the sense of colonization. In the characterization of the colonial economy there are three elements pointed out by Caio Prado: large property, monoculture and slave labor.

Like Simonsen, he presents a cyclical view of the colonial economy, moving
from the sugar cycle to the gold cycle and the coffee cycle. The fall in the price
of sugar with the Antillean competition causes a crisis in Brazilian production
and the colony transfers its resources to mining. The same occurs in the transition from mining to the coffee cycle. Even after independence, the Brazilian
economy would have retained its colonial form, directed by the class of landowners, but subordinated to foreign interests.

From this interpretation of Brazil in the light of the colonial formation, the
author derives two conclusions about the Brazilian political situation of the
1940s, shortly after the dictatorship of the Estado Novo. First, the distinction
between export and subsistence agriculture, advocating agrarian reform to
improve the conditions of food production. And second, the political consequences of large property, implying a concentration of power that corrobo-
rates authoritarianism.

Back in Brazil after his doctorate, he was informed of the position at ECLAC
and goes to Santiago de Chile in February 1949. The years in the commission
were of profound importance in Furtado's trajectory, forming his understanding of Brazil and Latin America. He works with Raúl Prebisch in the
first surveys of the region's economies and realizes Brazil's relative backwardness. There he writes the article *Características Gerais da Economia Brasileira*
(General Characteristics of the Brazilian Economy, 1950), published in the
Revista Brasileira de Economia (Brazilian Journal of Economics).

This article is Furtado's first work after joining ECLAC and already shows
the influence of Prebisch, which would grow from then on. However, it is
noteworthy that it does not use the concept of periphery, but that of colonial economy. Here is a mixture of the theory of development of ECLAC with

the interpretation of Brazilian historical formation, a distinctive mark of the author's thought and his great contribution both to ECLAC and to Brazilian economic thought.

Furtado gives centrality to the deterioration of the terms of trade of primary products, a trend in the international division of labor. This would be the origin of the external imbalances that spread through currency devaluation and inflation. Since the colonial economy was essentially monoculture and with the political dominance of large landowners, the tendency of export prices to fall was combated with exchange rate devaluation, in order to sustain the price in national currency and guarantee the producer's profit. Consequently, the loss of exporters is transferred to the entire population, extremely dependent on the import of consumer goods, since the exchange rate devaluation makes the imported product more expensive, generating inflation. This procedure is called socialization of losses by the author, and is analyzed within the dynamics of cyclical fluctuations of the colonial economy.

The condition of colonial economy would be overcome in the interwar period, with a turning point in the 1929 crisis – the ECLAC argument of external shocks. The 1930s depression changed relative prices in favor of the Brazilian industry, with less foreign exchange inflows and currency devaluation, creating a barrier to imports and favoring the industry unintentionally. The Second World War would consolidate the industry's position, generating market protection and production expansion.

Furtado evaluates that industrialization had a positive effect on the economy, making it less dependent on cyclical fluctuations of the prices of primary products. Agriculture underwent modifications: the colonial monoculture system for export was gradually replaced by polyculture for the domestic market. The industrialization and urbanization processes have economically integrated the regions of the country. If, in the colonial past, the Brazilian economy developed through export cycles, now it would do so through the domestic market, concluding the process of national formation.

> As Brazil entered its new phase of economic development, it not only ended its colonial cycle, but still merged all previous 'cycles' into an integrated economic unit, and completed the historical process of its national formation.
>
> FURTADO, 1950, p. 31

An important moment of Furtado's passage through ECLAC is the direction of the ECLAC-BNDE Mixed Group (1953–1955), in the recently founded *Banco Nacional de Desenvolvimento Econômico* (National Bank for Economic

Development, BNDE).[12] There he published the book *A Economia Brasileira* (*contribuição à análise do seu desenvolvimento*) [The Brazilian Economy (The contribution to the analysis of its development)] in 1954. In it he makes a first attempt at a theoretical formulation of underdevelopment and consolidates his interpretation of the crisis of the coffee economy and the process of industrialization by import substitution, presenting an interpretation of the structural imbalance of the Brazilian economy.

The book synthesizes the convergence between the historical interpretation of Brazil and the theory of development. A change in the approach of history is observed, privileging the analysis of income flows and cyclical fluctuations, with a clear influence of Keynes. ECLAC's reflection began to give the author autonomy to distance himself from his main sources in economic history: Roberto Simonsen and Caio Prado Jr.

In the colonial economy, investment was driven by external demand, with no link between the productive system and local consumption. "It is in this sense that the colonial economy does not, properly speaking, constitute an 'economic system', but rather a dependent part of a system" (Furtado, 1954, p.63). The profit of the owning class was the only local income and their consumption expenses were linked to imports. Therefore, there was no internal income flow to the slave colonial economy, the flow was established between the productive unit and the outside, making the internal market unfeasible.

The coffee expansion of the late 19th century involved European immigration and introduced wage labor. The external impulse remained the dynamic element, but now it was multiplied by wage earners' consumption expenditures, moving domestic production. There is, then, an internal income flow that exceeds the export impulse. Although it made possible the formation of the domestic market, the multiplication of the external impulse generated imbalances in the balance of payments, since the growth in demand also increased imports, which tended to exceed the availability of foreign exchange. This trend was intensified by the worsening of the trade relations of primary products, causing exchange devaluation and inflation.

At the beginning of the 20th century, the defense of coffee growers' interests, through exchange rate policy and the purchase of unsold stocks, sustained the profitability of exports in crisis and guaranteed the maintenance of employment and income levels in the economy. The crisis of 1929 would break this situation, combining two crises: crisis of overproduction and crisis of

---

12   Working group organized in partnership between ECLAC and BNDE. It aimed to train
      technical staff in economic planning and produced a study that later subsidized the elab-
      oration of the *Plano de Metas* by Juscelino Kubitschek.

demand. There was, then, a change in the coffee defense policy. In the midst of
the crisis, unable to obtain external loans, the retention and burning of stocks
was financed through the expansion of credit in national currency. Before, the
financing with external loan guaranteed the entrance of foreign exchange,
now, the maintenance of the level of employment and income through credit
sustained the demand without foreign exchange coverage.

Sustained demand put pressure on imports and increased the external imbalance, causing exchange rate devaluation. This caused a significant
change in relative prices, compressing the import coefficient. There is import
substitution, making the domestic market a dynamic element of the economy
and giving industry the leadership in capital formation. The dynamic center
was shifted to the interior of the economy, attracting coffee capitals to the
industry. According to Furtado, the defense of exporters favored the industry,
unintentionally, through an anti-cyclical policy.

The post-war regularization of trade and the liberal policy adopted led to
an increase in imports. In view of the fear of exchange devaluation increasing inflation, the external imbalance was combated, from 1948 onwards, by the
policy of selective control of imports, favoring industrialists twice: controlling
the entry of consumer goods with similar national products and defining a
special exchange rate for importing capital goods. At the same time that it
reduced foreign competition, it allowed the re-equipment of industry.[13]

In 1956, working for ECLAC in Mexico, Furtado met Nicholas Kaldor, a
Cambridge professor, who invited him to spend a year as a visiting researcher.
Furtado reports that he already felt constrained at ECLAC, hence his interest in seeking new spaces of reflection (Furtado, [1985] 1997). The season in
Cambridge was remarkable, making contact with university intellectuals,
participating in courses and seminars on economic dynamics and economic
history.

Furtado's best-known work was written in Cambridge between 1957 and
1958, synthesizing more than a decade of research on *Formação Econômica do
Brasil* (Economic Formation of Brazil). Published in 1959, the book is a moment
of consolidation of the historical-structural method and of the structuralist
interpretation of the historical formation of Brazil.

The first part of the book, on the economic foundations of territorial occupation, makes a synthesis of the colonial period. Expanding the perspective on
the world capitalist system, he understands the colony as an integrated part

---

13   Even so, the author goes on to affirm that this policy did not have the direct intention of
      promoting industry.

of the European reproductive economy, that is, the Portuguese would apply techniques and capital in agricultural production for sale in the European market. The first agricultural colonial enterprise was successful because it relied on Portugal's previous experience in producing sugar in the Atlantic islands, ensuring mastery of production techniques. Furtado argues that Portugal counted on the contribution of the Dutch, who organized the distribution and commercialization of the product in Europe, and also financed production – holding part of the sugar business. Finally, the Portuguese insertion in the African slave market provided the necessary number of workers to carry out such an enterprise.

These factors gave Portugal a monopoly on sugar, later lost with the disarticulation of the system. Holland's independence from the Spanish empire, concomitant with Portugal's annexation to this empire, turned Dutch cooperation into competition. The war between Spain and Holland would affect Portugal,[14] which saw its sugar-producing colony being invaded by the Dutch. After the end of the Iberian Union in 1640, the Dutch are expelled from Brazil, but they took their production techniques with them, installing a competing industry in the Antilles and breaking the Portuguese monopoly.

In the 1948 thesis, he had argued that the introduction of sugar production in the Antilles changed its characteristic from a settlement colony to a colony of exploitation. Broadening the analysis, he assesses the relationship between Antillean export agriculture and the settlement colonies of North America. He argues that a triangular trade was formed between the USA, the Antilles and Europe. Once the sugar monoculture was established in the Antilles, local food production became unviable, shifting demand to imports. England, in the midst of the civil war, was unable to meet demand, and the United States began to sell food, timber and cattle to the Antilles.

These historical circumstances provided, in the USA, a completely strange phenomenon to the colonial system: an economy with low concentrated property, producer of subsistence goods, without distinction between export and domestic consumption production, where the lower concentration of income allowed the development of the intern market. The author also points out social differences, arguing that the ruling classes in the USA, by controlling

---

14   The current Holland was part of the Kingdom of Spain until 1581, when it gained its independence, after decades of war with Spain. However, in 1580 the Iberian Union took place, when Portugal lost its political autonomy and became governed by the king of Spain. Thus, Portugal and Holland, which were important trading partners, become war enemies. This resulted in the Dutch invasion of Portuguese colonial territories, including Brazil.

trade, became aware of the divergence of interests with the metropolis, while in the colonies of exploitation there was a communion of interests between the ruling class and the metropolis.

The second part of the book presents the slave economy of tropical agriculture in the 16th and 17th centuries, analyzed from the perspective of the income flow. The author characterizes the sugar economy: high income concentration, structural rigidity to cyclical fluctuations and income flow between the production unit and abroad. He argues that cattle ranching was formed, along with exports, to supply the mills. The relation between the sugar economy and cattle ranching defines the formation of the Northeastern economic complex. When the sugar crisis begins, Furtado presents a scenario of reduced income and a reversal of cattle ranching into a subsistence economy.

The third part of the book deals with the slave mining economy that was formed in the center-south region in the 18th century. Mining is a point of great influence by Simonsen in Furtado's thought, distancing it from Caio Prado's interpretation, especially with regard to the organization of gold production and the economic integration of southern cattle ranching. Very profitable, mining concentrated all available resources, resulting in enormous productive specialization. Thus, the demand for food and transport animals was directed to the ranching regions: the northeastern hinterland and the southern region. Mining, the new dynamic core of the economy, would have provided the economic integration of the different regions of the colony from its consumer market.

Furtado highlights some elements of mining that enabled it to form an internal market and to develop manufacturing, however, this was practically null. Among the reasons, the author minimizes the prohibition of manufacturing in the colony in 1785. The main cause would have been the technical incapacity of the Portuguese metropolis: weak manufacturing in Portugal meant little development of the colony. The relationship between Portugal and England would explain the setback of Portuguese industrialization, since the Methuen Treaty (1703)[15] had reduced Portugal to a condition of agricultural dependence on England. The treaty created a trade imbalance in favor of England and Brazilian gold came to cover Portuguese deficits. Without achieving endogenous development, gold production would be disjointed with the exhaustion of the deposits, quickly regressing into a subsistence economy.

---

15   Under the treaty, Portugal committed to buy English cloth, in exchange for opening the English market to Portuguese wines.

The fourth part of the book deals with the transition economy to wage labor in the 19th century, when wages would allow the formation of the internal market.[16] Political independence was achieved, but economic dependency on England was established, opening the market to English goods. The effects of liberalism in independent Brazil led many interpreters to ask if a protectionist policy was possible in the early 19th century. Furtado argues that it was not feasible to follow the steps of the United States towards industrialization, and explains the central motto of the research and of the book:

> The assumption that it would be within Brazil's reach – in the event of total freedom of action – to adopt a policy identical to that of the USA, in this first phase of the 19th century, does not resist a close analysis of the facts. This problem is of particular interest and can be summarized in a question that many men of thought have been asking themselves in Brazil: why did the USA industrialize in the 19th century, catching up with European nations, while Brazil evolved to become a vast underdeveloped region in the twentieth century?
>
> FURTADO, [1959] 2003, p. 100

The comparison between Brazil and the USA and the attempt to understand why they took such different paths are the main concern of Furtado – and, in general, of the interpreters of Brazil. The author highlights the economic and social differences between the two countries in the first half of the 19th century. Unlike the USA, Brazil did not have a developed technical base that would allow industrialization. Furthermore, the differences between the ruling classes implied different economic policies. While the USA was controlled by large urban traders and small farmers, in Brazil, the dominance of large exporting slave farmers was expressed in the adoption of liberal policies in foreign trade and in the dependency on Europe.

This situation would only be reversed in the middle of the century, when there is an important change in the Brazilian economy. Along with the expansion of coffee exports, there is an inflection in trade policy, with an increase in import tariffs in 1844. Another milestone is the end of the slave trade in 1850, putting the abolition debate on the agenda and leading to the introduction of wage labor. The gestation of the coffee economy leads to the formation of a

---

16   The link between wage labor and the formation of the internal market is a clear influence of Marx (Paula, 2009).

ruling class that is more conscious of the export business as a whole. The proximity of the capital made it possible for coffee growers to instrumentalize the State, when the imperial government organized and financed the immigration of European workers to the coffee plantation in São Paulo.

By the end of the 19th century, there was a differentiation between Brazilian regions, accentuating the process of economic concentration in the center-south. If there is a vertiginous growth in coffee production in the southeast, absorbing part of the subsistence economy and raising overall productivity in the region; there is also a slow disarticulation of export production in the northeast, with reversion to subsistence economy, characterizing the Brazilian regional inequality.

The fifth part of the book analyzes the transition economy to the industrial system in the 20th century, which emerged precisely from the coffee crisis and its defense mechanisms. This theme was already developed in the 1954 book, the novelty in FEB would come in the last chapter, when the author glimpses the perspectives for the next decades. If the displacement of the dynamic center removed from foreign trade its central role in determining the income level of the economy, on the other hand it increased its importance for capital formation. That is, once industrialization started, it is up to foreign trade to make the foreign exchange necessary for the assimilation of technical progress through capital goods. Hence, Furtado emphasizes the change in the composition of imports, increasing the external dependency for the expansion of production.

Another feature highlighted by the author was the increase in regional inequalities. If the formation of the internal market and the displacement of the dynamic center allowed the articulation of the regions in a common system, they also encouraged the concentration of income in the Southeast, clustering industrial activity in São Paulo. Left to free market forces, the economy tends to reproduce regional and social concentration and inequalities. The book's conclusion clarifies Furtado's political view: the need for State intervention to complete industrialization, reducing external dependency and combating regional and social inequalities.

It is no coincidence that upon his return to Brazil in 1959, he took on a special board at BNDE to guide the *Working Group for the Development of the Northeast* and prepared the project *Operation Northeast*. These works support the proposal, taken over by President Juscelino Kubitschek, for the creation of the *Superintendência do Desenvolvimento do Nordeste* (Northeast Development Superintendence, *Sudene*), still in 1959, having Furtado as superintendent. During the João Goulart administration, Furtado inaugurated the Ministry of

Planning and was one of the main leaders of the reform movement. With the 1964 coup, he was revoked by Institutional Act 1 and went into exile.[17]

However, based on a petty-bourgeois worldview, as a member of the State bureaucracy and acting in the main positions of the State, Furtado will not propose any kind of radical break with the capitalist system. On the contrary, it will identify with and defend the interests of the industrial bourgeoisie, understood as a carrier of social progress. The author's position is clear when he sees in the industrialization and the rise of the industrial bourgeoisie at the command of the State elements of overcoming the agro-exporting society. Reformism, which supports industrialization with greater economic and political participation by the working class, is affirmed as his political horizon.

5   Review of the Controversy

Having made this effort to synthesize the interpretations, it becomes possible to evaluate this controversy on economic history of Brazil. Simonsen, Caio Prado and Furtado share some features in common, which distinguish them from the historiography produced until then. Perhaps the main one is the characterization of the Brazilian colonial economy as capitalist, in opposition to the prevailing feudal theses. Another common point is the comparison between the development trajectories of Brazil and the USA. However, their interpretations are different, especially regarding the political program defended.

Roberto Simonsen represents the transition of the Brazilian bourgeoisie between coffee exports and industry. He was an organic intellectual of the industrial bourgeoisie, at the historic moment of consolidation of its hegemony. He acted in class organizations and in the State, especially after the political centralization of the *Estado Novo*. He produced studies on the formation of the Brazilian economy, founding the Free School of Sociology and Politics of São Paulo, where he inaugurated the discipline of economic history of Brazil.

Based on the worldview of the ruling class, always legitimizing the established power. This is expressed in the way he organizes economic history, structured by production cycles, making transversal cuts in history to analyze each cycle. His political program defends profit and industrialization, through State planning, protectionism and association with foreign capital. State action

---

17   Institutional Act 1, published on April 9, 1964, was the first institutional act by the civic-military dictatorship to remove political rights from its enemies, among them, Celso Furtado.

would be subordinated to the interests of the industrial bourgeoisie, creating infrastructure for the expansion of private capital and practicing protectionist policies. Foreign capital would be demanded for heavy industry, where the need for capital and technology would be beyond the capacity of the national private initiative. The author's objective with the industrialization planned by the State was the affirmation of the São Paulo industrial bourgeoisie, increasing the economic concentration and the power of São Paulo in the federation.

Caio Prado has a social origin very close to Simonsen, however his worldview was deeply influenced by the Brazilian Communist Party and the action of the working class. This is how he moves away from the political position of his class of origin to produce a Marxist interpretation of Brazil, criticizing the "official history" of the ruling classes and defending the socialist revolution. His interpretation seeks to capture the economic structure and the organization of production, social stratification and political disputes between classes. His central categories of analysis are the sense of colonization and the great rural exploitation. The sense of colonization can be understood as a search for historical totality, determining the path of the country, linked to the objective of producing tropical goods for export. This would define the colonial economy, commanded by external interests and dependent on the world market.

The author emphasizes the conservative character contained in the independence and in the Republic, perpetuating the colonial system by other means: by liberalism in the Empire and by imperialism in the Republic – preventing the transition of the colonial economy into a national economy. In this context, the import substitution industry would be subordinated to the external interests of imperialism and the Brazilian economy would be subject to colonial reversal. To overcome the colonial system and complete the transition into a national economy, he defends State planning for industrialization. However, his goals are different from Simonsen's: a national economy should produce to satisfy the needs of the population.

Celso Furtado has the world view of the petty-bourgeoisie, with social insertion in the State bureaucracy, as a public servant and international officer. He inaugurates the structuralist interpretation of Brazil, applying ECLAC's Latin American structuralism. Furtado takes Simonsen's interpretation of production cycles and Caio Prado's interpretation of the colonial economy as sources, in order to then make a dialectic overcoming: process of conservation, negation and new synthesis.

Formação Econômica do Brasil is the moment of synthesis of his structuralist interpretation of Brazil. The blend of historical interpretation and development theory is his distinguishing feature – the historical-structural method. The political proposal also differs from the others. By identifying the disequilibrium of the balance of payments and the social and regional concentration of income as characteristics of Brazilian industrialization, the author proposes State planning to conduct this industrialization. The central objectives would be to break external dependency and reduce social and regional inequalities, operating economic deconcentration through structural reforms.

The consensus around the State planning of industrialization has led historians of economic thought to assert a hegemony of developmentalist ideology in Brazil between 1930 and 1964. In fact, these authors express the direction of the transformation observed in the country with the emergence of the urban-industrial society, defending it. However, it is necessary to highlight that, although the planned industrialization is in fact consensual, there are significant differences between the objectives of this industrialization. Differences originated in the distinct worldviews and that are made explicit in the historical interpretation and political position of the authors.

Bibliographic References

Bielschowsky, Ricardo. Pensamento econômico brasileiro: o ciclo ideológico do desenvolvimentismo. 4ª ed. Rio de Janeiro: Contraponto, 2000.

Borja, Bruno. A formação da teoria do subdesenvolvimento de Celso Furtado. Tese (Doutorado em Economia Política Internacional) – Instituto de Economia, Universidade Federal do Rio de Janeiro, Rio de Janeiro, 2013.

Carone, Edgar. Seleção, notas e bibliografia. In: Simonsen, Roberto. Evolução industrial do Brasil e outros estudos. São Paulo: Editora Nacional e Editora da USP, 1973.

Coutinho, Carlos Nelson. A imagem do Brasil na obra de Caio Prado Júnior. In: Coutinho, Carlos Nelson. Cultura e sociedade no Brasil: ensaios sobre ideias e formas. São Paulo: Expressão Popular, [1988] 2011, pp. 201–220.

Freitas Filho, Almir Pita. A historiografia sobre a formação econômica do Brasil e a problemática do modo de produção escravista colonial: notas de aula. Texto Didático n.35, FEA/UFRJ, 1988.

Furtado, Celso. Economia colonial no Brasil nos séculos XVI e XVII: elementos de história econômica aplicados à análise de problemas econômicos e sociais. São Paulo: Editora Hucitec / Abphe, [1948] 2001.

Furtado, Celso Características gerais da economia brasileira. In: Revista Brasileira de Economia, vol. 4, n.1, p.7–37. Rio de Janeiro, 1950.

Furtado, Celso A economia brasileira (contribuição à análise do seu desenvolvimento). Rio de Janeiro: Editora A Noite, 1954.

Furtado, Celso. Formação econômica do Brasil. São Paulo: Cia Editora Nacional, [1959] 2003.

Furtado, Celso. As aventuras de um economista brasileiro. In: Furtado, Celso. Obra Autobiográfica de Celso Furtado, tomo II. Rio de Janeiro: Paz e Terra, [1972] 1997.

Furtado, Celso. A fantasia organizada. In: Furtado, Celso. Obra autobiográfica de Celso Furtado, tomo I. Rio de Janeiro: Paz e Terra, [1985] 1997.

Iglésias, Francisco. Um historiador revolucionário. In: Iglésias, Francisco. (org.). Caio Prado Júnior – história. São Paulo: Ática, 1982, pp. 7–44.

Paula, João Antonio de. A formação do mercado interno e a superação do subdesenvolvimento em Celso Furtado. In: Coelho, Francisco; Granziera, Rui. (orgs.). Celso Furtado e a formação econômica do Brasil. São Paulo: Atlas, 2009.

Pericás, Luiz Bernardo; Wider, Maria Célia. Caio Prado Júnior. In: Pericás, Luiz Bernardo; Secco, Lincoln. Intérpretes do Brasil: clássicos, rebeldes e renegados. São Paulo: Boitempo, 2014, pp. 193–214.

Pinheiro, Filipe Leite. Revisiting the origins of the controversy on the Brazilian revolution: a debate between Octavio Brandão, Mario Pedrosa and Lívio Xavier. In: Malta, Maria; León, Jaime; Curty, Carla; Borja, Bruno (eds.). Controversies on history, development and revolution in Brazil: economic thought in critical interpretation. In this book, 2021.

Prado Júnior, Caio. Evolução política do Brasil. São Paulo: Brasiliense, [1933] 2007.

Prado Júnior, Caio. Formação do Brasil contemporâneo. São Paulo: Brasiliense, [1942] 1995.

Prado Júnior, Caio História econômica do Brasil. São Paulo: Brasiliense, [1945] 1970.

Ricupero, Bernardo. Sete lições sobre as interpretações do Brasil. São Paulo: Alameda, 2008.

Saes, Flavio Azevedo Marques de. A historiografia econômica brasileira: dos pioneiros às tendências recentes da pesquisa em história econômica do Brasil. Rev. Territórios e Fronteiras, v.2 N.1 – Jan/Jun, 2009, 182–203.

Secco, Lincoln. Tradução do marxismo no Brasil: Caio Prado Júnior. In: Pinheiro, Milton. (org.). Caio Prado Júnior: história e sociedade. Salvador: Quarteto, 2011, pp. 57–72.

Simonsen, Roberto. História econômica do Brasil (1500/1820). São Paulo: Editora Nacional, [1937] 1978.

Simonsen, Roberto. Aspectos da história econômica do café. In: Simonsen, Roberto. Evolução industrial do Brasil e outros estudos. São Paulo: Editora Nacional e Editora da USP, [1938] 1973.

Simonsen, Roberto. Evolução industrial do Brasil. In: Simonsen, Roberto. Evolução industrial do Brasil e outros estudos. São Paulo: Editora Nacional e Editora da USP, [1939] 1973.

Szmrecsányi, Tamás. Sobre a formação da Formação Econômica do Brasil de C. Furtado. Estudos Avançados, 13 (37), 1999.

Szmrecsányi, Tamás. Retomando a questão do início da historiografia econômica no Brasil. Nova Economia, v.14, n.1, p.11–37. Belo Horizonte, janeiro-abril, 2004.

Teixeira, Aloisio; Gentil, Denise. O debate em perspectiva histórica: duas correntes que se enfrentam através do tempo. In: Teixeira, Aloisio; Maringoni, Gilberto; Gentil, Denise. Desenvolvimento: o debate pioneiro de 1944–1945. Brasília: Ipea, 2010.

PART 2

Revolution, Development and Democracy: The Story of a Brazil That Could Have Been

∴

CHAPTER 4

Revisiting the Origins of the Controversy on the Brazilian Revolution

A Debate between Octavio Brandão, Mario Pedrosa and Lívio Xavier

Filipe Leite Pinheiro

1   Introduction[1]

A widespread hypothesis in the historiography of Brazilian economic thought attributes to Caio Prado Jr. the pioneering spirit in the elaboration of a Marxist portrait of the Brazilian reality. According to his supporters, Caio Prado was the first author to establish a correct articulation for the historical transition of Brazilian economic and social formation from the colony to the present day from a Marxist theoretical framework. For this reason, the Caio Prado Junior is awarded the title of founder of the Marxist tradition of thought in Brazil. This hypothesis suffers from a frequent misunderstanding in the historiography of thought: it uses as a criterion of demarcation for the origin of Brazilian Marxism only factors of a theoretical nature, forgetting the material conditions that enable the existence of such interpretations.

In this chapter I intend to argue in the opposite direction, defending the hypothesis according to which the Marxist interpretations of the Brazilian reality arise not with the more or less correct theoretical synthesis of one or another author, but with the confrontation of different theoretical and political formulations of organic intellectuals of the Brazilian working class who had the purpose of intervening politically in the here and now. This confrontation occurred in the last years of the Oligarchical Republic (1889–1930), under the influence of the momentum to the political organization of the working class provided by the Russian Revolution and the economic and political crisis of the republican regime dominated by the coffee oligarchies. In the course of these historical events, the debate between Octavio Brandão, Mario Pedrosa and Lívio Xavier occurred. These were authors who sought to understand the

---

1   This chapter is an adapted version of the paper "The origins of the controversy on the Brazilian revolution: a debate between Octavio Brandão, Mario Pedrosa and Lívio Xavier", published in issue 51 of the *Revista da Sociedade Brasileira de Economia Política* (Journal of the Brazilian Society of Political Economy).

direction of the Brazilian historical process to transform the present at that time in a socialist direction. A theoretical itinerary that culminates in the elaboration of Marxist portraits of Brazil, to use the terminology employed by Coutinho (2011a; 2011b) to address the works of Caio Prado Jr. and Florestan Fernandes.

To demonstrate the validity of this point of view on the origin of Brazilian Marxism, I begin by presenting the view of Octávio Brandão (1896–1980), a theoretical and political formulator of the *Partido Comunista Brasileiro* (PCB) Brazilian Communist Party. In *Agrarismo e industrialismo: ensaio marxista leninista sobre a revolta de São Paulo e a guerra de classes no Brasil* (Agrarianism and industrialism: Leninist Marxist essay on the São Paulo uprising and the classes war in Brazil) – 1924 ([1926] 2006), his main work, Brandão characterizes the Brazilian bourgeoisie as liberal and industrialist, and the opposition between the agrarian structure and industrialism as a basic contradiction of Brazilian economic and social formation. At the same time, a process of proletarianization of the petty bourgeoisie took place, a consequence of the economic policy that aimed to sustain the domestic income of coffee farmers from successive exchange devaluations. The low permeability of the political regime to the demands of the petty bourgeoisie led to its political radicalization, something that can be observed in the two *tenentistas*[2] uprisings of 1922 and 1924. Thus, the Brazilian revolution would be characterized by Brandão as petty bourgeois democratic. That is, the revolution would have a bourgeois democratic content, while it would have in the petty bourgeoisie its main driving force.

Then, I address the view of Mario Pedrosa (1900–1981) and Lívio Xavier (1900–1988), formulators of the *Grupo Comunista Lenin* (GCL) – Lenin Communist Group –, a Trotskyist group critical of the PCB's position. In their *Esboço para uma análise da situação econômica e social brasileira* (Outiline for an analysis of the Brazilian economic and social situation) ([1931] 2015) the authors inaugurate the characterization of the Brazilian bourgeoisie as agrarian and anti-liberal and dependent. Which galvanizes an alliance with urban sectors of the bourgeoisie in order to subordinate the urban and rural working classes. Rather than forging their political unity around liberal principles in a struggle against feudalism, the Brazilian bourgeoisie forges its unity in the struggle against the working classes, using a fundamentally conservative

---

2 As stated in the "Introduction and warning to the reader", in this book, *tenentista* is an adjective derived from the word *tenente* (lieutenant in Portuguese), that named a movement of uprisings of Brazilian military in the 1920's.

ideology. Consequently, the Brazilian revolution would be characterized as a socialist revolution, having in the working class its main driving force.

I conclude my argument with some considerations about the controversy that corroborate the hypothesis defended here about the study of this controversy as a materialist starting point to narrate the history of Brazilian Marxism. Furthermore, I point out relations between this foundational debate of Brazilian Marxism and the later theoretical formulations in the field of Marxist interpretations of Brazil.

2   Octavio Brandão's Portrait of Brazil

Result of the exhaustion of the cycle of strikes that occurred between 1917–1921,[3] the PCB would be founded, in 1922, from a split between "Bolsheviks" and "pure anarchists" in the union movement. Without having any previously established Marxist or socialist tradition,[4] let alone a thriving bourgeois political culture, with which to engage in dialogue, anarchist militants emulated Bolshevik organizational methods, under the influence of the Russian Revolution (Antunes, 1995, p. 27). The communists saw the need for the political and electoral organization of the working classes, but at the same time, due to the union origin of the majority of their cadres, they saw in these organizations the ideal place to gather workers and form a revolutionary vanguard (Mattos, 2009, p. 50).

These militants and intellectuals were trained in a cultural broth in which Marx was just another reference associated eclectically to a myriad of other anarchist thinkers, such as Bakunin and Kropotkin, or positivists, such as Comte and Spencer (Aricó, 1987, p. 422; Batalha, 2014, p. 12). Positivism was influential in these media as a tool to analyze the historical, economic, political and national scenario, and it paradoxically assumes, in this configuration,

---

3 The second cycle of strikes of the Oligarchical Republic took place between 1917 and 1921. According to Mattos (2009, p. 53), there occurred in Rio de Janeiro: in 1917 – 13 strikes; in 1918 – 29; in 1919 – 26; in 1920 – 26; in 1921 – 4. It can be noted that the slowdown of strikes coincides with the IV Comintern Congress analysis of the on the loss of strength of the world revolution. That is, the PCB already emerges at a time of influx of the workers' movement and of the Comintern's turn to the single front line.

4 There were attempts to organize a socialist union movement in Brazil in the late nineteenth century and the early decades of the 1900s. Mattos (2009, p. 46) attributes the bad fortune of the socialists to their emphasis on political struggle at the expense of union struggle.

the role of a progressive worldview,[5] in a context of predominance of conservative thought (Zaidan, 1985, p. 19–20).

Octavio Brandão embodies the typical trajectory of his peers, pioneers in the construction of the Brazilian communist movement (Bianchi, 2012, p. 136). Born in the town of Viçosa on September 12, 1896, a well-known sugar cane region in the center of the state of Alagoas, located near *Quilombo dos Palmares*, its landscape and its people served as inspiration for novels by his classmate in elementary school, Graciliano Ramos (Brandão, 1978, p. 58). The realism of his trajectory could easily belong to Graciliano's novels, and his introduction to Marxism and Communism bears the marks of a worldview theoretically founded on positivism and politically founded on anarchism.

A trained pharmacist, Brandão studied in Recife between 1912 and 1914, a time when the city's political and intellectual environment was undergoing a cultural renovation with the assimilation of positivism (Zaidan, 1985, p. 33). In Recife (in the state of Pernambuco), Brandão would make his first contact with positivism and evolutionary materialism, which he soon applied to the problems of Brazilian reality, as in the paper *Aspectos Pernambucanos nos Fins do Século XVI* (Aspects of Pernambuco at the end of the 16th century). The text reveals the assimilation of Buchner, Haeckel, Humboldt and Darwin, ideas used to "describe the natural landscapes and the historical, economic and social conditions of Pernambuco at the time" (Brandão, 1978, p. 75).

Brandão is simultaneously interested in the natural and historical sciences, which he regards as dealing with qualitatively similar forms of being, articulated in a continuous evolution. In his first full-lenght work, *Canais e lagoas* (Channels and lagoons) ([1919] 2001), the author describes the land and people of the Lagoons of Manguaba and Mundaú, in the state of Maceió. Inspired by Euclides da Cunha, the book marks the maturation of his youth worldview, covering in a single theoretical framework the land and people of the lagoons, and dealing with geological, botanical, anthropological and social aspects in 12 evolutionary cycles (Lacerda, 2015, p. 15).

From this research, Brandão gave two lectures in 1917 in Maceió, in which he explained the geological processes that had produced the Lagoons of Mundaú

---

5   The examples of the relationship between Marxism and positivism go far beyond Brandão's formulations. For example, Leônidas de Rezende, author of *A formação do capital e seu desenvolvimento* (The formation of capital and its development) ([1932] 2011), and Edgardo de Castro Rebello, author of *Mauá e outros estudos* (Mauá and other studies) ([1931] 1975), both influential professors in the formation of Mario Pedrosa and Lívio Xavier at the *Faculdade Nacional de Direito* (FND) – National School of Law. They were adepts of a positivist interpretation of Marxism.

and Manguaba. These processes indicated that the sediments accumulated in the lagoons and in their channels of connection with the sea were indications of the possibility of discovering marketable oil. Brandão's scientific explanation for the formation of the lagoons, based on geology, deeply displeased the Catholic Church, which was extremely influential in the local social scene, while his national-popular political positioning, deeply displeased the local elites, aligned with imperialism.[6]

Participating in the struggle for the reduction of working hours and of pay increases with peasants and workers from Alagoas, Brandão would be the target of police harassment. The publication of an article in the newspaper *A Semana Social* (The Social Week) with a position contrary to the entry of Brazil in the World War I, an imperialist war, would lead to the closing of the newspaper by order of the federal government, and would aggravate this situation. Brandão would be sworn to death by a hitman, who, if executed Brandão, would receive the post of police chief (Moraes, 2014, p. 16–17).

Hiding on a ship, Brandão would flee to Rio de Janeiro in 1919, where he took the front line of union struggles, writing articles in the press, holding conferences for workers, leafleting at factory doors and giving speeches at rallies.[7](Del Roio, 2004, p. 119). The approach to the PCB would be a tortuous process: his dhesion would be linked to the conclusion that the crisis of the second strike cycle resulted from the organizational weaknesses of anarcho-syndicalism. An organizational form capable of facing the police methods employed by the bourgeoisie was needed, and this form was Bolshevism.[8] Upon joining the PCB, Brandão was assigned to the tasks of theoretical formulation,

---

6   In the words of the author: "It is time to open our eyes to our wealth and trust it rather than the classic indecent loans or the false promises of our intended Latin brothers or British friends, who are, after all, insatiable leeches" (Brandão, [1919] 2001, p. 133; emphasis added).

7   In 1919 the PCB was first founded, an organization that basically followed the anarchist molds and dissolved with the dissemination of news about the true content of the Russian revolutionary process. The text of Helio Negro and Edgard Leuenroth dates from that period, *O que é o maximismo ou bolchevismo. Programa comunista* (What is Maximism or Bolshevism. Communist Program) ([1919] 2017) and *Princípios e Fins* (Principles and Purposes) (1919), by José Oiticica. Such texts tangent the problem of the Brazilian revolution, without, however, taking an analysis of the historical-social formation as a basis. For this, see Bandeira et al. (1967, p. 280–284).

8   On the political persecution of workers throughout the Oligarchical Republic, see Pinheiro (1991, ch. 5). In this chapter, the author discusses police methods of repression of the working class, highlighting deportation and exile to concentration camps, such as Clevelândia, in Oiapoque. Workers were often arrested for loitering, or chosen at random, among the personal enemies of police authorities. The conditions of transportation to the camps, as well as the inhuman living conditions witnessed, made exile, in practice, a death sentence.

elaborating a defense of the international communist movement and the Russian Revolution (Konder, 2009, p. 181).

Among these, two contributions stand out. The first is the writing of *Rússia Proletária* (Proletarian Russia) (1923), a transitional work, in which a passionate defense of the Russian Revolution is made. Published by the newspaper *A Voz Cosmopolita* (The Cosmopolitan Voice), the work is divided into two parts, the first dealing with indigenous people, "prehistoric elements" in Brandão's terms, and the second dealing with "historical elements". The latter is subdivided into four evolutionary cycles: Primitive, Medieval, Medieval-Modern and Modern. This evolution culminates in a final stage, the Communist Revolution, which had yet to occur, but had already been established. With the exception of the latter, the dictatorship of the proletariat, all other cycles have a division between exploiting classes and exploited classes, which, in Brandão's perspective, are dynamic contradictions in Brazilian historical evolution. Brandão presents theoretical advances in *Rússia Proletária*, such as the introduction of the concepts of social class and imperialism, which now share space with the concepts of people and nation. However, the application of evolutionary cycles and the monist view of historical and social reality remain in his analysis, bringing in the embryo of the interpretation presented in *Agrarismo e Industrialismo*.

Another important contribution associated with Brandão's work is the first complete translation of The Communist Manifesto, published in 1924 in the newspaper *A voz cosmopolita*. Brandão's work in promoting Marxism is rarely remembered as an important aspect of his work. Even Konder, unsympathetic to the Marxist from Alagoas, recognizes that: "Apparently, no other Brazilian Marxist, at that time, had a baggage of knowledge comparable to Brandão" (Konder, 2009, p.182). Some of the scarce Marxist literature (written by Marx and Engels), available only in foreign languages, were: *Poverty of philosophy*, *Anti-Dühring*, *Ludwig Feuerbach and the end of classical German philosophy*, *The Class struggles in France, 1848–1850*, and the Carlos Cafiero's summary of *Das capital*.

Finally, it is worth menting Lenin's decisive influence on Brandão's embrace of Marxism, through texts such as *The State and the Revolution* and *Imperialism, the highest stage of capitalism*. Such an influence would even appear in the title of *Agrarismo e Industrialismo*, which even before the term Marxism-Leninism was adopted,[9] was already intended as a Marxist-Leninist essay of historical

---

9   Commentators disagree about the first use of the expression Marxism-Leninism. While Moraes (2007, p. 41–43) states that Deborin first employed the expression in March 1928, and that Stalin only authorized it in 1930, Bianchi (2012, p. 138) diverges, stating that the

interpretation. Persecuted by the political police during Arthur Bernardes' state of siege, and hidden in the house of a comrade,[10] Brandão was closely following the *tenentista* uprising of 1924, which began locally, as well as the uprising of the 18 of Copacabana Fort in 1922, to then gain national magnitude, originating the *Coluna Prestes* (Prestes Column).

2.1 A Marxist-Leninist Analysis of Brazilian Economic and Social Formation

Impacted by the *tenentista* uprising that would trigger the *Coluna Prestes*, Brandão began to writing what would become the first Marxist essay to interpret Brazilian national reality. Brandão's objective was to understand the meaning of the *tenentistas* uprisings from a totalizing viewpoint, for which he resorted to the "Marxist-Leninist" theoretical framework. The influence of the lieutenants' movement is reflected in its first paragraphs: "While the battle continues in the inland cities, through guerrillas, we will try to analyze these struggles from the point of view of Marxism-Leninism" (Brandão [1926] 2006, p. 25).

But *Agrarismo e Industrialismo* is not limited to the theoretical analysis of the object, but also bringing a call to action of the working class in the political events that followed, so that the text oscillates between an essay on historical interpretation and a pamphlet of political agitation. His style is straightforward, trying to reach his target audience, the working masses and the urban petty bourgeoisie, but "he was nevertheless confused, dispersed and pretentious" (Bianchi, 2012, p. 139), lacking in the form of presentation, disposition and development of the argument.

This has to do with the way it was written. The first part of the book, which contains its fundamental elements, was completed in August 1924, and served as the basis for formulating the theses of the II PCB Congress,[11] in 1925. The last

---

expression was used by Zinoviev, in 1927, in his theses on the Chinese revolution, and Stalin would not employ it until 192. The point here is that all dates are after *Agrarismo e industrialismo* was published, endorsing Brandão's "pioneer" use of the term.

10   "In clandestinity, Octavio Brandão, on July 28, 1924, was at the home of journalist Rodolfo Mota Lima, when news arrived in Rio that Isidoro's troops had evacuated São Paulo. Rodolfo Mota Lima enters the house completely desperate for news of the defeat. Brandão had just read a French translation of *Imperialism, the highest stage of capitalism*; sitting at the back of the dining room, he began to write a study about the 1924 upsiring, following the Marxist interpretation" (Dulles, 1977, p. 222)

11   Even though it served as a basis for writing the theses of the II PCB Congress, there is no mention of *Agrarismo e Industrialismo* in *A formação do PCB* (The formation of the PCB), by Astrojildo Pereira. Narrating the II Congress, the author summarizes Brandão's argument without citing Brandão's book (Pereira, [2012] 1962, p. 92).

two parts, which complement the previous discussion, were written respectively in 1925 and 1926. The absence of a clear exposition of his theses and the construction of the argumentation by enumeration, raising facts and data apparently without any internal connection for giving strengh to the argument, obscure many points of the work, hindering a proper understanding of the author's formulations.

The Marxist-Leninist method used by Brandão was harshly criticized. Aristides Lobo, commenting *Agrarismo e Industrialismo* in the newspaper of the *Liga Comunista Brasileira* (LCB) – Brazilian Communist League –, considers that the work would have been "the most serious, most meticulous and even most heroic attempt" (Lobo [1931] 2015, p. 75) to deal with the Brazilian situation until then, but, at the same time "the most anti-Marxist and disastrous [...] a bazaar of theoretical monstrosities" (Lobo [1931] 2015, p. 76). Among Brandão's work commentators, Konder (2009, p. 183) insists on the mechanism of the author's thought, which understands Marx's dialectic as the use of the triad thesis-antithesis-synthesis for the explanation of historical development, having an understanding of dialectics that is closer to Aristotle than to Marx. Others, like Moraes (2006, p. 15), consider it unfair to criticize Brandão for these mistakes, given the conditions of his analysis, emphasazing Brandão's correct treatment of specifically historical and concrete subjects. Even Konder is forced to assume, apparently begrudgingly, that, in these moments, Brandão makes "some empirical observations not without interest regarding Brazilian society" (Konder, 2009, p. 184).

Although he has a mechanical understanding of dialectics and a monist and evolutionary philosophical basis inherited from his education – which compromises his analysis at higher levels of abstraction – Brandão undoubtedly advances in the analysis of Brazilian specificity. This is true both for Brazilian Marxism, which took the first steps in this debate with the contribution of Brandão, and for Brazilian social thought, in which, in general, naturalistic determinism and the racism of Social Darwinism prevailed.[12] (Silva, 1997, p. 44).

---

12   Leandro Konder states that "Even racial prejudices emerge from Brandão's thought. He regrets that Brazil is hampered by the proliferation of 'intermediaries'. The intermediaries – Brandão explains – are "types that, generally, do not possess the qualities of the extremes, having only defects of both" (Konder, [1988] 2009, p. 185); Ângelo José da Silva, on the other hand, disagrees: "Studies based on race, in the physical and geographic environment etc., although they appear in *Agrarismo e industrialismo*, do not compose the focus of the work. In other words, at the very least I affirm that the work in question is a rupture with everything that had been done until then, as an attempt to interpret Brazilian society" (Silva, 1997, p. 44).

Brandão starts from the historical predominance of the agrarian forces, sometimes designated as feudal or semi-feudal, sometimes designated as an agrarian bourgeoisie, the terminology used oscilating throughout the text and editions of the work. Such forces would be consolidated through the tripod: Catholic Church, army and State. Externally, they would associate themselves with British imperialism, first, through Portugal, and later, through British direct domination. Throughout the Brazilian Empire and the Brazilian Republic British rule would be established by the State's indebtedness to the British Bank, making Brazil a colony of British capitals. Loans, finances and concessions were dominated by the Rothschilds, allies of the landowners, who, in exchange for their support, gave the landowners management positions in these companies. In addition, politically, they tried to impose the British development agenda for Brazil in those years, summarized in the *Relatório Montagu* (Montagu Report).[13]

For Brandão, dominated by "economic agrarianism ... Brazil had to be dominated by political agrarianism, a direct consequence of that" (Brandão, [1926] 2006, p. 36). Political agrarianism is the political domination of large landowners, who take the State as a tool "employed for their selfish, individual benefit, in order to multiply their profits, although the State and people are sacrificed" (Brandão, [1926] 2006, p. 28). All political decisions of the State were directed to the interests of the agrarian bourgeoisie: external indebtedness to finance the policy coffee valorization policy, the use of exchange rate devaluations as a support mechanism for coffee farmers' incomes and the absence of taxes on property land ownership.

The World War I would shake British domination, posing the struggle for supremacy in the Brazilian market, which throws the English and American bourgeoisies into a deadly war. According to the periodization proposed by the Brandão

A deadly struggle, with ebbs and flows, thus unfolds between the two great imperialisms: 1822–1891 supremacy of England, 1914–1922 supremacy of the United States, 1923–1924 Anglo-American imperialist rivalry, tipping the scales for the side of England.

BRANDÃO, [1926] 2006, p. 94

---

13   English economic mission (1923–1924) sent by the Rothschilds, and directed by Lord Montagu, to evaluate the financial conditions of Brazil and the guarantees to foreign capital, aiming to concretize the external debt rollover.

Associated to American imperialism, a politically liberal and industrialist urban industrial bourgeoisie. Until then suffocated by agrarian hegemony, these forces dispute the direction of the State and the definition of economic policy, hitherto ruled by coffee farmers. However, for Brandão, the turning point of imperialist rivalry to the British side externally, and the resistance of the agrarian forces internally with the Arthur Bernardes government, contributed to the industrialist bourgeoisie political disorganization.

According to Brandão, "There is a large petty-bourgeoisie – rural, commercial, industrial, bureaucratic – always trying to reconcile: in the countryside, the interest of peasant-servants with those of the landowners; in the cities, the interests of workers with that of the great industrial bourgeois" (Brandão, [1926] 2006, p. 33). In the countryside and in the cities, the petty bourgeoisie demands the improvement of its economic situation and greater political participation. In the foreground, there is the process of proletarianization of this class fraction, as a result of successive exchange devaluations to guarantee coffee growers' export income, which in the framework of an agrarian-export economy, with a high import coefficient, causes an increase in the cost of living. These conditions also aggravated problems such as the lack of urban infrastructure, basic sanitation and the housing deficit.[14]

On the political level, there is "[the] disillusionment of the petty bourgeoisie, to obtain improvements through the competent means; that is, through legal, juridical, pacifist, reformist means" (Brandão, [1926] 2006, p. 26), pointing to the low permeability of the democratic political system to the demands of the various social sectors and the impossibility of reconciliation. In the Brandão's words: "The petty-bourgeoisie disintegrates. Economically rolling into misery. Politically, hesitating between the proletariat and the great bourgeoisie" (Brandão, [1926] 2006, p. 143). This factor would explain the gradual political radicalization of this fraction, something attested by the *tenentistas* uprisings of 1922 and 1924, the first of which was local, and the second of national magnitude, which led to the formation of the *Coluna Prestes*.

The incipient industrial development originated a numerically reduced urban proletariat, which, according to Brandão, will seek to organize itself politically. The final part of the book presents a history of the Brazilian proletariat divided into three parts:

---

14   Mattos (2009, p. 43) presents a chart that points to a detachment of the wage and cost of living index after 1917, taking 1914 per base year. The index moves from 128, in 1917, to 167, in 1921. The author concludes: "You worked a lot, you earned little and you paid dearly to live poorly. The descriptions of the workers' housing places at the beginning of the century lead us to miserable, unhealthy and overpopulated realities" (Mattos, 2009, p. 43).

1st, The history of slavery of Indigenous and African. 2nd, The history of
servitude of the rural worker (in the first edition: rural proletarian). 3rd,
the history of the wages (proletariat).

BRANDÃO, [1926] 2006, p. 113

The task of revolutionary intellectuals in this sphere would be to deal with
the second and third stages, insofar as the bourgeois historians " have occupied themselves with the first part, though toning down the hues"[15](Brandão,
[1926] 2006, p 113). According Brandão, the struggle of the rural worker and
his servitude would still be an obscure page waiting for a historian. The history of the industrial proletariat, addressed by Brandão, begins with the strikes
that occurred after 1889, with the arrival of European immigrants, bringing the
anarchist seed.

This organizational process reached its peak with the workers' strikes of
1917–1919, a context in which the anarchist movement was drained, and the
PCB was first founded. In the following years, an ideological dispute between
communists and anarchists would take place, allowing us to understand
that: "A new idea and a new method were needed. Thus, on November 7, 1921,
the fourth anniversary of the Russian revolution, twelve comrades laid the
foundations for the *Partido Comunista do Brasil* (PCB) – Communist Party of
Brazil –, founded in March 1922" (Brandão, [1926] 2006, p. 116).

Throughout the 1920s, together with the process of political organization of
the proletariat, the PCB would strengthen within the union movement, weld-
ing a bond between the party and the working class. Brandão narrates this evolution over seven evolutionary cycles that unfold in a mechanical dialectics.

In short, in Brandão's perspective, there would be a fundamental clash
between, on one side, the conservative agrarian forces associated with British
imperialism, and, on the other, the progressive forces that would compose a
bloc headed by the industrial bourgeoisie, petty-bourgeoisie, proletariat and
rural workers associated with US imperialism. This agrarian order would have
as a central element of its disaggregation the *Tenentista* insurgent movement
and the political radicalization of the petty bourgeoisie, in the face of the disorganization and economic and political weakness of the industrial bourgeoisie.

---

15   Still in this regard: "Let us create a revolutionary tradition, writing the history of proletar-
      ian struggles in Brazil, the history of militants and martyrs, of victories and defeats, of the
      ideas and feelings of the mass and the vanguard and, mainly, extracting the appropriate
      tactical lessons. Let us study in depth Brazil in its thousand aspects – economic, politi-
      cal, moral and mental, historical and ethnographic, physical and social – because it is in
      Brazil that we have to carry out the work of Leninism" (Brandão, [1926] 2006, p. 130).

Despite the organizational weaknesses, the proletariat should take sides in the ongoing petty-bourgeois uprisings, both in the second Tenentista uprising (in the years of writing the book, still open), and in the organization of a third uprising, should one occur.

2.2 The Petty-Bourgeois Democratic Strategy for the Brazilian Revolution

As his "portrait of Brazil" articulates the historical transition of economic and social formation, Brandão's analysis of the social formation already contains the outlines of the analysis of the revolution: its bourgeois-democratic, anti-feudal and anti-imperialist content, the characterization of the industrial bourgeoisie as politically liberal, and the political radicalization of the petty-bourgeoisie as the driving force of the disruption of the agrarian social order. The proletariat should insert itself into this process and guide it, especially through the radicalization of the petty bourgeoisie, which would make the content of the socialist process. The petty-bourgeois democratic revolution appears not as a necessary step in the revolutionary process, previously framed in an abstract scheme, but as its antechamber, removing obstacles to class struggles within the framework of a concrete social and economic formation[16] (Bianchi, 2012, p. 129–130).

Still in the final part of *Agrarismo e Industrialismo,* whose writing was completed in 1926, Brandão considers that the possibility of a proletarian revolution is conditional on the realization of a third *tenentista* uprising. Along the lines of the triad thesis-antithesis-synthesis, the author attributes the thesis to the first *tenentista* uprising, still local, the second uprising, already national, would be its antithesis, and a third uprising, carried out by the proletariat, would be its synthesis. From this analysis Brandão deduces some tactical guidelines:

> Let us strive to push the petty bourgeois revolt to the limit, putting pressure on it, transforming it into a permanent revolution in the Marxist-Leninist sense, prolonging it as long as possible, in order to stir up the deepest layers of the proletarian crowds and lead the insurgents to broader concessions, creating an abyss between them and the feudal past. Let us push the revolution of the industrial bourgeoisie – [...] – to its last limits, in order that, once the stage of the bourgeois revolution

---

16   Thus, any possibility of Brandão's inclusion in what Caio Prado Jr. ([1966] 2014, p. 39) designated as "the consecrated scheme of a democratic-bourgeois revolution", distancing itself from "the theses about Latin American history that that were beginning to be outlined by the Comintern" (Bianchi, 2012, p. 139).

has passed, the door of the proletarian communist revolution may be opened.

BRANDÃO, [1926] 2006, p. 133

Besides *Agrarismo e Industrialism*, Brandão addresses the theme for the III PCB Congress (1928 and 1929). In *O proletariado perante a revolução democrática pequeno-burguesa* (The proletariat before the petty-bourgeois democratic revolution) ([1928] 1985), published in issue 8 of the magazine *Autocrítica* (Self-criticism), discussion forum for the III PCB Congress,[17] the characterization of the revolution outlined in Agrarianism and industrialism is deepened. In this article, besides detailing the characterization of the content and tasks of the revolution, the conception of permanent revolution is reaffirmed, by linking the petty-bourgeois stage to its socialist outcome.

Brandão initially separates two complementary complexes from problems: "1st.) The problem of the petty-bourgeois democratic revolution unfolding in a semi-colonial country in the current phase of imperialist capitalism; 2nd) the problem of the proletarian revolution in that same country" (Brandão, [1928] 1985, p. 121). A victorius proletarian revolution in Brazil would follow the petty-bourgeois way, triggered by a third *tenentista* uprising:

> [...] the proletarian revolution seems to us to be the natural consequence of a petty-bourgeois democratic revolution, born of a third uprising, aggravated by a coffee crisis [...] and radicalized by the combat against imperialism and, mainly, by action armed and urban masses.
>
> BRANDÃO, [1928] 1985, p. 122

For Brandão, the insertion of the proletariat in this process is fundamental. The proletariat should prepare itself from then on for the third uprising, thus being able to act in a politically independent manner throughout the process, without going along with the petty-bourgeoisie movement:

> Therefore, the current problem is that of the attitude of the proletariat and its party towards the petty-bourgeois democratic revolution, a fleeting prelude to the proletarian revolution, if the proletariat and its party

---

17   The version of *O proletariado perante a revolução democrática pequeno-burguesa* to which I refer to throughout this section came as an appendix to Michel Zaidan's (1985) book, *PCB (1922–1929): na busca das origens de um marxismo nacional* [PCB (1922–1929): in search of the origins of a national Marxism].

are actually prepared, organically and ideologically, with due advance, that is, from now on.

BRANDÃO, [1928] 1985, p. 122–123

However, in order to the proletariat to enjoy the potential for autonomous action, it was necessary to develop a policy of consistent alliances with such a strategic objective. Lenin is influential in this formulation, insofar as the policy of alliances was fundamental in the Russian revolutionary process. According to Brandão:

> [...] no doubt is possible: according to Lenin's own words in one of his fundamental books on tactics, the industrial proletariat and its party have to seek allies not only in the period after the proletarian revolution, but also in the previous period (which is our case). It doesn't matter that they are hesitant, unreliable allies. We must look for them: that is one of our fundamental problems.
>
> BRANDÃO, [1928] 1985, p. 124

Brandão then considers the need to establish alliances with the liberal industrial bourgeoisie and the radicalized petty bourgeoisie, in order to form an anti-agrarian block to take over the agrarian State. The formation of a united front with the enemy forces of the agrarian State is accompanied by a series of tactical guidelines that value the parallel action of the proletariat in the elaboration of independent forms of organization and action. The task of the proletariat would be to transform the petty-bourgeois revolution into a proletarian one:

> [...] the best way to work for the proletarian revolution is to look for means to transform the petty-bourgeois democratic revolution into a proletarian revolution. [...] One of our fundamental works must be to strive for the petty-bourgeois democratic revolution to be placed on an inclined plane that makes it roll in the direction of the depth of the workers' revolution.
>
> BRANDÃO, [1928] 1985, p. 131

Despite presenting a concrete basis for identifying the specificities of the Brazilian case, Brandão's formulation would be rejected by the Third Comunist International after the defeat of the Shanghai uprising,[18] and the holding of

---

18   The defeat of the Shanghai uprising in 1927 culminated in the massacre of the Communists on the orders of Chiang Kai-shek, the Kuomintang's main leadership. This event would mark the Kuomintang's final break with the Chinese Communist Party.

its VI Congress, with the adoption of the "class against class" line in detriment of the united front strategy. With the intervention of the *Secretariado Sul-americano* (SSA) – South American Secretariat –, the Comintern for the first time imposed its historical interpretation guidelines on the PCB. The "salutary neglect" of the Comintern with the PCB was broken, which allowed the development of an evidently limited interpretation, but which was familiar with national specificities, to be replaced with a theory as or more limited, and completely alien to the historical and concrete specifics[19] (Antunes, 1995, p. 30–31; Zaidan, 1985, p. 50).

Through the intervention of the *Secretariado Sul-americano* (SSA) in Brazil, Brandão and other members of the *Comissão Central Executiva* (CCE) – Central Executive Commission –, such as Astrojildo Pereira, were removed after the III PCB Congress in 1928 and 1929 accused of menshevism. That is, accused of making alliances with the petty bourgeoisie, which was equivalent to being accused of being a traitor. With the removal, Brandão would be erased from the party's history and memory. His formulations about the particularity of Brazilian national reality would be ignored, divorcing it from the analysis of the communists. Exiled to the Soviet Union in 1930, Brandão would remain isolated even after returning to Brazil, living as an exile within his own country. The author departs definitively from the PCB in 1957. When he died in 1980, those years would mark the resumption of the study of Brandão's work and the beginning of his intellectual rehabilitation.[20]

3   Mario Pedrosa and Lívio Xavier's Portrait of Brazil

In 1930, with the foundation of the *Grupo Comunista Lenin*(GCL) – Lenin Communist Group –, the PCB would watch the emergence of the first dissent formed from its cadres, to act in the same political field (Karepovs et al., 2014, p. 237). The history of its foundation has been narrated in an anecdotal way

---

19   Lobo declares that: "Having condemned '*Agrarismo e Industrialismo*' as a Menshevist deviation, it was not for that reason that it was a matter of doing anything better. Only one other document, reissuing old opportunistic errors, has emerged to make the situation even more confusing, to further obscure the spirit of the working class and the mass of the party" (Lobo, [1931] 2015, p. 76).

20   In the 1980s, with the emergence of the working class as a relevant political actor in the process of redemocratization, the history of the Brazilian working class and its political role in the country's history is raised as a question. In the midst of this process, there are several studies on the workers' movement of the Oligarchical Republic and on the Brazilian working class. On this, see Costa (2014, p. 135–138) and Moraes (2006, p.17–18).

through Mario Pedrosa's illness, which would have made him stay in Paris in 1927, when he was on his way to the Leninist School in Moscow. During his stay, Pedrosa reportedly made contact with members of the *Partido Comunista Francês* (PCF) – French Communist Party – close to Trotsky, taking Trotsky side in his rupture with the Comintern in 1928 – after its VI Congress – and founded a political organization without any social or party base, by means of an epistolary letter addressed to Lívio Xavier in Brazil.

Even though it is an important element in the formation of the GCL, Mario Pedrosa's letter to Lívio Xavier integrates a more complex plot of events, engendered by three types of disagreements in the PCB: (i) political disagreements about the strategy for the Brazilian revolution; (ii) disagreements over the union unity policy; (iii) disagreements over the presence of intellectuals in the party, the result of Bolshevization and the strengthening of a workerist political culture.[21]

Political disagreements over the PCB program would begin even before the party's III Congress, at a CCE meeting in 1927, at which the alliance with Prestes and *Tenentismo* would be deliberated. Making a review of the policies put into practice by the PCB until then, the CCE found that these would have been too partisan, defending the approach with the *Tenentismo*. Joaquim Barbosa and Rodolpho Coutinho, members of the commission, claimed "that joining the *Coluna Prestes*, a 'petty-bourgeois movement' would be the same as betraying the proletariat and 'all the lessons of Marx and Engels'" (Dulles, 1977, p. 282). While Barbosa abstained from the vote, Coutinho was the only member who would vote against the alliance with Prestes, the reason for his removal from the PCB.

As for union politics, the controversy was related to the work of the PCB in unions. The main complaint also came from Barbosa, who at the head of the *Federação Sindical Regional do Rio de Janeiro* (Regional Union Federation of Rio de Janeiro), found that the PCB insisted on complete submission of the union to the party to obtain electoral results from the *Bloco Operário e Camponês* (BOC) – Workers and Peasant Block – in 1928, instrumentalizing unions for this purpose. Barbosa considered that: "the party leaders were distorting union action, turning it into a political instrument" (Dulles, 1977, p. 286). In addition, criticisms were made of the communists' policy of union unity, which, paradoxically, at the same time that it proclaimed unity in the union movement, fiercely fought the "yellow" or reformist unions. (Zaidan, 1985, p. 116–117). his

---

21   *Obreirismo* (Workerism) is a trend in leftist parties, especially communist parties, which argues that only cadres with a proletarian background can lead the struggle for the transformation of society.

divergence would lead Barbosa and the *célula 4R* (4R cell) that he led, composed of about forty workers, mostly tailors, to leave the PCB.

Dulles states that at the time of this split of the PCB "a group of intellectuals with no direct contact with the masses split with the leadership of the PCB for different reasons" (Dulles, 1977, p. 286–287), emphasizing the absence of direct contact of the group with the mass movement; but, on the other hand, the coincidence of those splits, "recognized by some historians to be the antechamber of the opposition" (Karepovs et al., 2014, p. 239), points to the existence of some relation between these intellectuals and the movement.

Finally, there is a hostile climate towards intellectuals established in the PCB after the Bolshevization process, in 1928 and 29. According to Dulles: "According to Rachel de Queiroz, in Rio de Janeiro, intellectuals who wished to join the PCB had to pass a thousand tests to show that they were part of the proletariat" (Dulles, 1977, p. 404).[22] Compared to the PCB, "[the] *Liga Comunista dos trotskistas* (Trotskyists' Communist League) was a pleasant haven for communist intellectuals ..." (Dulles, 1977, p. 405).

With Pedrosa's return to Brazil, Lívio Xavier and other militants such as Rodolpho Coutinho, Aristides Lobo and Plínio Gomes Mello articulate the *Grupo Comunista Lenin* (GCL) – Lenin Comunist Group –, *Liga Comunista Brasileira* (LCB)– Brazilian Communist League – from 1931, a "Bolshevist-Leninist" faction in the dispute for the PCB's political direction, a branch of the *Oposição de Esquerda Internacional* (OEI) – International Left Opposition – in the party. This stance would be abandoned in 1934 with the change in the OEI line, leading to the founding of the *Liga Comunista Internacionalista* (LCI) – Communist Internationalist League –, the main organization of the first generation of Brazilian Trotskyists, which lasted until 1939 (Karepovs et al., 2014, p. 237). My analysis is restricted to the period between 1931 and 1934, when the Trotskyists sought to make internal opposition in the PCB within the scope of the LCB, producing in this dispute a Marxist debate on Brazil.

Another contribution of the branch would be in the diffusion of Marxism in Brazil, with the translation of several works for publication by *Editora Unitas*

---

22 Dulles reports a censorship by the party leadership of the writer's second novel, *João Miguel*. The manuscript of the work was already in the editor's hands when the party leadership asked for a copy. A month later the writer was called to the leadership of the PCB: "the Party considered the work to be a reactionary and petty-bourgeois story. As it was the party denied him the *imprimatur* (perimission for printing). And, as Rachel de Queiroz did not agree with the ideas dictated by the Party, which would bring about a change in the narrative and in 30 characters in the novel, she found herself expelled from the PCB" (Dulles, 1977, p. 404–405).

(Unitas Publishing), in São Paulo, among which: Lenin's *The State and the Revolution*, translated by Aristides Lobo, and Trotsky's *Revolution and counter-revolution in Germany*, translated by by Pedrosa. In general, the members of the GCL had a high cultural level and mastered foreign languages. To stay only with the authors addressed in this analysis, Pedrosa had completed high school in Switzerland, was fluent in German and had studied economic theory in Germany, while Xavier was fluent in French (Castro, 2013, p. 5).

Both born on the same day in 1900 in Brazil's Northeast – Pedrosa in Timbaúba (Pernambuco State) and Xavier in Granja (Ceará State) – they would live in the same boarding house and joined the *Faculdade Nacional de Direito* (FND) – National School of Law of the *Universidade do Brasil* (University of Brazil) together. On this occasion, they would have their first contact with Marxism in the classes of Professor Edgardo de Castro Rebello,[23] close to the GCL. Consolidating a companionship relationship that was to be long-lasting, they joined the PCB in 1927. Their interest in Marxism would be related in Pedrosa's case to art criticism and in Xavier's to literary criticism, areas in which they established themselves. Not so coincidentally, both would be founders of the GCL, and would assume the collective task of formulating an interpretation of Brazilian reality that would guide the Group's political practice (Candido, 2001, p. 13; Neto, 2001, p. 86).

3.1   An Outline for a Marxist Interpretation of Brazil

Based on the internal discussions of the GCL, Pedrosa and Xavier wrote *Esboço para uma análise da situação econômica e social brasileira* (Outline for an analysis of the Brazilian economic and social situation) ([1931] 2015), published in issue six of the newspaper *A Luta de Classes* (Class struggle), the GCL press agency, in October 1930. The text had little circulation due to the confiscation of the print during the armed movement of 1930. It was rediscovered in a footnote to Pedrosa's *A Opção Brasileira* (The Brazilian option), which referred to the publication of the text in La *Lutte de Classes* (Class struggle), an institution of the French communist opposition, published between February and March 1931, from which it was translated back into Portuguese and published in Brazil

---

23   Edgardo de Castro Rebello (1884–1970), he was a professor at the FND since 1914, becoming a professor of commercial law in 1931. He embraced Marxism in the late 1920s, forming the first group of Marxist intellectuals at a university in the years 1930, together with Hermes Lima and Leônidas de Rezende. His main work is the collection *Mauá e Outros Estudos* (Mauá and other studies) (1975). The assimilation of Marxism together with Auguste Comte's positivism is characteristic of the group, that sought to reconcile Marxism with evolutionism – in a very similar way to Brandão.

in the 1980s. According to Abramo, the outline "constituted, for much of the 1930s, the basis for the international direction of the Trotskyist movement in its discussions on the Brazil" (Abramo, 2015, p. 14).

Despite being only fifteen pages long, the *Esboço* reveals great theoretical accuracy in the treatment of Brazilian economic and social formation, advancing in the analysis, especially when compared to the "Marxism-Leninism" of the 1920s. The structure of the argument, whose clarity contrasts with Brandão's confused style, one can see the profound understanding of Marx's Capital, an advantage over Brazilian marxists up until then, since text was nonexistent in Portuguese. Pedrosa and Xavier also had the advantage of focusing on the dissolution of the Oligarchical Republic in its colapse, certainly a privileged observation point.

The starting point of the *Esboço* are chapters 24 and 25 of Marx's *Capital*, in which Marx presents respectively the primitive accumulation of capital and the theory of systematic colonization.[24] According to Pedrosa and Xavier, Capitalism was exported from the metropolises to the New World, and in the colonies the excess of land was converted into private property and an individual means of production – as a consequence, the transition is a simple change of form. Colonial Brazil is a vast agricultural exploration, characterized by the presence of latifundium, of enslaved labor, and of "production directed by landlords with their clientele, urban bourgeoisie and a small portion of free workers, both in cities and in the countryside" (Pedrosa & Xavier, [1931] 2015, p. 64). Another point emphasized by Pedrosa and Xavier is the absence of a peasantry in the strict sense of the term, basing their argument on the absence of free land in Brazil, so that here we do not know the figure of the free settler. Therefore, colonial agricultural production was already oriented to the world market, and the roots of the bourgeoisie are agrarian, anti-liberal and authoritarian.

The State is endowed with a class system, based on local elites, who ascend in the various economic cycles: sugar cane, gold, etc. With the emergency of coffee production, the transition to capitalism began, and with this, the São Paulo State faction of the bourgeoisie imposed the republican political form on the various local oligarchies. Such imposition aimed to "operate, without very serious impacts, capitalist development in the old regions united by purely political links, but in compensation, separated by an almost unparalleled diversity

---

24   In just one passage, Pedrosa and Xavier characterize the colonial economy as a peculiar form of feudalism, in which "everyone came to explore the workforce of the adjusted indigenous and imported African" (Pedrosa & Xavier, [1931] 2015, p. 64).

of economic possibilities" (Pedrosa & Xavier, [1931] 2015, pp. 65–66). Political centralization would be a prerequisite and a stimulus for the development of coffee production, a typically capitalist development.

This development was based on the colonial productive structure, taking advantage of all the conditions gathered by it: "virgin lands, absence of land incomes, greater possibility of specialization in production, in a word, possibilities of monoculture production" (Pedrosa & Xavier [1931] 2015, p. 66). The development of trade, of the mortgage debt and credit system, consolidates a national capitalist foundation. The problem of the wage labor force necessary to operationalize the valorization of coffee capital, is solved by the ruling classes through the mass immigration of European workers.

The flourishing of the coffee production transforms the most backard productive bases, subordinating them formally and effectively to capitalism, and promoting the unequal development of the different regions, which stresses the federative political form. This also deepens Brazil's relations with imperialism, integrating Brazil more and more into the world economy, entering the imperialist attraction realm. With the World War I, industrial growth was accentuated, complicating class relations under the government of Epitácio Pessoa:

> The policy of the bourgeoisie was, until then, aimed at maintaining the monopoly of coffee production on the world market. With the rise of industry and greater capitalist infiltration, the main problem was complicated by the problem of creating domestic markets. [...] For the development of internal markets all means are good and strong centralized government is an essential condition.
>
> PEDROSA & XAVIER, [1931] 2015, p. 68

The need to build internal markets and strengthen its national capitalist foundation makes the State's intervention a condition for industrial development. Thus, an increasingly strong and centralized State was needed, which strained the federative structure itself. Imperialism, in turn, accelerates and aggravates this picture of economic contradictions and class contradictions:

> Imperialism constantly changes the economic structure of the colonial countries and the regions subjected to its influence, impeding their regular capitalist development, not allowing this development to take place formally within the confines of the State. For this reason, the national bourgeoisie does not have stable economic foundations that would allow to build a progressive political and social superstructure. Imperialism

does not allow time to breathe and the specter of proletarian class struggle takes away the pleasure of a calm and happy digestion.
PEDROSA & XAVIER, [1931] 2015, p. 68

Caught between the external and internal contradictions of capitalist development, the national bourgeoisie, when it appeared in the historical arena, was
already conservative and reactionary, with corrupt democratic ideals. In this
context, "liberal slogans, even the most banal ones, have a subversive character
for the government" (Pedrosa & Xavier, [1931] 2015, p. 70). At the same time,
there is also no commitment on the part of the bourgeoisie to the construction of a liberal and progressive political superstructure. This is something that
appears in the patrimonial nature of the State, built from successive maneuvers over the bourgeoisie, as well as in the absence of an active civil society and
a fully established democratic order.

To the extent that the State is constituted from above, moments in which
the very continuity of the material existence of the bourgeoisie's material existence makes it necessary to sacrifice its general class interests are not rare. In
this way, Pedrosa and Xavier characterize the Brazilian bourgeoisie as having
agrarian roots and an authoritarian political tradition inspired by Bonapartism.
This would be a bourgeoisie that "only begins to acquire class consciousness
with the dread of the social revolution" (Pedrosa E Xavier, [1931] 2015, p. 72),
since this is not forged in the struggle against reactionary ruling classes, but
rather in the struggle against the dominated classes. The State must be strong
enough even to materially guarantee dominance over subordinates, using coercion if necessary. The Brazilian bourgeoisie is already born old and reactionary,
with corrupt democratic ideals, building, through successive maneuvers from
above, a State closed to popular demands.

Observing the corrosion of the bourgeois order in the Oligarchical Republic,
Pedrosa and Xavier considered two possibilities: either an even stronger centralization of the State, which would delay the solution of the contradictions
between the different national factions of the bourgeoisie, or the implosion
of the federative system and the rupture national unity. They end up betting
on the first option, with the central executive being empowered over regional
fractions through the establishment of an agreement. Shortly afterwards, the
"1930 revolution" would give reason to the authors' interpretation.

3.2   *The Brazilian Revolution as a Socialist Revolution*

With this analysis Pedrosa and Xavier diverged from the characterization of
the Brazilian revolution proposed by the PCB. Considering the primitive accumulation of capital, the great exploitation, and the agrarian and authoritarian

roots of the Brazilian bourgeoisie, the authors note the impossibility of making an alliance with such segments, disregarding the possibility of an anti-agrarian bloc. The Brazilian revolution has a socialist content and poses as a task the organization of an autonomous party for the proletariat. To address this, in addition to the *Esboço para uma análise da situação econômica e social brasileira*, I analyze *Mensagem aos trabalhadores do Brasil* (Message to workers in Brazil) ([1931] 2015), text published in the *Boletim da Oposição* (Opposition Bulletin).

Starting from a characterization of the Brazilian colonial economy as a capitalist development, the authors attest to the agrarian origins of the Brazilian bourgeoisie, as well as its seigniorial tradition. The weakness of the national base of capitalism and the pressures imposed by the penetration of imperialism obstruct the possibility of a liberal project being implemented by the bourgeoisie, which would put its own existence as a class in jeopardy. Thus, this bourgeoisie has no appreciation or commitment to democratic values, assuming a counter-revolutionary stance in the face of the most hesitant and incipient democratic or popular tradition.

These points are reaffirmed in *Mensagem aos trabalhadores do Brasil*, LCB document subsequent to the *Esboço para uma análise da situação econômica e social brasileira* – published in paragraph 1 of the *Boletim da Oposição de Esquerda* (Left Opposition Bulletin) – in which the positions resulting from this interpretation are developed in terms of political strategy. In the message, LCB states:

> *No fraction of the bourgeoisie, however liberal its label, can carry out democratic promises.* The class struggle is more powerful than the abstractions of political liberalism. In the imperialist phase of capitalism, bourgeois democracy – formal democracy – is nothing more than mystification. The bourgeoisie no longer has a direct interest in the realization of democratic demands.
>
> ABRAMO & KAREPOVS, 2015, p. 58 my emphasis

The absence of any commitment by the bourgeoisie deriving from its conservative political ideology points to the democratic tasks unfulfilled by the bourgeoisie, political tasks that would be inherited by the proletariat:

> *Only the proletariat can fight for democratic demands, because only it has a vital interest in the conquest of democracy.* In the face of the proletariat, as a class, all fractions of the bourgeoisie have no disagreements and, conservative and liberal, face a united front. When the proletariat demands

the most basic slogans, the heavy hand of bourgeois reaction tries to muf-
fle the workers voice.

ABRAMO & KAREPOVS, 2015, p. 59 my emphasis

Therefore, for the first Brazilian Trotskyists, there would not be a block of anti-
agrarian classes, but a block composed of several bourgeois class fractions, especially the agrarian and industrial bourgeoisie, galvanized in the fight against the
subaltern classes. Thus, the revolution in question would not be a nationalist
democratic-bourgeois revolution, whatever the specificity of its driving force,
but a socialist revolution capable of placing the proletariat as the subject of
social transformation, that is, the revolutionary dictatorship of the proletariat.
For this, it was urgently necessary to create a proletarian mass party, which
would allow the class to accomplish its historical task: "the establishment of
the proletarian dictatorship and the safeguard of national unity through the
organization of the Soviet state" (Pedrosa & Xavier [1931] 2015, p. 74).

4   Final Considerations

Throughout this chapter I have argued that the controversy on the Brazilian
revolution has its origin in the confluence of two factors: the Russian
Revolution and its unfolding at the international level, as well as the economic
and political crisis that marks the disruption of the Oligarchical Republic at
the domestic level. Analyzing the Brazilian economic and social formation
with the intent of substantiating a revolutionary strategy, in their theoretical
itinerary the studied authors approach the themes that constitute a Marxist
portrait of the Brazilian reality. These themes are the characterization of the
singularities of the colonial economy and its transition to capitalism, the characterization of the State, the characterization of politics, the characterization
of social classes and their respective fractions; under which tactical guidelines
for a feasible revolutionary strategy are articulated.

Organic intellectuals from political parties associated to the working class,
the treated authors reflect in their interpretations the conditions and limits of
this collective experience. From their respective political organizations, these
authors launched a totalizing look at the history of Brazil, taking as a reference
from historical analysis the historical process that leads to the formation of the
present, to then envion its possibilities of political transformation in a socialist
perspective.

According to Brandão, Brazil has historically been dominated by agrarian
forces associated with British imperialism. After the World War I, this domain

was jeopardized, and there was an increase in American influence in Brazil, leading to the emergence of a liberal industrial bourgeoisie associated with the US. This bourgeoisie was not able to establish its domination due to the reaction of the agrarian, who made use of the State and the economic policy to curtail their organization. The petty bourgeoisie becomes proletarian and radicalized by this policy, leading the bourgeois revolution, while the proletariat should force the process to deepen in a socialist perspective. The petty-bourgeois democratic formulation of the revolution guided the PCB in the 1920s, until the intervention of the *Secretariado Sul-americano* (SSA) – South American Secretariat – of the Third Communist International (Third International), after the VI Congress of the Comintern, and the III *Congresso* (III Congress) of the PCB (1928 and 1929).

The VI Congress would consolidate the Bolshevist process of the communist parties around the world and would originate the first Stalinist influence in the PCB. Breaking the salutary neglect hitherto prevailing, the Comintern would then establish a policy for these parties. The intervention removed the entire leading group from the PCB, including Brandão, accused of *Menshevism*.

Another consequence of this process would be the final expulsion of Trotsky. This event reverberated in the PCB even before its consummation, influencing members of the party – such as Mário Pedrosa and Lívio Xavier – who diverged from the leading core in relation to the alliance with the bourgeoisie and the Bolshevinism. The *Grupo Comunista Lenin* (GCL) – Lenin Communist Group was formed –, a Bolshevist-Leninist dissent from the PCB referred to in the *Oposição de Esquerda Internacional* (OEI) – International Left Opposition –, which, in this dispute, created an alternative "portrait of Brazil".

This appears in the paper *Esboço para uma análise da situação econômica e social brasileira* (Outline for an analysis of the Brazilian economic and social situation) ([1931] 2015), by Pedrosa and Xavier. Starting from the categories of primitive capital accumulation and systematic colonization, the authors present Brazilian agricultural production as a great exploitation based on enslaved labor subordinated to capital. The transition to capitalism would be a simple change of form, emphasizing the agrarian base of the Brazilian bourgeoisie, which explains its authoritarianism and conservatism at the political level, making political alliances unfeasible. This leads to the characterization of the revolution as socialist, the strategy being the construction of a mass party from the base.

The debate that took place in the 1920s expresses in an embryo of the positions of the subsequent debate, concentrated in the 1950s, 1960s and 1980s. In these periods, the positions of Brandão, Pedrosa and Xavier are echoed, which makes it unavoidable to consider their contribution as a starting point for the debate. Brandão's formulation is close to that proposed by Nelson Werneck Sodré, with Sodré's peculiar characterization of the transition from colonial economy to capitalism starting from a Brazilian-style feudalism and Brazilian revolution following the classic model of a bourgeois-democratic revolution. The formulation of Pedrosa and Xavier anticipates aspects of Caio Prado Jr. and Florestan Fernandes, such as the capitalist basis of the colonial economy and the agrarian and conservative origins of the Brazilian bourgeoisie, that result in its pattern of authoritarian political domination, in the patrimonialism of the State and in the absence of a commitment of these classes with the constitution of a conservative political superstructure.

Considered as the starting point of the debate, the study of such reflections can not only contribute to a reappraisal of the formulations of the debate's classics, but also contribute to the contemporary resumption of discussions on the topic, which is necessary, above all, due to the economic conditions and policies of current Brazil. This resumption, in turn, requires an urgent update of these formulations, both in relation to economic and social formation, and in relation to the Brazilian revolution. In this sense, although they come from a debate held about a hundred years ago, Brandão, Pedrosa and Xavier's formulations about the Brazilian reality remain current.

Bibliographic References

Abramo, Fúlvio. Apresentação. *In*: Abramo, Fúlvio; Karepovs, Dainis. (org.) Na Contracorrente da História. Documentos do trotskismo brasileiro (1930–1940). São Paulo: Sundermann, 2015, p. 13–17.

Liga Comunista Brasileira. Mensagem aos trabalhadores do Brasil. *In*: Abramo, Fúlvio; Karepovs, Dainis. (org.) Na Contracorrente da História. Documentos do trotskismo brasileiro (1930–1940). São Paulo: Sundermann, [1931] 2015, p. 54–61.

Antunes, Ricardo. Os Comunistas no Brasil: As repercussões do VI Congresso da Internacional Comunista e a primeira inflexão stalinista no Partido Comunista do Brasil (PCB). Cadernos do AEL, Campinas: n° 2, 1995, p. 12–34.

Aricó, José. O marxismo latino-americano nos anos da Terceira Internacional. *In*: Hobsbawm, Eric. (org.). História do marxismo – volume VIII: o marxismo na época da terceira internacional: o novo capitalismo, o imperialismo, o terceiro mundo. Rio de Janeiro: Paz e Terra, 1987, p. 409–460.

Bandeira, Luiz Alberto Moniz et al. O Ano Vermelho. Rio de Janeiro: Brasiliense, 1980.

Batalha, Claudio H. M. A difusão do marxismo e os socialistas brasileiros na virada do século XIX. In: Moraes, João. Quartim de (org.) História do Marxismo no Brasil – Vol. 2 – Os influxos teóricos. Campinas: Editora Unicamp, 2014, p. 9–42.

Bianchi, Alvaro. Octavio Brandão e o Confisco da Memória: nota à margem da história do comunismo brasileiro. Crítica Marxista, São Paulo: Editora UNESP, n° 34, 2012, p. 133–149.

Brandão, Octavio. Agrarismo e industrialismo: ensaio marxista leninista sobre a revolta de São Paulo e a guerra de classes no Brasil – 1924. 2ª edição. São Paulo: Anita Garibaldi, [1926] 2006.

Brandão, Octavio. Canais e Lagoas. Maceió: EDUFAL, [1919] 2001.

Brandão, Octavio. Combates e Batalhas. Memórias. 1° volume. São Paulo: Alfa-Ômega, 1978.

Brandão, Octavio. O Proletariado Perante a Revolução Democrática Pequeno-burguesa. In: Zaidan, Michel. PCB (1922–1929): na busca das origens de um marxismo nacional. São Paulo: Global, [1928] 1985, p. 121–132.

Brandão, Octavio. Rússia Proletária. Rio de Janeiro: Voz Cosmopolita, 1923.

Brandão, Octavio. Uma Etapa da História de Lutas. In: Brandão, Octavio. Agrarismo e industrialismo: ensaio marxista leninista sobre a revolta de São Paulo e a guerra de classes no Brasil – 1924. 2ª edição. São Paulo: Anita Garibaldi, [1957] 2006, p. 189–196.

Candido, Antônio. Um socialista singular. In: Neto, José Castilho de Marques (org.) Mario Pedrosa e o Brasil. São Paulo: Editora Fundação Perseu Abramo, 2001, p. 13–18.

Castro, Ricardo Figueiredo de. Mario Pedrosa, Lívio Xavier e a história do marxismo no Brasil. Blog Marxismo 21, 2013. Available at: <http://marxismo21.org/mario-pedr osa-e-livio-xavier-2/> Acess: June, 26th, 2017.

Costa, Emília Viotti da. A nova face do movimento operário na Primeira República. In: A dialética invertida e outros ensaios. São Paulo: Editora Unesp, 2014, p. 135–156.

Coutinho, Carlos Nelson. A imagem do Brasil na obra de Caio Prado Jr. In: Coutinho, Carlos Nelson. Cultura e sociedade no Brasil: ensaios sobre ideias e formas. São Paulo: Expressão Popular, 2011a, p. 201–220.

Coutinho, Carlos Nelson. Marxismo e imagem do Brasil em Florestan Fernandes. In: Coutinho, Carlos Nelson. Cultura e sociedade no Brasil: ensaios sobre ideias e formas. São Paulo: Expressão Popular, 2011b, p. 221–241.

Del Roio, Marcos. Octávio Brandão nas origens do marxismo no Brasil. Crítica Marxista, São Paulo, Ed. Revan, v.1, n.18, 2004, p. 115–132.

Dulles, John Foster. Anarquistas e Comunistas no Brasil. 2ª edição. Rio de Janeiro: Nova Fronteira 1977.

Karepovs, Dainis. et al. Trotsky e o Brasil. In: Moraes, João Quartim de. (org.) História do marxismo no Brasil – Vol. 4 – Os influxos teóricos. Campinas: Editora Unicamp, [1995] 2014, pp. 229–253.

Konder, Leandro. A Derrota da Dialética: A recepção das idéias de Marx no Brasil, até o início dos anos trinta. Rio de Janeiro, Campus, 2009.

Lacerda, Felipe Castilho de. A Transição de Octávio Brandão ao Marxismo: os livros Canais e Lagoas e Rússia Proletária. In: XXVIII Simpósio Nacional De História,

Anais Eletrônicos. Florianópolis, 2015. Available at: <http://www.snh2015.anpuh .org/resources/anais/39/1427837065_ARQUIVO_snh-2015_felipe-lacerda.pdf> Acess: June, 26th, 2017.

Lobo, Aristides. A Situação Brasileira e o Trabalho para o seu Esclarecimento. *In*: Abramo, Fúlvio; Karepovs, Dainis. (orgs.) Na Contracorrente da História. Documentos do trotskismo brasileiro (1930–1940). São Paulo: Sundermann, [1931] 2015, pp. 75–82.

Mattos, Marcelo Badaró. Trabalhadores e Sindicatos no Brasil. São Paulo: Expressão Popular, 2009.

Moraes, João Quartim de. A influência do leninismo de Stalin no comunismo brasileiro. *In*: Moraes, João Quartim de; Reis, Daniel Aarão. (org.) História do marxismo no Brasil – Vol. 1 – O Impacto das Revoluções. Campinas: Ed. Unicamp, 2007, pp. 47–88.

Moraes, João Quartim de. Octávio Brandão. *In*: Pericás, Luiz Bernardo; Secco, Lincoln (org.). Intérpretes do Brasil: clássicos, rebeldes e renegados. São Paulo: Boitempo, 2014, p. 13–28.

Moraes, João Quartim de. Um Livro Fundador. *In*: Brandão, Octavio. Agrarismo e industrialismo: ensaio marxista leninista sobre a revolta de São Paulo e a guerra de classes no Brasil – 1924. 2ª edição. São Paulo: Anita Garibaldi, 2006, p. 11–18.

Negro, Hélio; Leuenroth, Edgard. O que é o maximismo ou bolchevismo. Programa comunista. São Paulo: Entremares, [1919] 2017.

Neto, João Castilho de Moraes. O jovem intelectual e os primeiros anos de militância socialista. *In*: Neto, João Castilho de Moraes. (org.) Mario Pedrosa e o Brasil. São Paulo: Editora Fundação Perseu Abramo, 2001, p. 83–98.

Oiticica, José. Princípios e fins do programa anarquista-comunista. Spartacus, Rio de Janeiro, 16 ago. 1919.

Pedrosa, Mario; Xavier, Lívio. Esboço para uma análise da formação econômica e social brasileira. *In*: Abramo, Fúlvio; Karepovs, Dainis. (org.) Na Contracorrente da História. Documentos do trotskismo brasileiro (1930–1940). São Paulo: Sundermann, [1931] 2015, p. 62–74.

Pereira, Astrojildo. Formação do PCB – 1922–1926. 3ª edição. São Paulo: Anitta Garibaldi, [1962] 2012.

Pinheiro, Paulo Sérgio. Estratégias da Ilusão: A revolução mundial e o Brasil 1922–1935. São Paulo: Cia das Letras, 1991.

Pinheiro, Filipe Leite. As origens da controvérsia da revolução brasileira: um debate entre Octavio Brandão, Mario Pedrosa e Lívio Xavier. Revista da Sociedade Brasileira de Economia Política, n. 51, p. 98–120, 2018.

Pinheiro, Filipe Leite. A crítica à teoria consagrada de Caio Prado Jr. atinge Octavio Brandão? Aparando as arestas para uma (re)interpretação das origens do marxismo brasileiro. Revista História Econômica e História de Empresas, v. 23, n. 1, p. 197–228, 2020.

Prado Júnior, Caio. A Revolução Brasileira. São Paulo: Cia das Letras, [1966] 2014.

Rebello, Edgardo de Castro. Mauá e Outros Estudos. Rio de Janeiro: Livraria São Jose, 1975.

Silva, Ângelo José da. Agrarismo e industrialismo: uma primeira tentativa marxista de interpretação do Brasil. Revista de Sociologia e Política, Curitiba, n. 8, 1997, p. 43–55.

Silva, Ângelo José da. Tempo de Fundadores. In: Moraes, João Quartim de & Del Roio, Marcos. (org.). História do Marxismo no Brasil – Vol. 4 – Visões do Brasil. Campinas: Editora Unicamp, 2014, p. 135–160.

Zaidan, Michel. PCB(1922–1929): na busca das origens de um marxismo nacional. São Paulo: Global, 1985.

CHAPTER 5

Visions of the Brazilian Revolution

Nelson Werneck Sodré, Caio Prado Jr. and Florestan Fernandes

Bruno Borja, Carla Curty and Jaime León

1   Introduction

The controversy on the Brazilian revolution gives birth to the first and main Marxist interpretations of Brazil, written by Nelson Werneck Sodré, Caio Prado Junior, Florestan Fernandes and their precursors of this controversy.[1] This being one of the main in the history of Brazilian economic and social thought in the 20th century. As pointed out by Pinheiro (2021), in the previous chapter, this debate presents itself as an attempt to particularize the theory of revolution for the specificity of the Brazilian social formation, it has been greatly influenced by the Soviet revolutionary experience of 1917, also it has been guided by the debates that took place at the meetings of the Communist International, under the leadership of the Communist Party of the Soviet Union. In this way, the controversy unfolded following the guidelines of the international movement, not only in theoretical terms, but also in its political practice. At the same time, it is articulated with the historical reality experienced by a Brazil that becomes republican and which begins the process of formation of its working class.

It is possible to organize the evolution of the discussion in historical terms, following a periodization that takes this relationship between the international communist movement and the Brazilian as a reference. Thus, a first wave of revolutionary ideas spread with the creation of the Communist International (IC), the 3rd International, in 1919 and the profusion of communist parties founded since then: in our case, the founding of the Communist Party of Brazil in 1922. A turning point was the 6th IC Congress in 1928, which defines the character of the revolution in colonial, semi-colonial and dependent countries.[2] At

---

1   See, in this book, Pinheiro (2021).

2   At the 6th IC Congress, held from July to August 1928, the following issues were debated: the capitalist development of the time, imperialist contradictions, the problem of fascism and, more particularly for the analysis of this chapter, the prospect of revolution in the countries under imperialist rule, colonial, semi-colonial and dependent countries. The debate around these countries was held with China as the main focus and parameter, but the situation in

this same congress, Trotsky was expelled and the first major split occurs in the international communist movement. A break that also occurs in Brazil, when the leading group of the PCB is removed at the 3rd Congress of the party in 1928/1929.[3] This is the period of greatest political centralization, when there is the Stalinist standardizing of the PCB. Another inflection would occur only in the 1950s, with Stalin's death in 1953, Kruschev's declaration in 1956 and the March 1958 Declaration of the PCB. These are marks of the great world rift of the international and Brazilian communist movement.

In this way, the first controversy about the Brazilian revolution can be drawn during the "Tenentismo" in Brazil, but this debate has not ended either internationally or in Brazil, and it is linked to the interpretation of the process of the Brazilian economic and social historic formation. Brazilian. Thus, it was in the third great moment of inflection of the international movement, in the context of the crisis of the leadership of the communist parties, that the controversy of the Brazilian revolution resumed, but not only due to issues specific to the movement.

At the end of the 1940s, there was a peak of the cold war, with a great expansion of communism after the Chinese revolution of 1949, the Korean war of 1950 –1953 and the Cuban revolution of 1959. The latter brought the feeling that the revolution was an urgent matter, since it had arrived in Latin America, influencing the imagination of Brazilian militants. The revolutionary flame remained lit and the controversy intensified in Brazil. The development of cities and the industrial growth of the country, the legalization of the union movement and the progressive implementation of laws that guaranteed workers' rights with the Consolidação das Leis do Trabalho (CLT) – Consolidation of labour Laws – and the development of social struggles reinforced class organizations.

Social tensions were increasing in the 1950s, especially during the second Vargas government (1951–1954). In the years that followed, the country advanced in its industrialization under the aegis of national developmentalism, with the tripod of financing composed of State investment – international

---

India, Indonesia, North Africa and Latin America was also analyzed. The focus of the struggle in the Latin American region should be the "peasant-workers' government", within the framework of anti-imperialist resistance and against the latifundium. From the 6th Congress came general decisions that would guide all PCs who should try to adapt the guidelines to the concrete conditions of their realities.

3   On the debate in the 1920s and the political changes in the PCB, see The origins of the controversy of the Brazilian revolution: a debate between Octávio Brandão, Mario Pedrosa and Lívio Xavier.

capital – national capital. Despite this development of urbanization and modernization, especially in the south-central part of the country, the dream of overcoming underdevelopment was not achieved. Thus, in the early 1960s, the advance of Brazilian capitalism brought with it a deepening of its contradictions. On the one hand, establishing the strengthening of organized workers' struggles, capable of representing themselves in a broad labor movement, but also with communist wings, putting pressure on governments for distributive changes, improvement in working conditions, control of remittance of profits abroad and land reform. On the other hand, the Brazilian bourgeoisie did not see in that movement the birth of allies for a national or anti-imperialist revolution, on the contrary, it articulated itself with the international bourgeoisie and with conservative sectors of the armed forces in a preventive counter-revolution, giving rise to the coalition policy that delivered the 1964 coup.

Despite the fact that the coup implied violent persecution of left-wing organizations, the thought of the Brazilian revolution and the possibilities for a democratic and socialist future was still alive, especially when it came to the understanding of the nature of the bourgeois revolution in Brazil and the possible steps of resistance and reaction of the Marxist camp. Among the discussions on the Brazilian future, the theme of the revolution was taken up by the hands of three exponents of Brazilian Marxism: Nelson Werneck Sodré, Caio Prado Junior and Florestan Fernandes.

Our contribution in this chapter is to present those authors as representatives of different political currents in the spectrum of the Brazilian communist movement after the third great divide in the international communist movement and during the civil-military dictatorship in Brazil. Nelson Werneck with a position remarkably close to the line of the central direction of the PCB, Caio Prado making the internal criticism to the dominant interpretation in the party and Florestan Fernandes representing an external criticism to the party, a dissent that expresses the decentralization of the debate with the cracks of the communist movement.

The criterion of our cut for the construction of the controversy between these authors, in addition to the specific situation in which they carry out their analysis, is the fact that they are interpreters of Brazil in the sense that we have been using methodologically in this book (Curty & Malta, 2021), that is, authors who have a study on the economic and social formation of the country, which generated a position on the current production mode in the conjuncture when they wrote and its constitution process, in order to propose a reflection on the political practice for the revolution. Regarding specially the theory of revolution and the concrete analysis of the revolutionary situation, these authors based themselves on the work of Marx, Engels and Lenin, seeking to assess the objective and subjective conditions for the realization of the revolution in Brazil in the second half of the 20th century. Thus, the authors are engaged in an attempt to characterize the current mode of production in Brazil, evaluate the policy of viable class alliances in the Brazilian context and point out the paths of the Brazilian revolution.

Nelson Werneck Sodré characterized the mode of production as Brazilian feudalism, where a political alliance of workers with the national bourgeoisie against feudal landowners and imperialism would be feasible in order to carry out a bourgeois democratic revolution, a necessary stage for the eventual construction of socialism in the country. Caio Prado Junior maintained, since the 1930s, a capitalist characterization of the mode of production in Brazil, and did not consider an alliance with the national bourgeoisie viable, given its character associated with imperialism, being the fundamental alliance to carry out the revolution the one between rural and city workers, the democratic-bourgeois principle, to move gradually towards socialism. Florestan Fernandes, on the other hand, presented an interpretation of Brazilian dependent capitalism that left no room for a strategic alliance (even though there is a tactical gap) between workers and the bourgeoisie, since it exercises an autocratic and imperialist-dependent class domination, therefore, bet on the organization autonomy of workers as the only viable path to revolution in Brazil.

2   Nelson Werneck Sodré: The Bourgeois Democratic Revolution

Nelson Werneck Sodré was one of the most important names of the communist militancy in Brazil and his analyses had a great influence on the debates and formulations of the PCB. He has authored more than 60 titles about Brazil, covering economic history, military history, history teaching and Marxist interpretations of Brazil. He was an important articulator of the Instituto Superior de Estudos Brasileiros (ISEB) and formed a generation of communists in Brazil. Unlike Caio Prado Junior and Florestan Fernandes, Nelson Werneck Sodré does not present in his work a more theoretical-abstract analysis specifically for the question of the revolution, in which it is possible to explicitly identify his theoretical references on the question of the Brazilian revolution. His texts on this issue are organized around the specific historical questions of the Brazilian reality. Although the author does not make explicit references to theoretical debates in these texts, it is possible to perceive nuances of the influence of Marx, Engels, Lenin and contemporary debates on revolution in the scope of the PCB and the IC.

When introducing the thesis of the predominance of the feudal mode of production in the Brazilian formation, Sodré simultaneously rejects both the intepretations that attributed a capitalist character to the relations of production in Brazil, that of Caio Prado Jr. (1933; 1942; 1945) and Roberto Simonsen (1937) and that of Varnhagen (1854) and Capistrano de Abreu (1907), who understood colonization as the direct transplantation of feudalism from Portugal to Brazil without making the necessary mediations.[4]

In *Formação Histórica do Brasil* – Historical Formation of Brazil – (1962), Werneck Sodré puts the existence of a feudal monopoly on land as a central explanatory factor about the mode of production in Brazil, postulating the existence of a feudal regression process, originated from the decomposition of colonial slavery.

The feudalism developed by Sodré is the result of the need to understand the specifics of the Brazilian historical process. When placing the focus of the analysis on the internal conditions of production and the relations of possession and property in force in Brazil, Sodré observes that the Brazilian mode of production cannot be characterized neither as capitalist, nor of a capitalist sense – in direct criticism of Caio Prado Junior's formulation – for having a land monopoly and non-waged labour relations. Like Caio Prado Jr., Sodré sees the colonization process in Brazil as an unfolding of the process of primitive capital accumulation in Europe, the colonial system being the lever of this accumulation process. However, for the author, this did not mean, contrary to what Caio Prado thought, that the colonization process of Brazil, as it derived from the emergence of the capitalist system, implied on a colonial capitalist production, even though the slave production is endowed with this meaning. Sodré's criticism lies in the fact that, during the process of primitive accumulation, capitalist production would not have occurred even in Portugal, insofar as in this stage of the historical process the dominant form of capital was commercial capital, still unable to expand on its own bases, and which, therefore, would not be fully capitalist (Sodré, 1962; 1980).

For Sodré, the development of capitalism in some regions of Europe took place in order to place different forms of non-capitalist production at the service of its logic. For the author, the process of accumulation of mercantile capital, which took place in the sphere of circulation, coexisted with feudal

---

4 Caio Prado's contribution lies in Formação do Brasil Contemporâneo – Formation of the Contemporary Brazil – (1942); Roberto Simonsen's lies in História Econômica do Brasil – Economic History of Brazil – (1937); Varnhagen's lies in História Geral do Brasil – General History of Brazil – (1854); that of Capistrano de Abreu lies in Capítulos da História Colonial – Chapters of the Colonial History – (1907).

relations of production and strengthened them in some places, while it acted as one of the ways to constitute the capitalist mode of production in others. The existence of feudal relations in some parts of Europe, such as Portugal, was functional for the development of capitalist relations of production in others, such as England. The determining factor for the consolidation of the capitalist mode of production is taken as something internal to the dynamics of the local economy.

Sodré's main criticism of the current that understands Brazil as capitalist since its colonial era lies in the confusion, which according to Sodré this current incurs, between commercial capital, which achieves its surplus in the sphere of circulation, and the capitalist mode of production itself. Sodré states that the commercial bourgeoisie that emerges from this process cannot be confused with a hegemonic bourgeois class (Pinheiro et al, 2015). In this sense, he presents a position quite different from what he had formulated in 1944 in *Formação da Sociedade Brasileira* (Formation of the Brazilian Society) (Sodré, 1944). In 1962, Sodré disputes the bourgeois character of the Avis Revolution that he had previously presented and which until then was the vision established in historiography – the Avis Revolution was the process that triggered the early unification of Portugal in 1385. For Sodré this would have been a process of struggle within the framework of feudalism to expel the Moors. Plus, the institutions and the State that were constituted in this process have no capitalist content. At the same time, this is already marked by the rise of commercial capital that works by dissolving established feudal relations.

In other words, there was feudalism in Portugal, but it was a decadent feudalism, endowed with some characteristics. The implementation of a commercial group in Portugal, at the stage of political centralization, was not a sufficient condition for the implementation of capitalist relations of production in Brazil. This would then be one of the keys to understanding what is happening with the Brazilian formation (Grespan, 2006). Sodré criticizes those who saw capitalism in Portugal from 1385 onwards, being the origin of the mistake the confusion between commercial capital and capitalist production method itself.

The Brazilian colonization process was an enterprise of Portuguese commercial capital that had an absolutist State as its institutional legal framework. It is in this context that commercial exploitation of the Brazilian coast takes place in the first years of colonization. Moreover, it was back to this time that the hereditary captaincy system, which failed in a few years, was inserted. Although it did not leave significant legacies at the institutional level, since the General Government would be instituted in 1549, the captaincies left a legacy which Sodré points out that would be permanently reinstated in the history of

Brazil, the feudal monopoly of the land. The royal monopoly on access to land and the land use concessions made by the Crown would have already started a land distribution concentrated both in the enterprises aimed at the world market and in the primary activities necessary for the reproduction of the colonial economy, that is, the activities aimed at the domestic market. Such land distribution originating from feudalism would reproduce permanently in the Brazilian historical reality.

Regarding the existing mode of production in Brazil, Sodré also states that the one installed here had no direct connection with indigenous production, for the slavery implanted here was a total and direct rupture with the primitive communism characteristic of the organization of production for these people. Although in some areas the indigenous labor force has been enlisted as slave labor or subsumed to work by religious coercion, this is not the typical case of the labor force used, the black African. In this way, the production method installed here is transplanted. There is no continuity between indigenous primitivism and slavery. In the latter, Africans come in the condition of enslaved dominated and the Portuguese as dominators, both conditions that did not exist before in Brazil. The slavery that is implanted here is structured with slave labour of African origin based on elements of European productive and social organization. That is,

> [...] the so-called colonization is born from the transplantation of African and European human elements: the former provided the mass of the dominated class, which competed with the work; the latter provided the absolute majority of those who competed with the property, the dominant class.
> SODRÉ, 1980, p. 136

Another important aspect of the Brazilian social formation is the existence of uneven development and how this uneven development is manifested in Brazilian history. For the author, the fact that the historical existence of Brazil is treated based on the act of "discovery" needs to be reassessed. The "discovery" took place at a time when feudalism was declining in Western Europe, with the commercial revolution and the great navigations as its landmarks, thus defining a world market, in which different social formations are inserted in different ways.

The Brazilian social formation would be marked by heterochrony, that is, by the presence of modes of production that characterize different historical times in the same economic and social structure, characteristic of the uneven development of this structure. For Sodré, primitive communism, slavery, and feudalism coexist in Brazil as modes of production; the advance of production over indigenous areas and the decline of slave production led to the dominance of feudalism over others. These different modes of production coexist simultaneously, but in his understanding, it is feudalism that characterizes the main mode of production in this structure. In the author's view, one of the problems caused by this heterochrony at the theoretical level would be the use of categories based on the analysis of other concrete situations and historically associated with previous periods to try to explain the Brazilian case, which according to Sodré would be a problem inherent to his notion of feudalism itself.

Heterochrony, a characteristic present in the Brazilian historical reality as a result of the process of uneven development, unfolds, in turn, in the presence of different historical stages in the same geographic territory, what Sodré called the *contemporaneidade do não-coetâneo* (contemporaneity of the non-coeval). In other words, for the author, this phenomenon is an internal reflection of heterochrony:

> Brazil has presented, and still presents – today, in fact, with already considerably reduced effects – different stages of development, to apply a generalized and harvested concept of the economy. Uniformity is still, among us, a trend that has been accentuated, no doubt, but that heterochrony exists and works, conditioning communities and societies. This is another aspect – now particular, because it is Brazilian – of uneven development.
>
> SODRÉ, 1980, p. 135

When analyzing these different stages coexisting in the Brazilian economic-social structure, other authors, such as Ignácio Rangel, work with the same terms "contemporaneity of the non-coeval" that Sodré presents, but they bring other interpretations about the Brazilian social formation. According to Oliveira Filho (2000), many ISEB authors had in their analysis the notion of contemporaneity of the non-coeval. For Rangel (1957), the contemporaneity of the non-coeval would be one of the characteristics of the basic Brazilian duality, a type of specifically Brazilian mode of production. The contemporaneity of the non-coeval for Sodré would be another characteristic of the uneven development in Brazil.

From his point of view, being colonized by a feudal country after the accumulation of mercantile capital, Brazil would have inherited a feudal productive structure, which, when faced with the material conditions of the new world, would once again regress to the slave mode of production. "The economic, demographic and political predominance of slavery is undoubted until the late 19th century, associating slaveholding landowners with large traders on the world market" (Del Roio, 2000, p.88).

The heterochrony presented by Sodré is the starting point of the idea of feudal regression presented by the author, since, in the same economic-social structure, slavery and feudalism coexist, and the decomposition of the former implies, for the author, the dominance of the latter. With the decomposition of slavery, the feudal regression characteristic of the oligarchic Republic would take place. The maintenance of the land monopoly and the various labour relations that are established in the countryside, instituted in the figures[5]of the partner, sharecropper or resident, were predominantly non-wage relationships, which led Sodré to characterize the current mode of production in Brazilian reality as feudalism. With the feudal regression, the country's land structure is preserved. However, before thinking about European feudalism,[6] it is necessary to highlight that it is a truly Brazilian form of feudalism, since the author perceives through the category what he believes to be the specificity of the mode of production in Brazil, the concentration and monopoly of the lands. The dominant mode of production is feudal because the land monopoly is the basis on which the production and reproduction of material life is organized.

When drawing a parallel between these relations of production and feudal ones, Sodré is always careful to establish the appropriate mediations to capture the specifics of the Brazilian case. It is in this sense that it can be said that Nelson Sodré builds feudalism in a Brazilian way. Such an explanation is not simply an adaptation of the Soviet and IC-incorporated formulations on the issue. It is important to remember that the term feudalism to characterize the

---

5   The production systems with partners, sharecroppers, residents were systems that involved agreements between landowners and the peasants who lived and produced on that land, the landowners gave up the use of the land in exchange for the division of production carried out by the peasants. In many cases, in the agreements there was also some type of debt between the peasant and the owner, such as the payment of travel by migrant peasants, which should be reimbursed for the production carried out by the peasant. They were relations of production based on the political, legal, military power of the owners over workers, based on personal relationships and non-economic forms of coercion. Nelson Werneck Sodré highlights the importance of these production relations in Brazil, highlighting their non-capitalist character.

6   In fact, it is important to highlight that in historiography there is a debate about the nonexistence of a single case of European feudalism, but of several feudalisms, which would not be possible to speak of a feudalism of the classical type. In general, Sodré questions in his argument the very idea that feudalism would be a uniform mode of production, placing the existing differences in European feudalism itself.

mode of production in Latin America was a usual term in the field of historical debates until the 1960s. Sodré, when making his analysis of this feudalism to the Brazilian case, makes use of the term disseminated at his time, bringing a unique and in-depth analysis of the characterization of the mode of production in Brazil.

With the interpretation of the Brazilian historical process in the light of the idea of feudal regression, Sodré carries out a rigorous Marxist foundation from the national democratic program formulated by the PCB based on the so-called March 1958 Declaration.[7] If the interpretation of the Brazilian social formation until then had been carried out through the official Marxism-Leninism of the 3rd International, with concepts considered as universal for colonial, semi-colonial and dependent countries, mechanically imported into the Brazilian reality, it is based on Sodré's contribution that this analysis acquires outlines historically based on the specificities of the Brazilian social formation.

The concept of feudal regression elaborated by the author justifies the political tactic of a broad popular front so that, fighting the remnants of feudalism, fully realize the bourgeois revolution in Brazil. This broad front would include the working class, urban and peasant, and the national bourgeoisie, which oscillated between nationalism and imperialism, but which according to Sodré, had material nationalist interests, manifested, for example, in supporting the Brazilian State in the industrialization process . Here it is worth considering the use of the national bourgeoisie category in Sodré's work. The author considers the use or not of the national bourgeoisie category to refer to the bourgeoisie in Brazil, more specifically, in the chapter O problema da burguesia (The problem of the bourgeoisie) of the book Introdução à revolução brasileira (Introduction to the Brazilian revolution) (Sodré, 1958), from 1958, Sodré refers to the national bourgeoisie as that fraction of the bourgeoisie that

---

7   In the March 1958 Declaration, the party publicly abandoned the position of armed struggle, assumed after its entry into illegality in 1947, and readmitted the institutional route as a tool of political struggle, with its strategy embodied in the national democratic program. Synthetically, the perception contained in the national democratic program was that the bourgeois revolution in Brazil was still to be done, requiring an anti-feudal and anti-imperialist agenda. The characterization of the existing capitalist development in Brazil in this document identifies it as unequal – due to the combination of capitalist methods of production with the monopoly of land and social relations of semi-feudal production – and that was forged within the framework of imperialist dependence and influence. From this diagnosis, it became necessary to eliminate the feudal reminiscences in the Brazilian formation, which would be dulling the possibilities of developing a thriving capitalism, understood as a necessary stage for the transition to socialism. For the full March 1958 Declaration, see PCB: twenty years of politics 1958–1979 (documents) (PCB, 1980, p. 3–27).

resists imperialism and that would have a role in the process of the Brazilian revolution, differentiating it from the fraction of the bourgeoisie associated with imperialism and that would have no role in the Brazilian revolution. Thus, he defends the use of the category to refer to this fraction of the bourgeoisie in Brazil.

Sodré's argument about the Brazilian revolution has as its central element the perception of the atrophy and the non-realization of the bourgeois revolution in Brazil. For Sodré, when breaking with the oligarchic Republic, the 1930 Revolution would have kept many features of the oligarchy, this bourgeois revolution would only be completed with a rupture conducted by the national bourgeoisie, aiming to overcome the archaic features inherited from the colonial period.

In this context, the complete non-realization of the bourgeois revolution means that there was an opposition between the nation that was being formed and imperialism and its internal agents. Soon, it became necessary to form a coalition of nationalist forces in order to overcome the double obstacle to national economic development: the feudal monopoly of the land and imperialism.

The feudal monopoly of the land, the latifundium, characteristic of the feudalism that Sodré identifies in the Brazilian mode of production, has its production based on the logic of the interests of the foreign market. Besides it constitutes an extremely concentrated and unproductive land structure. According to Pinheiro et al. (2015) this structure, for Sodré, would lead to the scarcity of foodstuffs supplied to the urban masses in Brazil and to permanent inflationary problems, in addition to generating a chronic surplus of workforce in the countryside, thus curbing the constitution of an internal market in its breadth, which would be important for the development of the thriving national economy.

Imperialism manifested itself as an obstacle to the development of vigorous national capitalism due to Brazil's peripheral insertion in the international context, subordinated to imperialism, especially the United States, through the external strangulation of the Brazilian economy, the payment of the external debt and the constant remittances of international capital installed in the Brazilian economy. These elements would be major obstacles to the development of the national economy in Brazil autonomously.

In this way, the alliance between the working class and the national bourgeoisie should conduct an anti-feudal, anti-imperialist, national and democratic revolutionary process, in order to overcome this double obstacle. This overcoming should be done through an agrarian revolution and a national revolution, in addition, it would be necessary to complete the process of industrialization of the Brazilian economy. The Brazilian revolution would therefore be a bourgeois one. This would be fundamental for the development of strong and dynamic national capitalism, a necessary stage for the subsequent transition to socialism.

In this way, Werneck Sodré's analysis also placed him in the field of the national democratic program for the Brazilian revolution that would be in discussion. The expectation was to form a coalition of nationalist forces in order to finally develop the nation in democratic terms, overcoming the feudal land monopoly and imperialism. Such hopes would only be diluted with the 1964 coup, which, by curbing the historical possibilities of its implementation of the nationalist alliance, highlighted the historical-political limits of its proposal.

3   Caio Prado Junior: Criticism of the Democratic Bourgeois Revolution

Caio Prado Junior was a historic militant of the PCB, affiliated to the party in 1931, who never abandoned it. However, he was always far from the leadership and from the dominant theoretical line of the party, systematically criticizing its theoretical-political position.[8] Since his first book, *Evolução Política do Brasil* (Political Evolution of Brazil) (1933), he has expressed a different formulation about the characteristics of Brazilian social formation, diverging even from the majority positions worldwide, propagated by the IC since 1928.

In the 1933 book, the author affirmed the capitalist character of Portuguese colonization over Brazil, pointing out the specificities of large-scale production carried out in the large rural exploration typical of the colony. He also presented the internal class contradictions that led to independence, as well as analysing the scenario of great political instability in the empire, especially during the regency period, in which he pointed out the difficulties of the revolts in achieving lasting successes. In *Formação do Brasil Contemporâneo: Colônia* (Formation of Contemporary Brazil: Colônia) (1942), Caio Prado continued his reflection on the Brazilian social formation, becoming recognized as one of the first Marxist interpreters to characterize the sense of colonization as commercial and capitalist, going against the defended feudal thesis, in the left field, by the PCB.

This position – distinct from that defended by the PCB, as we have seen in the works highlighted above – remained until its last great work, *A Revolução*

---

8   For a more detailed analysis of Caio Prado Jr.'s political and intellectual trajectory, see in this book: Borja (2021), Controversy on Economic History: Roberto Simonsen, Caio Prado Jr. and Celso Furtado.

Brasileira (The Brazilian Revolution) (1966) – including the balance that it makes of it in the text *Perspectivas em 1977* (Perspectives in 1977). This all confirms that *A Revolução Brasileira* is not a fortuitous book, in circumstance, in response to the 1964 coup. It is evident that the main motivation of the book is to present an interpretation and a political position in the face of the coup, however, this is done in total coherence with the formulations long developed by the author. Thus, *A Revolução Brasileira* presents itself as a book summarizing Caio Prado Junior's theoretical-political trajectory.

As the author himself points out, the central thesis of the book revolves around the political implications for the left, for the communists in particular, derived from a mistaken theory of the Brazilian revolution.[9] In other words, the book is part of a great controversy on the direction of the Brazilian revolution. That was a fundamental controversy in the field of the left, which until then was hegemonized by the PCB formulations, according to the IC program. The central elements of the debate are related to the characterization of the current mode of production in Brazil, the revolutionary political forces and the character of the revolution. In other words, we could say that the controversy presents itself as a typical debate of interpreters of Brazil, that is, historical interpretation, conjuncture analysis and political transformation program.

At the opening of the book, Caio Prado questions the concept of revolution:

> In the sense in which it is ordinarily used, "revolution" means the use of force and violence to overthrow the government and seize power by some group, social category or any other force in the opposition. "Revolution" has the meaning that most appropriately fits the term "insurrection". But "revolution" also has the meaning of transforming the social-political regime that it can be and as a rule has historically been triggered or stimulated by insurrections. But that is not necessarily so. The proper meaning is concentrated in the transformation, and not in the immediate process through which it takes place.
>
> PRADO JR, [1966] 1978, p. 11

Thus, the author already demonstrates a very particular position on the subject. He is aligned with those who defend the procedural character of the revolution: "a historical process marked by successive economic, social and

---

9   As the author argues in the article Addendum to the Brazilian Revolution, published in Revista Civilização Brasileira nº 14, 1967 (Prado Júnior, 1967). It has been written in response to the critical article by Assis Tavares published in a previous issue of the magazine, the addendum was later incorporated into future editions of the book.

political reforms and modifications, which, concentrated in a relatively short historical period, will lead to structural transformations of society" (Prado Jr, [1966] 1978, p.11). Therefore, the great debate carried out in the book deals with the transformations sought and the social forces capable of bringing them about.

It is in this way that the author will directly confront what he calls the consecrated theory of the Brazilian revolution, read: the theory of the PCB revolution. Caio Prado traces an itinerary of importing the Marxist theory of revolution which, derived from the concrete analyses of Marx and Lenin, would have spread as a closed and universal program for the cases of colonial, semi-colonial and dependent countries after the 4th Congress of the Communist International, held in Moscow in the year 1928. And then transmitted to the PCB.

As pointed out above, this consecrated theory of the Brazilian revolution presents Brazil – and all other colonial, semi-colonial and dependent countries – as a feudal social formation, where the feudal latifundium and social relations of the same character would predominate. Thus conceived, the generalizing historical interpretation, derived from European models and Lenin's interpretation of Russia, addresses the first central element of the Brazilian revolution: the anti-feudal struggle, as an agrarian revolution led by peasants in search of land ownership.

In this classic model, another element was added, distinctive of colonial, semi-colonial and dependent countries, that is, imperialism. The strength that the foreign capital of the great powers has in these countries would be one of the main obstacles to be overcome by the revolution. However, the consecrated theory focuses on the competition that imperialism acting on the domestic market does to national capital, thus this main theory sees a contradiction between imperialism and a "national bourgeoisie". Here we would have another central element of the Brazilian revolution: the anti-imperialist struggle, as a national revolution led by the bourgeoisie against foreign competition.

It should be noted that, in light of this theory, the typical stage of the Brazilian revolution to be sought would be the democratic-bourgeois revolution, led by the so-called "national bourgeoisie" and the peasantry. Elaborated and disseminated in the 1920s, this European-inspired theory was still in force and it was dominant in the Brazilian left of the 1960s. It is against such an established theory that Caio Prado raises all his indignation, pointing out the idealism and formalism contained in it. In short, a theory foreign to the history of formation and to the concrete reality of the Brazilian situation, and, therefore, inefficient for the political conduct of its revolutionary process.

The theory of the Brazilian revolution, to be something effectively practical in conducting the facts, will be simply – but not simplistically – the interpretation of the current situation and the historical process that results. This process, which, in its future projection, will fully answer the outstanding questions. This is what the dialectical method fundamentally consists of. *Method of interpretation*, not prescription of facts, dogma, framing the historical revolution within pre-established abstract schemes.

PRADO JR, [1966] 1978, p. 19

With this, the need to elaborate an interpretation of Brazil is affirmed and, from it, the need to derive a theory of the Brazilian revolution. Caio Prado identifies the biggest problem of the consecrated theory in the mechanical transposition of the social categories of European reality, the Russian one in particular, for the Brazilian case – as the author understands to have been done by Nelson Werneck Sodré, to whom he addresses harsh criticisms. He especially questions the identification between the great Brazilian landowners and the feudal nobility, and between the workers of the Brazilian countryside and the European peasant. This abstract identification would not find a match in the reality of Brazilian social formation.

This theme had been addressed by the author in his works on the history of Brazil – *Evolução Política do Brasil* (Political Evolution of Brazil) (1933), *Formação do Brasil Contemporâneo – colônia* (Formation of Contemporary Brazil – colony) (1942) and *História Econômica do Brasil* (Economic History of Brazil) (1945) – and then resumed and deepened in his intervention in the debate on the agrarian question in the early 1960s. Consistent with his interpretation, Caio Prado maintains the belief that the Brazilian colonization originated from the capitalist impulse of European commercial expansion and that there was no reason to talk about feudalism in Brazil.

The sense of tropical colonization would differ greatly from feudalism, inasmuch as the objective of selling to the external market was essential. In addition, the colonization's economic and social structure itself would have very peculiar characteristics, where in the latifundium there was production based on the collective work and cooperation of a large number of enslaved people under the sole direction of the owner. This means that neither the social relation of production was serfdom, since slavery predominated, nor was the production system organized on a peasant basis, such as European feudalism. Furthermore, the determinant was not the title of property itself, but the ability to invest large sums of capital to organize a single large-scale production for the world market.

It is evident that, for the author, there has never been feudalism in Brazil. The alleged fight against "feudal remains" defended by the PCB and by Nelson Werneck Sodré's analysis was mistaken. What there was left were slave remains, which implied terrible working conditions in the Brazilian countryside. Hence the importance of a correct interpretation of Brazil, since it has serious political consequences. According to Caio Prado, the political objective of the struggle in the countryside was not the struggle of peasants for owning land, but better working and living conditions.

Another central element criticized was the supposed contradiction between imperialism and the so-called "national bourgeoisie". Again, relying on his classic works on Brazilian history, the author criticizes this perspective of the PCB, affirming the absence of a national bourgeoisie with revolutionary potential. The Brazilian bourgeoisie would bring with it a conciliating element with imperialism, since it has been formed in the process of Portuguese colonization with its capitalist character. Since the 1940s, in *História Econômica do Brasil* (Economic History of Brazil), Caio Prado has already drawn attention to the association between the Brazilian and foreign bourgeoisies. A community of interests that became apparent with heavy industrialization and the need for foreign capital to boost Brazilian industrialization.

Far from the contradiction of interests propagated by the consecrated theory, there was the dependence of the Brazilian bourgeoisie on foreign investments to guarantee the production of durable consumer goods. Especially after the Juscelino Kubitschek's *Plano de Metas* (Goals Plan), this would be the nucleus of the growth dynamics of the Brazilian economy, growth that benefited the local bourgeoisie by opening new business opportunities. There, the generalization made to colonial, semi-colonial and dependent countries was quite different, since the latter, in the case of Brazil, had a social formation in which the supposed national bourgeoisie benefited from foreign investments, without offering them greater resistance, let alone a revolutionary character.

Within the framework of this historical interpretation, we can understand what Caio Prado calls colonial reversal. For the author, in Brazilian history there was a perpetuation of the colonial system by other means. Even after achieving political independence from Portugal, Brazil would have immediately placed itself in the condition of dependence on England, especially through liberalism in the 19th century. In the 20th century, in the context of the Republic and the affirmation of US domination, it would the colonial system be perpetuated by the action of imperialism, controlling the direction of Brazilian industrialization. Thus, the "import substitution industrialization" was extremely fragile for the author, now threatened by a return to the typical model of primary export, now handled by the interests of imperialism.

This configures what Caio Prado qualifies as the central nucleus of the Brazilian revolution, still in progress in the 1960s: the difficult transition from the colonial economy to the national economy. The colonial economy would be the constant objective of Brazilian economic production turned to the outside and controlled by external interests. While the national economy would have as its final objective the economic production for the consumption and subsistence of its population, and which would be controlled by national interests.

> In the concrete instance of the Brazilian historical evolution that now occupies us, we observe, in the most general plane that we are given to observe it, that what is found as an expression of the whole process is the progressive transformation and overcoming of the colonial Brazil that comes from the past and it constitutes the complex of situations, structures and institutions in which the Brazilian colonization took place. Transformation and overcoming that, driven by the game of contradictions that are configured in the same situations, structures and institutions, are taking them to a new and different feature that means and will mean more and more the national integration of Brazil. That is to say, the configuration of a country and its population essentially focused on themselves, and organised economically, socially and politically according to their own needs, interests and aspirations.
>
> PRADO JR, [1966] 1978, p. 134

Within this framework, and this perspective of transformation, the author analyzes the conjuncture of the 1960s. This would be characterized by the rise of the struggle and organization of rural workers, however in a context of little autonomy for urban workers in the face of the opportunism of labor governments. As for the so-called "national bourgeoisie", there was no expectation of a direct confrontation with imperialism. Caio Prado considered that, at most, there would be one or another competition problem, but that these would be resolved within the framework of dependent capitalism, without any revolutionary perspective of the so-called national bourgeoisie, generally associated with imperialism.

Therefore, in the face of such a situation, the political problem of the Brazilian revolution, that is, the mobilization of revolutionary social forces, would consist in building an autonomous organization of urban workers, so that the central alliance in the Brazilian revolutionary process was made viable: the alliance between rural and urban workers. The old motto of the proletarian-peasant alliance should be better qualified in the Brazilian case, since in the author's interpretation there would not be exactly peasantry in Brazil, but workers in the field. For Caio Prado this analogous condition of workers fighting for better working conditions, whether in the countryside or in the city, would be the central element for the unity of the revolutionary struggle.

As for the character of the revolution and its practical program, the author is somewhat ambiguous. He says the debate about the character of the revolution is unproductive, and it is impertinent to classify it as democratic-bourgeois or socialist. As a Marxist, Caio Prado defends the ultimate goal of socialism. But in making explicit his revolutionary program, it is evident that he proposes elements typical of the democratic-bourgeois revolution, although not fully restricted to them.

In the Brazilian historical context of the 1960s, living under a dictatorship, the author asserts that it was up to the revolutionary movement to fight for the return to democratic normality. This would make it possible for communists and the trade union movement to go underground and proceed with a more efficient organization of rural and city workers. The return to democracy and the more effective organization of the workers' movement could allow the dispute of the bourgeois State, pressing for the adoption of policies aimed at revolutionary interests.

Restricted to the horizon of institutional reforms and State planning, the author does not clearly present how certain measures, defended by him, would go beyond the democratic-bourgeois program, such as: the restriction of free private initiative, without eliminating it; the State monopoly on foreign trade; the control of the remittance of profits by foreign companies. For Caio Prado, it was all about the organization of workers and their struggle for better working and life conditions in the countryside and in the city. Moreover, it would be the rise of the political force of the working class within bourgeois democracy that would allow the progressive transformation of the system as a whole, including the socialist sense of this transformation.

Thus, Caio Prado Jr, despite being critical of the PCB's dominant view of the Brazilian revolution, remained within the scope of the national democratic program. The author pointed out the permanence of the difficult transition from the colonial economy to the national economy as a fundamental element of transformation necessary for the creation of revolutionary conditions in Brazil, articulating an anti-imperialist struggle. At the same time, the struggle for democracy was fundamental to the organization of the left in the context of criticism of Stalinism at the international level and of the civil-military dictatorship in Brazil.

4   Florestan Fernandes: Permanent Revolution and
     Counterrevolution

Florestan Fernandes was considered, by default, founder of the School of
Sociology at the University of São Paulo (USP) and father of Brazilian sociology. Politically, he was affiliated with the *Partido Socialista Revolucionário*
(PSR) – (Socialist Revolutionary Party) between 1942 and 1953 and, later,
with the *Partido dos Trabalhadores* (PT) – (Workers' Party), party to which he
contributed critically to the formation and for which he was a federal deputy twice between 1987 and 1995, having participated in the constituent. Like
Nelson Werneck Sodré and Caio Prado Jr., he was part of the Brazilian communist tradition influenced by the Russian revolutionary process that took place
throughout the 20th century.

Florestan's thought, however, has a greater influence from the 4th
International, yet the author is still quite referred to Leninism-Marxism.
Among the main influences of revolutionary theory and practice that the
author suffered, *Estado e Revolução* (Lenin's State and Revolution) (Lenin, 1918)
stand out; the concept of permanent revolution introduced by Marx & Engels
(1850), and which would be developed by Trotsky (1930); and, finally, the concept of uneven and combined development[10] also formulated by Trotsky, composing a very solid conceptual basis for his participation in the controversy of
the Brazilian revolution.

However, Florestan Fernandes created a very original, critical and systematized interpretation of the peculiarity of the bourgeois revolution in Brazil,
as a corollary of Latin American dependent capitalism and this made him take
part of the controversy on the Brazilian Revolution in a critical and external
way to the PCB staff, represented both by Sodré's majority view and by Caio
Prado's minority view. Thus, Florestan Fernandes did not share the PCB's
national democratic program.

---

10   According to the sociologist, following the logic of Trotsky's theory of uneven and com-
      bined development, the *uneven* development of capitalism at the international level
      means that in countries considered backward the development of capitalism has its own
      historicity that assimilates the modern elements of societies considered advanced, adapt-
      ing them to archaic cultural and material elements, typical of backward societies. The
      combined element is explained by this superposition of the culture, politics and inno-
      vations of the advanced nations with the pre-capitalist social relations verified in back-
      ward countries and it is this factor that determines the possible subjects of the unfinished
      social revolutions.

As indicated, Florestan glimpsed the main debates of the national democratic program through his militancy in a Trotskyist party.[11] After having left the PSR, he would academically insert himself into the debate by following Caio Prado Jr.'s critical line. Although he pointed out some limits to the interpretation of Brazil by the geographer and historian, such as the undersizing that Caio Prado had given to the reach of post-war Brazilian industrialization and the lack of a sociological analysis of the meaning of Brazilian colonization, Florestan agrees with that author with regard to the character of the Brazilian bourgeoisie and the orientation of the Brazilian revolution that must be a process guided by the proletarians and which promotes better living conditions for the mass of the population (Fernandes, 1995).

Thus, it can be said that when treading Caio Prado's interpretation, Florestan Fernandes went further by providing a critique from outside the PCB and for being one of the founders of the Brazil program that replaced the national democratic program: the popular democratic program, always with the permanent revolution as a guiding principle on the horizon. The popular democratic program highlights the impossibility of articulating the political coalition with the weak and associated Brazilian bourgeoisie, in the struggle for the creation of the nation and elaborated the question of the revolution as a permanent process in search of a socialism that would be reached through a growing political participation of the population: an effective mass democracy.

The object of study that runs through Florestan's work is the possibility of a social revolution that breaks with the bonds of what the author defines as the double articulation of dependent capitalism: external dependence and internal social segregation. This, according to the author, would be the mark that Brazil has brought since colonial times and which would be intensified with the structuring of society into classes based on the abolition of slavery, the proclamation of the Republic and the slow process of urbanization of a "competitive social order" at the turn of the 19th to the 20th century.

Influenced by the principle of uneven and combined development, he gives centrality to the specificity of a country dependent on the global order. In *Sociedade de Classes e Subdesenvolvimento* (Society of Classes and Underdevelopment) of 1968, one year before of having his political rights revoked by AI-5, he states:

---

11   The dissent of the PCB would give rise to what Karepovs et alli (1995) called 1st and 2nd generation of Trotskyists in Brazil. Florestan Fernandes would be the representative of the latter and would join the PSR at the invitation of Hermínio Sacchetta in 1942.

Therefore, an underdeveloped society, which is at the stage of dependent capitalism, not only has a capitalist market economy, in the modern sense. Your own economic order is a capitalist order. In this respect, it reproduces several essential conditions for the existence, functioning and growth of the social regime of capitalist production. Perhaps due to this, some authors were tempted to focus on it as if it constituted a miniature replica of the original model and were thus in an inevitable but transitory stage in the normal evolution of capitalism. However, this view distorts reality on a fundamental point. Insofar as the structure and historical destiny of such societies is linked to dependent capitalism, they embody a specific situation, which can only be characterized through a doubly polarized capitalist market economy, devoid of self-sufficiency and possessing, at most, limited autonomy.

FERNANDES, 1968, p. 36

In *A Revolução Burguesa no Brasil* (The Bourgeois Revolution in Brazil), his main work, Fernandes shows in detail how the process of the bourgeois revolution was slow and controlled. Started with the 1930 coup in a context of increasing urbanization and industrialization, this process transformed the country's economic structure and political superstructure. Overcoming the panorama of the Oligarchic Republic without making a radical break, the dominant and aristocratic classes, coming from the colonial regime and oriented by the "business sense", merged with the emerging class of petty-bourgeois traders combining the archaic element of Brazilian society with the modern element of Western industrial society.

Thus, the pace, meaning and intensity of capitalist development in Brazil came under the strict control of the ruling classes that resorted to the State as the center of their political, economic and ideological domination. It happens that, under dependent capitalism, the bourgeois revolution would have a peculiarity: even before consolidating its economic domination over the "semi-integrated" and "condemned of the system"[12] on modern bourgeois bases, the

---

12   The sociologist analyzes the social structure of Brazilian society in a society of classes and underdevelopment (Fernandes, 1968). There is a presentation, inspired by Weber, of what the convicts of the system would be (those who have no chance of participating effectively in the possible democracy in dependent capitalism); the semi-integrated (those who manage to enter the market, even if it is in the form of temporary, informal or underemployment jobs) and the integrated ones of the system (people who can appreciate themselves either through the formal labor market or through the possession of goods).

ruling classes already had the political control of society using the State as a strong instrument of domination.

Therefore, the bourgeois revolution in the context of Latin American dependent capitalism, would lead the bourgeoisie to abandon the "ideology and utopia" of the English, American and French liberal revolutions because they did not need it. They were able to conceal their particularistic, selfish and patrimonial class interests as if they were the general interests of a "nation", of an integrated collectivity. By centralizing their power in the State, these bourgeoisies acted in an oppressive and repressive manner in moments of historical disjunctive when the status quo, that is, their class situation as a ruling class, was threatened. In Brazil, this resulted in the redefinition of the social issue in terms of a police issue, showing the ultra-authoritarian, anti-social and anti-national character of our bourgeoisies that, in times of crisis, carry out preventive counter-revolutions.

In Brazil, the bourgeois revolution took place in a peculiarly autocratic way with the intensification of the double articulation between internal social segregation and external dependence. Moreover, in the period of the monopolistic social order of total imperialism of the 1960s, there was a bourgeois crisis derived from the peculiarity of the double character of the Brazilian bourgeoisies (omnipotent inward and subservient to the outside) that would lead to a radical solution: the concretization of the bourgeois revolution in Brazil with the establishment of the 1964 civil-military regime. From the perspective of capital, or of the ruling classes, the issue of national formation would be swept away from the scene definitively through what Fernandes (1975) defined as a permanent counterrevolution, the institutionalization of oppression and repression as a bourgeois solution to the crisis of bourgeois hegemony via the unification and centralization of the ruling classes in the State, a political super-entity.

It turns out that, as the author himself pointed out, this solution was temporary, as the bourgeois solution carried seeds of contradictions that would lead to the relaxation of the authoritarian regime, at least in the ultra-reactionary and unified form present in the 1964 regime. From *A Revolução Burguesa no Brasil* (The bourgeois revolution in Brazil), the sociologist envisions the combination of a double possibility in the period of political transition that began in the late 1970s: the marriage of the intensification of the bourgeois autocratic regime with the emergence of the political form of co-optation democracy. To proceed, a digression must be made to understand co-optation democracy as a process of revolution in the techniques of counterrevolution.

In 1981, in the context of the political distension of the military regime in Brazil, Florestan Fernandes considered the counterrevolution from the co-optation in *O que é revolução?* (What is a revolution?):

If a rigorous analysis is carried out, taking into account the developments that took place in the central capitalist societies, it is discovered
that the bourgeoisie not only learned to live with the class struggle – it
went further and bent the socialist movement itself, first, and the communist movement, then, forcing them to define as their political axis
the bourgeois form of democracy (that is, it forced them to renounce
the class struggle and the violent, "non-democratic" means of conquer-
ing power) [...] the bourgeoisie learned to use globally the techniques
that are appropriate for class struggle and dared to incorporate these
techniques into a gigantic institutional network, from the company to
the employers' union, from the State to the continental and world capitalist organizations. While the socialist movement and the communist
movement opted for "tactical" and "defensive" options, the bourgeoisie
advanced strategically, at the financial, state and military levels, and pro-
ceeded to a true revolution in the techniques of the counter-revolution.
It even opened up new spaces for itself, exploring the functions of legitimizing the State to tie the working classes to the security of order and to
weld unions or workers' parties to the destinies of democracy.

> FERNANDES, 1981, p. 10

Therefore, the idea of co-optation democracy is linked to the development of
instruments to maintain the status quo by the ruling classes. Its hallmark is the
fact that it constitutes a hidden counter-revolution, that is, without the single use of force with oppression and repression. The methods of co-optation
democracy are varied, but the objective is clear: to transform revolutionaries
into reformists and to guarantee the gradual and continuous absorption of the
contradictory elements that emerged in the class struggle within the scope of
political society and civil society. This form of democracy implies the "intrinsic
and inevitable" corruption of the power system.

For Florestan Fernandes, in an effective mass democracy, it would imply
the use of tolerance as a form of conflict resolution. However, in the Brazilian
context of the 1960s, the autocratic State prevented this. In addition, the way
in which the transition from that regime to the democratic form took place
in the mid-1980s in Brazil ensured that this blockade on the use of tolerance
was perpetuated. It is, then, a restricted democracy that configures the closed
circuit, under which only "the most equal", the dominant elites and the middle
classes, participate in the decision-making process of political, economic and
social life.

Co-optation democracy, in addition to the process of transforming the radical sectors of the middle class more and more into bourgeois fractions as well

as the leaders of the labour movements, is a type of democracy that, at least in appearance, could "open downwards" by allowing the incorporation, into the competitive social order, the working class in a tutelary way. However, this opening downwards would not go beyond the limits of an oligarchic democracy of an autocratic State, where the rules of the game apply only to the most equal (those inserted in the current social order). As the author explains, co-optation in Brazil was born during the period of the civil-military dictatorship, during the so-called "economic miracle" between 1968–1973:

> With all its limitations and inconsistencies, the composite and articulated pattern of bourgeois hegemony can demonstrate, then, all its usefulness as a "bridge" between national and foreign bourgeois classes and class strata, a flexible link, which facilitates the distribution of all in the "revolutionary" political space and the unequal enjoyment of power or advantages among the most equal. Thanks to it, the middle strata gain in the apportionment and are privileged far above their own social prestige, moving the levers of the State apparatus that are in the hands of the bureaucratic, technocratic and military bourgeoisie. At the same time, also thanks to it, the "truly strong interests" and the "predominant interests" face, in short, their ideal political environment, being able to impose themselves at will, from "top to bottom", and flourish without restrictions. If there ever was a bourgeois paradise, it exists in Brazil, at least after 1968.
>
> FERNANDES, 1975 p. 416

Florestan himself at the conclusion of his main work shows how the democracy of co-optation was incipient and uncertain even in the second half of the 1970s. According to him, this political form was born weak, as it was conceived in the context of the amalgam of two antagonistic revolutions that were fruits the bourgeois consensus on authoritarian domination: a revolution of economic acceleration that preached capitalist modernization as a means of legitimizing the autocratic State and another in the form of a preventive counter-revolution that had the strategy of maintaining order and freezing the social issue. In a country of dependent and poor capitalism with an extreme concentration of wealth and power, there is little room for the purchase of stable alliances and loyalties. Thus, co-optation democracy ends up

> [...]exacerbating the contradictions intrinsic to the class regime, leading to explosive points of effervescence that further weaken that strengthen

the autocratic state, compelled to function under extreme permanent
and self-destructive tension, of insurmountable armed peace.

FERNANDES, 1975, p. 424

Thus, with the bourgeois revolution understood as already carried out,
Florestan Fernandes indicates the need to build an alternative that is guided
by the interests of the workers, since dependent capitalism only allows a
restricted democracy, not opening space for solutions within the order. A revolution out of order would be necessary, whose historical subject can only be
the working class.

In *O que é Revolução?*, (What is Revolution?) Florestan seeks to work on the
identification of this historical subject, as well as explaining his conceptions
of people and nation. To this end, the Communist Manifesto is brought up to
date, citing the three elements of the proletarian revolution: 1) the formation
of the proletarian class as a class independent of the capitalist class, a true
class in itself and aware of its challenges; 2) confrontation with the bourgeois
class for political hegemony, which demands an organized party and 3) the
effective takeover of the State.

We are calling attention to the fact that Florestan was aware of the fact that
a "revolution is not made to order". Even though he was one of the exponents
of the popular democratic program during the birth and rise of the PT in 1980,
the author made several criticisms of the contradictions that this highly heterogeneous party contained in itself. For this reason, the sociologist takes up
in *Nós e o marxismo* (Marxism and us) the importance of Lenin's category
"revolutionary situation", the only moment when revolution is possible, and
which depends on a set of objective and subjective circumstances that must
be combined. The objective conditions are i) a summit crisis that prevents the
ruling classes from governing as before; ii) the growth of misery and anguish
intensely; iii) independent action by the masses. The subjective conditions are
the party's organizational capacity to lead the mass movement, with the task
of raising class consciousness and define strategy and tactics in conducting
revolutionary actions for the seizure of power.

Regarding this, Florestan realizes that one must avoid very common situations in Brazil: composition, amalgam, bourgeois radicalism and populism, as
they can lead to co-optation and framing "within the order" of the revolutionary process, running the risk of becoming something similar to the European
social democracy. Considering this reflection by Florestan and the political
conjuncture of the transition from dictatorship to the New Republic, the text
by Marx and Engels "Message from the Central Committee to the League of

Communists" (1850) helps us think about building a revolution out of order, in a permanent revolution movement.[13]

Florestan Fernandes makes his perception of permanent revolution clear when he distinguishes between "revolution within the order" and "revolution out of the order". In clear words, the first can be understood as "reform" while the second as structural change led by workers and oriented towards their interests.

In formulating that the ruling classes would seek to find new forms of State coercion, the author suggests that the spread of the co-optation democracy would imply the partial favoring of the subordinate classes. Thus, the possibility of vertical social mobility engendered by passivation and the alliance of classes in the reforms would have two consequences: 1) bourgeois sectors of the working and destitute classes, partially incorporated into the bourgeois order, generating protests within the order; but this same process would generate 2) a growing organization of pressures against the order, since the contradictions of class society would be exposed, an issue that cannot be solved within the framework of dependent capitalism.

Once constituted as a class in itself, with independent force in the face of the capitalist and politically organized class, the proletarians should organize the process of revolutionary social change. According to Florestan (1989), the example of the formation of the proletarian class in Brazil as a class in itself are the episodes of the strikes of 1978 in the ABC *Paulista*. There the workers would have shown themselves as an independent and organised class for the first time in the country's history, according to the sociologist.

The author assesses the deficiencies in the political form of co-optation democracy, by raising the tensions of dependent capitalism to a point of inexorable contradiction, which would serve as a trigger for the social revolution. It is not, however, an "accumulation of forces" necessary for capitalism as the PCB defended after March 1958, but the tactical form of a struggle that has a well-defined strategic objective, the emancipation of the working class in Brazil. Florestan was aware of the need for a program of his own, independent and with the bourgeois alliance only as far as it did not conflict with the proletarian cause (Fernandes, 1989).

---

13   In the authors' perspective, the proletarian party can make tactical alliances in a context of democratic-bourgeois revolution, provided that: it manages to maintain its own program; an independent organization that acts both legally and secretly and that, if necessary, takes up arms; be able to establish a double power; and, most importantly, to keep the revolution permanent or, in other words, to transform the bourgeois revolution into a proletarian social revolution.

Florestan's participation in the controversy of the Brazilian revolution high-lights the historical specificity of the Brazilian trench, the struggle for the end of the process of colonial submission, which defines the character of our bour-geoisie, business bourgeoisie, minor partners of international capital. At the same time, such ruling classes forged the character of the Brazilian State, as an instrument of domination by these bourgeoisies, which maintains the coun-terrevolution both in coercive and consensual forms:

> Those who repress and oppress these days, struggle to prevent the final short circuit, which for them turns out to be the disappearance of a State antagonistic to the Nation and the People, that is, a State that, like any elitist State, always has to "close the story" to those not in power.
>
> FERNANDES, 1976, p. 34

This Revolution cannot be national or associated with this bourgeoisie, it has to be a popular revolution to create a socialist democracy.

5   A Controversy in Permanent Revolution: by Way of Conclusion

In the history of Brazilian economic and social thought, the characterization of Brazilian social formation and its possibilities for transformation, that is, the controversy of the Brazilian revolution, was marked by important reflections on the theory and practice of the revolution in Brazil made by the authors who positioned themselves politically as socialists and who claimed the Marxist tradition. In rescuing this controversy, in its second edition, we present some of the main contributions to Brazilian Marxist thought in the 20th century to understand the Brazilian reality and think about its possibilities and meanings of change.

Nelson Werneck Sodré placed himself as one of the main references for the position of dominant Marxism in the PCB. It sought to analyse the internal relations of production and property to define the current mode of produc-tion in Brazil. To this end, he developed a historical interpretation that under-stands the colonization process under the command of commercial capital in the heart of Portuguese feudalism, in such a way that a capitalist mode of production would not have been constituted in Brazil. On the contrary, there would have been a regression in feudalism itself, leading to the installation of slavery in the colony. This would be a mode of production transplanted by the colonization process, progressively composing the heterochrony charac-teristic of the Brazilian economy, that is, the simultaneity of different modes of production, or, in Sodré's words, *a contemporaneidade do não-coetâneo* (the contemporaneity of the non-contemporary).

The decay of slavery in the second half of the 19th century would establish the predominance of the feudal mode of production in the Oligarchic Republic, founded on the land monopoly inherited from colonization. This would be Brazilian feudalism, different from the European one, but which would in any case present itself as an obstacle to the development of capitalism in the country. In fact, there would be a double obstacle, typical of a colonial country: the feudal monopoly of the land and imperialism.

Hence the author proposes a policy of alliances to form a broad front with urban workers, peasants and the national bourgeoisie – the fraction of the bourgeoisie in Brazil that is resistant to imperialism. This would be the political composition of the revolutionary movement, to carry out the democratic-popular revolution, as proposed by the central line of the Communist International and the PCB. Therefore, this stage of the revolution should be anti-feudal, anti-imperialist, national and democratic. In the author's conception, if this first stage of the revolution did not exist, it would not be possible to create the basis for the socialist stage of the revolutionary process.

Caio Prado Junior will exercise persistent criticism of the PCB's interpretation and revolutionary politics, from its affiliation in the 1930s to its last interventions. Especially in the 1960s, after the 1964 coup, the author will make a harsh criticism of what he refers to as the consecrated theory of the Brazilian revolution. Pointing in this theory a mechanical transposition of the typical categories of European society to the Brazilian reality.

Thus, he criticizes the interpretation of feudalism in Brazil, always placing the capitalist characteristic of the colonial enterprise, that is, the sense of colonization and the organization of production on the basis of great rural exploitation. Furthermore, he considers the analysis of the peasantry to be mistaken, stating that there is no such social category of smallholders in Brazil in the countryside. For the author, they would all be rural workers without any land ownership. Likewise, it does not distinguish a "national bourgeoisie" with anti-imperialist impulses, being, on the contrary, formed in Brazil a bourgeoisie associated with foreign capital, with affinity of interests, even when there is eventually some friction of capitalist competition.

For Caio Prado, the central core of the Brazilian revolution would be the overcoming of the colonial economy, making a transition to the national economy. For this, the fundamental political alliance would take place between rural and city workers, united by the similar condition of exploited non-owners. This unity of struggle should be consolidated in a broad mass movement, with a strong rural base, but under the leadership of the urban proletariat.

The author demonstrates a certain ambiguity when dealing with the character of the Brazilian revolution, as he proposes some characteristic elements of the democratic-popular revolution, but always affirming the ultimate goal of the socialist revolution. Thus, it is betting on a return to democracy as a way to enable a better organization of workers, gaining active political participation and influencing the direction of the country. This would be the way of progressive institutional reforms and State planning to bring about a procedural transformation towards the socialist revolution.

Florestan Fernandes, in turn, will always affirm the need for the social revolution to break with the double articulation characteristic of dependent capitalism, marked by external dependence and internal social segregation. The evolution of world capitalism on the basis of uneven and combined development would have generated a specificity for the bourgeois revolution in Brazil: the bourgeoisie would carry out its revolution without a utopian horizon, without concerns about the formation of the nation or the institution of a democratic society.

Supported by the autocratic domination of the State, the Brazilian bourgeoisie would opt for the repression of workers whenever there was any threat to their power, making the political actions of the subaltern classes unfeasible. Thus, the bourgeois revolution would not be able to break with the double determination typical of dependent countries. On the contrary, it would carry out the deepening of these determinations by the current practice of preventive counterrevolution.

When analyzing the turn of the 1970s to the 1980s, Florestan already pointed out the limits of the democratic transition, describing what he called co-optation democracy. This would be a revolution in the techniques of the counterrevolution, supposedly opening up the State to the political participation of workers but making its effective revolutionary practice unfeasible through the co-optation of the leaders inserted in the game of bourgeois democracy. In such a way, it bet on the maintenance of the political autonomy of the workers in front of the bourgeoisie, with the organization of its own party, with a revolutionary program under the leadership of the workers. The tactical alliance with the bourgeoisie should last as long as there is no contradiction of class interests in the revolution within the order.

We realized, then, that the theme of the Brazilian revolution is central and structures almost all debates in the Marxist field. We show that, far from having a consensus, the proposal for a Brazilian revolution was the center of intense political and academic controversies for important authors of the Brazilian Marxist tradition. We also show that many of these divergences in diagnoses and prognoses stem from the party orientation and the critical conception of

Brazilian social formation carried out by each of the analyzed interpreters. Especially in times of advancing neoliberal hegemony, it is essential to return to the controversy of the Brazilian revolution,

Bibliographic References

Curty, Carla & Malta, Maria. Methodological Elements for the Organization of the History of Brazilian Economic Thought. In: Malta, Maria; León, Jaime; Curty, Carla; Borja, Bruno (eds.). Controversies on history, development and revolution in Brazil: economic thought in critical interpretation. In this book, 2021.

Del Roio, Marcos. A teoria da Revolução Brasileira: tentativa de uma particularização de uma revolução burguesa em processo. *In:* Moraes, João Quartim de; Del Roio, Marcos. (orgs.). História do marxismo no Brasil, vol. 4: Visões do Brasil. Campinas: Unicamp, 2000, p. 73–134.

Fernandes, Florestan. Sociedade de classes e subdesenvolvimento. Editora Zahar. [1968] 1981.

Fernandes, Florestan. A revolução burguesa no Brasil: ensaio de interpretação sociológica. Rio de Janeiro: Editora Globo, [1975] 2011.

Fernandes, Florestan. Circuito fechado: quatro ensaios sobre o "poder institucional". Rio de Janeiro. Editora Globo. [1976] 2010.

Fernandes, Florestan. O que é Revolução? São Paulo: Editora Brasiliense, 1981.

Fernandes, Florestan. Pensamento e ação: o PT e os rumos do socialismo. Rio de Janeiro: Editora Globo, [1989] 2006.

Fernandes, Florestan. Caio Prado Junior: a rebelião moral. Texto disponível em: https://pt.scribd.com/document/110625208/Caio-Prado-Jr-Rebeliao-Moral-Florestan-Fernandes. 1995.

Grespan, José Luís. O conceito de "modo de produção" em Nelson Werneck Sodré. In: Cunha, Paulo; Cabral, Fátima. Nelson Werneck Sodré: entre o sabre e a pena. São Paulo: Unesp, 2006.

Karepovs, Dainis. et al. Trotsky e o Brasil. *In*: Moraes, João Quartim de. (org.) História do marxismo no Brasil – Vol. 4 – Os influxos teóricos. Campinas: Editora Unicamp, [1995] 2014, pp. 229–253.

Lenin, Vladimir. O Estado e a Revolução. São Paulo: Expressão Popular, [1918] 2007.

Marx, Karl & Friedrich, Engels. Mensagem do Comitê Central à Liga dos Comunistas, 1850. Texto disponível em: https://www.marxists.org/portugues/marx/1850/03/mensagem-liga.htm. Acessado em 16/06/2017. Access on May 2020.

PCB. PCB: vinte anos de política 1958-1979 (documentos). São Paulo: LECH, 1980.

Oliveira Filho, Virgílio Roma de. A participação de Werneck Sodré no debate nacionalista da década de 1950. In: CUNHA, Paulo; CABRAL, Fátima (orgs.) **Nelson Werneck Sodré entre o sabre e a pena**. São Paulo: Editora da UNESP, 2000, p.245-263.

Pinheiro, Filipe. Revisitando as origens da controvérsia da revolução brasileira: um debate entre Octavio Brandão, Mario Pedrosa e Lívio Xavier. *In:* Malta, Maria; León, Jaime; Curty, Carla; Borja, Bruno. Controvérsias sobre história, desenvolvimento e revolução no Brasil: pensamento econômico em interpretação crítica. In this book, 2021.

Pinheiro, Filipe et al., *li.* Nelson Werneck Sodré: feudalismo e revolução à brasileira. *In:* Anais Colóquio Internacional Marx e o Marxismo 2015: Insurreições, passado e presente. Niterói, 2015.

Prado Júnior, Caio. Evolução Política do Brasil. 21ª edição. São Paulo: Editora Brasiliense, [1933] 2007.

Prado Júnior. Caio. Formação do Brasil Contemporâneo – colônia. 23ª edição. São Paulo: Editora Brasiliense, [1942] 1995.

Prado Júnior. Caio História Econômica do Brasil. 12ª edição. São Paulo: Editora Brasiliense, [1945] 1970.

Prado Júnior. Caio A Revolução Brasileira. 6ª edição. São Paulo: Editora Brasiliense, [1966] 1978.

Prado Júnior. Caio. Adendo a A Revolução Brasileira. In: Prado Júnior. A Revolução Brasileira. 6ª edição. São Paulo: Editora Brasiliense, [1967] 1978.

Prado Júnior. Caio. Perspectiva em 1977. *In:* Prado Júnior. A Revolução Brasileira. 6ª edição. São Paulo: Editora Brasiliense, [1977] 1978.

Simonses, Roberto. História Econômica do Brasil. São Paulo. Comp. Ed. Nacional. 1937.

Sodré, Nelson Werneck. Formação da sociedade brasileira. Rio de Janeiro: José Olympio, 1944.

Sodré, Nelson Werneck. Introdução à revolução brasileira. 2ª edição. Rio de Janeiro: Civilização Brasileira, [1958 (1963)].

Sodré, Nelson Werneck. Formação histórica do Brasil. Rio de Janeiro: Civilização Brasileira, [1962] 1976.

Sodré, Nelson Werneck. Modos de Produção no Brasil. *In:* Lapa, José Roberto do Amaral (org.) Modos de produção e realidade brasileira. Petrópolis: Vozes, 1980, p. 133–156.

Varnhagen, Adolfo. História geral do Brasil: antes da sua separação e independência de Portugal. Belo Horizonte; São Paulo. Itatiaia. USP. 1854.

Trotsky Leon. A revolução permanente. São Paulo: Expressão Popular, [1930] 2007.

CHAPTER 6

Underdevelopment and Dependency

An Analysis of Celso Furtado's Thought and Its Approach to Dependency Theory

Wilson Vieira

1   Underdevelopment and Dependency in the 1970s: Approximations between Celso Furtado and Dependency Theory

1.1   *Transformations in Furtado's Thought after the 1964 Coup*
From the 1964 civil-military coup, we observed in Furtado's reflection an ever greater expansion of his theoretical perspective, increasingly adopting the path of deepening the articulation between economic and political theory. This is shown in his formulation of the stagnationist diagnosis[1] and, more radically, from his works in the 1970s, through the critical overcoming of this diagnosis.

In fact, Furtado's reflections after 1964 reinforce what he had already perceived since 1960, that is, that industrialization was unable to resolve either economic or social issues in Brazil. This observation leads him, along with Prebisch (1964), to make his self-criticism and propose the inclusion of the need for social policies and income distribution to get out of underdevelopment, revealing a deep understanding of the political dimension of this phenomenon.

In order to proceed with the analysis of the transformations in Furtado's thought after the 1964 coup, it is necessary that we introduce in an introductory way the concepts of underdevelopment, cultural dependency and "modernization" in Furtado's vision, which we analyze in more detail throughout this section. .

Underdevelopmentis characterized as a situation in which certain countries are inserted in the international division of labor in a subordinate (and peripheral) manner in relation to developed countries (central, dominant of the capitalist system). The way in which this subordination occurs varies over time, but, roughly speaking, it can be said that, in the phase in which there is a predominance of a primary exporting sector (case of Brazil during the 19th and

---

[1]   The stagnationist diagnosis is found in Furtado (1966, 1968a, 1968b).

20th centuries until 1930), the terms of trade deteriorate[2]because exported primary goods have less added value than industrialized goods imported from central countries (and which first participated in the Industrial Revolution). In the phase in which Import-substituting industrialization (ISI) occurs (case of Brazil from 1930 onwards), underdevelopment is not overcome, as industry standards are imported from the capitalist center, seeking to feed consumer demand and with technology that is inadequate Brazilian reality.

The inadequacy of this technology is based on the fact that it saves labor and in the Brazilian reality, the diffusion of this new technological standard that is not the result of the internal process of accumulation and technical progress, will not be accompanied by the assimilation / demand of new goods consumption by the entire social body, but only by higher income elites, as there will be no incorporation of a large part of the population in the industrial workforce and most wages will remain in subsistence patterns.[3] Thus, what would be appropriate for the reality of the central countries, in which the diffusion of technical progress comes together with the assimilation of new consumer goods, is a producer of inequality for Brazil. All of this generates a situation of structural heterogeneity, in which two very different sectors coexist: a sector composed of a durable and capital consumer goods industry (more modern sector) and a sector composed of a non-durable consumer goods industry and a export-oriented agriculture – in addition to subsistence-oriented agriculture – with low capital intensity and extensive use of labor (traditional sector).

The failure to overcome underdevelopment, even with the presence of industry, is also characterized as a situation of cultural dependency, since the demand for consumer goods by the elites and the local middle classes obeys an imitation of the consumption patterns of the elites and middle classes in developed countries, characteristic of "modernization". The "modernization" corresponds to a process that incorporates technology and consumption patterns imported from the central economies, however, restricted to a small

---

2 Furtado uses Prebisch's analysis of the deterioration of terms of exchange. For more details, see Prebisch (1949) and Furtado (1985).

3 In Furtado's analysis, according to Borja (2011: 113): "The substitutive character of Latin American industrialization is expressed in the intention of national production to internally reproduce goods similar to those previously imported. This implied not only a redefinition of investment decisions, shifting away from primary export production and moving towards the consumer goods industry to the domestic market, but also an attempt to assimilate the productive processes in operation at the center of the world system, where labor-saving technology was in place – which intensified the concentration of income in underdeveloped countries. "

portion of the population. From this concept presented briefly, we now analyze in more depth how Furtado works with these concepts.

The 1968–1973 period is important for the change in Furtado's thought, when observing that the Brazilian economy has not remained stagnant. In fact, 1968 was the opening year for what would be called the Brazilian economic "miracle". In this period, Furtado receives the works of Tavares and Serra prepared at ECLAC in 1971 and published in 1972 (Tavares & Serra, 1972), reevaluates his previous reflections and innovates in his theory by elaborating the term "modernization", kept in quotation marks because it is not a modernization that leads to economic development, but that brings economic growth, and does not overcome the situation of underdevelopment. Furtado also innovates by including dependency in his reflections, denoting an approximation with DT.

The term "modernization" appears for the first time in the book Analysis of the Brazilian "Model" (1972). The word model appears in quotation marks to denote that it is not a model of economic development as it was proclaimed at the time both in Brazil and abroad, but a case of economic growth combined with a strong concentration of income, the result of economic reforms made by civil-military dictatorship in the period 1964–67 through the Government Economic Action Plan (PAEG). According to Furtado, this period clearly demonstrates that industrialization alone does not automatically bring about socioeconomic development.

To support his analysis of "modernization", Furtado initially draws attention to the economic development that took place after the Industrial Revolution, perceived in the forms it took: i) transformation of productive techniques, initially in manufacturing and in means of transport; ii) changes in consumption patterns. These transformations that occurred together characterize developed countries. In those countries where these transformations occurred only in the patterns of consumption (even of a minority of the population), we observe the phenomenon of underdevelopment. According to Furtado (1982, pp. 11–12):

> The history of underdevelopment consists, fundamentally, in the unfolding of this model of economics in which technological progress has served much more to modernize consumption habits than to transform productive processes. From the moment that the traditional system of international division of labor began to decline – that is, when the international demand for primary products started to grow relatively slowly – or, in the case of certain regions, easy-to-use natural resources were fully utilized – underdeveloped countries had to take the path of industrialization. (...) In the industrialization phase, the fundamental characteristic of underdeveloped structures is that the technological level corresponding to

> consumption patterns, that is, the level of modernization, it restricts the
> diffusion of technological progress, that is, its generalization to the set of
> productive activities. (...) In the language of Latin American sociologists,
> development is more exclusive.

Therefore, in (1982, p. 13 and 15), while in developed countries the flow of new products and the complex of technological innovations that accompany it are essential for the functioning of the capitalist economy, if we observe this fact worldwide, we realize that such factors preserve the relationships of domination and dependency (even if the periphery industrializes), pointing out underdevelopment as a situation of structural dependency, which can be translated by a narrow horizon of options in the formulation of own goals, in addition to reduced ability to articulate the economic decisions taken as a result of these objectives, denoting an approximation with DT by using the words domination and dependency, participating in the process of introducing a new "langue" in the "parole", as Pocock (2003) states.

Based on the definition and analysis of underdevelopment, which includes "modernization" and dependency in countries of the periphery, Furtado shows how this process occurs in the specific Brazilian case of the economic "miracle", as noted below.

The "miracle" was based on a strong concentration of income through wage compression, however, without being static, but dynamic, that is, because it also had the expansion of the consumer social group in the durable consumer goods market (including middle class in addition to the closed minority of proprietors of capital goods) through consumer financing in its various forms (consumer subsidies and transfers of bonds and credit). Such measures were taken to avoid difficulties in resuming the industrialization process (depression prevalent in important segments of economic activity) that would certainly occur if income concentration remained static.[4]

In the book The Myth of Economic Development (1974), especially in the second chapter Underdevelopment and Dependency: The Fundamental Connections, Furtado seeks to deepen the meaning of "modernization" and dependency for underdeveloped countries, by observing that they are inserted in the industrialization process, which is not oriented to form a national economic system, but to complete the international economic system. This industrialization is something specific to underdeveloped economies[5] and it counts,

---

4 Such an analysis is also made, but in a general way for Latin America, by Marini ([1973] 2000).
5 Here, although Furtado does not use the expressions imperialism and dependence, we can observe them in the way the periphery is industrialized.

in an ever stronger way, with the presence of large transnational companies, an aspect that reinforces the situation of dependency on the periphery (an important element of imperialism), as Marini and Dos Santos analyze, and that leads to the following consequences (felt mainly from the second half of the 1960s):

1) The process of unification of the central countries, which has led to an intensification of their growth.

2) Considerable widening of the gap between the center and the periphery.

3) Trade relations between central and peripheral countries (even more than between central countries) have gradually become internal operations for large companies.

In this process of peripheral industrialization, "modernization" is a manifestation of cultural mimicry (and dependency) on the periphery in relation to the center. According to Furtado (1974, p. 80):

> In order to capture the nature of underdevelopment, from its historical origins, it is essential to focus simultaneously on the *production process* (reallocation of resources giving rise to an additional surplus and the form of appropriation of that surplus) and the *circulation process* (use of the surplus linked to adoption of new consumption patterns copied from countries where the level of accumulation is much higher), which, *jointly, engender the cultural dependency that underlies the process of reproduction of the corresponding social structures.* (emphasis added)

In this passage, Furtado further deepens his interdisciplinary analysis by introducing the issue of cultural dependency, a point that would be developed in more detail in Creativity and Dependency in Industrial Civilization (1978). We can say that his analysis, despite being different from that made by DT (in its two approaches), is still a valuable complement to the analysis of dependency in the Marxist aspect.

Therefore, based on the reflection exposed above, Furtado (1974, pp. 81–82), deepens his notion of "modernization" and defines it as follows:

> We will call modernization this process of adopting sophisticated consumption patterns (private and public) without the corresponding process of capital accumulation and progress in productive methods. The broader the field of the modernization process (and this includes not only civilian but also military forms of consumption) the more

intense the pressure tends to be to expand the surplus, which can be achieved by expanding exports, or by increasing the "exploitation rate", that is, the proportion of the surplus in the net product. (...) Hence, there are increasing pressures, in terms of balance of payments, when the country reaches the point of decreasing income in traditional export agriculture and / or faces deterioration in terms of trade. (...) The importance of the modernization process, in shaping underdeveloped economies, it only comes to light fully at a more advanced stage when the respective countries embark on the industrialization process; more precisely, when they strive to produce for the domestic market what they have been importing. (...) By imposing the adoption of productive methods with a high capital density, this guidance creates the conditions for real wages to remain close to the subsistence level, that is, for the exploitation rate to increase with labor productivity. (emphasis added)

In Preface to the New Political Economy (1976), we observed the resumption of points analyzed in the works that we have exposed above, in addition to the addition of the following:

1) The ideology of progress is a strong driver of peripheral industrialization.
2) The penetration of the capitalist mode of production in the context of external dependency leads to tensions in the structure of internal domination (phenomenon of social insecurity) and social revolutions (which may occur occasionally). However, according to Furtado (1976, p. 60), "(...) the rule has been the relative growth of the authoritarian form of appropriation of the surplus, which tends to become hegemonic".
3) There is a double process of concentration of income: for the benefit of the central countries and, within each peripheral country, for the benefit of the minority that reproduces the lifestyle of the center.[6]
4) Furtado calls attention to important points to be studied, in order to better understand this process of "modernization": a) the groups that control the main economic activities in Latin American countries; b) the relations of national States with transnational companies.

---

6 Here, this analysis is also similar to that of Marini on the overexploitation of workers in the periphery (and more clearly, as we analyze later).

In the book Creativity and Dependency on Industrial Civilization (1978), which can be considered his most interdisciplinary book, Furtado reinforces the cultural and social aspects of "modernization" and dependency, calling attention to the importance of the internal social structures of the periphery for the understanding of dependent industrialization, but also to the fact of what Westernization also meant, that is, destruction of cultural values in various countries on the periphery without adequate substitution. According to Furtado (1978, p. 49):

> [It is] in the evolution of internal social structures that the specificity of dependent industrialization is clearly seen. Its close link with foreign trade can only be perceived in all its complexity if one takes into account that it has an important role in the reproduction of the social sectors that had access, albeit indirectly, to the material values of industrial civilization. This is the reason why this industrialization has as its axis the flow of imports, being less important its links with the pre-existing system of productive forces.

Despite this negative situation in the periphery, Furtado (1978, pp. 114–116) sees possibilities for overcoming it:

> The fight against dependency, therefore, involves an effort to modify the global conformation of the system. That this issue is currently being discussed – more precisely: that the global conformation of the system has been questioned – is a clear indication that the balance of forces is changing in favor of dependent countries. Right: in most peripheral countries, external dependency relations are introjected into structures of social domination. But, as we have already noted, this does not prevent the emergence of technobureaucratic power structures capable of exploiting the new situation that is being formed. (...) Among the power resources on which the so-called international economic order is based, they are particularly relevant: a) control of technology, b) control of finance, c) control of markets, d) the control of access to sources of non-renewable resources, and e) the control of access to cheap labor. These resources, gathered in considerable quantities and / or combined in different doses, give rise to positions of strength, which occupy states or large economic groups in the struggle for the appropriation of the surplus generated by the international economy. These positions of strength are of different weight and in their relationship, they tend to organize themselves,

producing a structure. The fight against dependency is nothing but an effort by peripheral countries to modify this structure. Country coalitions occasionally allow for obtaining the critical mass required to control a resource, or to articulate combinations of highly effective resources in generating power. Controlling a product's stocks is important, but even more important is to have financial resources to prolong this control. Having petroleum resources is a weapon, but the effectiveness of that weapon can increase considerably if the supply of oil on the international market can be organized globally.

Therefore, we observed in Furtado in the reflections from the Analysis of the Brazilian "Model" (1972), elements that show the situation of dependency of the periphery under the hegemony of the USA, also built by cultural conditions that are manifested in the phenomenon of "modernization", keeping similarity, and at the same time complementing, Dos Santos and Marini's reflections on imperialism and dependency in peripheral economies.

At the same time, Furtado, in thinking about international relations of power, dependency and submission, does not adopt the expression *imperialism*, a very important expression for dependentist thought, especially to denote the influence and interventions of the USA on Latin America, but the expression *hegemony*. This choice of lexicon can be seen in the second chapter of the book Underdevelopment and Stagnation in Latin America (1966),[7] which he republishes (with minor modifications) in the book The Hegemony of the United States and the Underdevelopment of Latin America (1973), which we analyzed in the paragraphs below.

In the chapter entitled External Obstacles to Development, Furtado shows that in order to overcome the inertia of underdevelopment, it is necessary to have a very clear definition of the external obstacles at that moment, in order to overcome them.

These obstacles stem from the cold war, a fact that led to an effort to define the areas of influence of the USA and the USSR. In this process, the USA proposed for its area of influence, where Latin America was inserted, a series of policies that include the "containment" of the USSR ", in the Eisenhower administration and the doctrines expressed in the document Aliança para o Progresso (Alliance for Progress – APP), already under the administration of John F. Kennedy.

---

7   We used the 1968 edition.

In the Eisenhower administration, government thought and action assumed that the USSR was not only exploiting the world revolution, but was also its creator. And it was in this context that the doctrine formulated by the technician staff of the Massachusetts Institute of Technology (MIT) was developed,[8] under the leadership of Rostow (late 1950s, early 1960s): US foreign policy objectives would be best achieved through well-targeted "foreign aid" to underdeveloped countries in order to achieve development and thereby eliminate the risks of social instability. The practical result was already in the Kennedy administration with the Alliance for Progress (APP), which was seriously criticized in a subsequent period within the US government on the grounds that development itself creates social instability, even if oriented from the outside.

From this criticism of the APP within the US state apparatus, we can understand the change in the policy of the US government in relation to Latin America, moving to the defense of the idea that we could not lose sight of the objective of US policy in relation to that region, that is, that of conserving its sphere of influence integrated, with the development of one country or another being a mean to achieve this objective. Aid would have to go to elite groups in those countries that are committed to keeping them out of communism and Soviet control. And within these countries, if necessary, military and police forces could be used to ensure stability during the implementation of programs along the lines of the APP.[9]

Therefore, in this analysis, the fundamental problem of the USA in the second half of the twentieth century is that of its "security" and that of Latin America is that of "development", one of the ways of building the nation. These are conflicting objectives, not at first sight, but in a more in-depth analysis, in which the role of US private companies cannot be ignored.[10] According to Furtado (1968, p. 42):

> From the moment that the "security" of the United States is defined as including the maintenance of the social status quo in the Latin American region, it is perfectly clear that the autonomy of the countries of that region (assuming that the peoples and States of the Latin

8   Observed in Rostow (1961) and Millikan & Blackmer (1963).
9   For more details, see Furtado (1968: 35–37).
10   This constitutes a great novelty in the construction of Furtado's stagnationist diagnosis, which he would deepen during the 1970s and 1980s and which he calls the capital's transnationalization, anticipating one of the elements of the analysis of the globalization of capital.

America are not confused with occasional power structures) to oversee development itself is reduced to little. It is implicit in this doctrine that decisions of a fundamental character must be taken at a higher level, probably in the political center of the sphere of influence, or in some "supranational" body, whose effective power constitutes a simple delegation of that political center. (...) [In this process], North American private companies have a basic role in Latin American development and that the implementation of the United States' "aid" policy must be mainly through these companies. (...) "Guarantee" agreements have been signed with Latin American governments by which US private companies, which operate in a certain country, now enjoy a privileged position in relation to identical companies operating in the United States. (emphasis added)

Therefore, in this view, nation building is at risk, as Furtado (1968, p. 44), in a critique of technocracy, which is deepened in his reflections from the 1980s, states:

This regional development "project", which tends to make the idea of nationality as the main political force in Latin America obsolete, presents a great attraction for important sectors of the local ruling classes, who see there a skillful formula to empty the "nationalism", to which attribute great responsibility for the present social unrest. In fact, if it is possible to extract from the State a large part of its substantive functions in guiding the process of economic and social development, it would be expected that the current political "fermentation", which characterizes many of the Latin American countries, will tend to be reduced., with governments now acting mainly on the "technical" level. (emphasis added)

The author, deepening his analysis, shows that implementing this project in the historical conditions of Latin America in the second half of the 1960s would be unfeasible, since the penetration of large consortia, characterized by high administrative inflexibility and great financial power, tends to cause structural imbalances difficult to correct, such as: greater disparities in living standards between population groups and a rapid increase in open and disguised unemployment. In this process, the reduction in the control capacity of national States leads to an increase in the concentration of economic activities in certain sub-areas, with the consequent worsening of the disparities in living standards between social groups and geographic areas, leading, therefore, to effective or potential rise of social tensions in Latin American followed by a repressive State action.

Despite this challenging diagnosis, Furtado (1968, p. 46) continues to believe in the construction of the nation under the leadership of the State, however, plus what may be the beginning of the defense of the radicalization of democracy in this process (which he would develop with more emphasis on 1980s):

> Economic development, in the difficult conditions currently facing Latin America, requires a cooperative attitude by large masses of population and the active participation of important sectors of that population. It is for this reason that the most difficult tasks are of a political rather than a technical nature. A difficult political action must be carried out, and this will only be possible with support in the current centers of national political power. Contrary to what is intended to convey, the principle of nationality is vital in the current phase of Latin American development. Every authentic development policy draws its strength from a set of value judgments in which the ideals of a collective are amalgamated. And if a community does not have the political bodies capable of interpreting its legitimate aspirations, it is not equipped to undertake development tasks. Thus, the principle of nationality is today, even more than in the past, of extraordinary functionality. Any measure that will be taken to weaken Latin American states as political centers capable of interpreting national aspirations and bringing people together around common ideals, will result in limiting the region's possibilities for development. Thus, Latin American economic integration is only justified if it is conceived as a definition of a common policy between national states, and not as an articulation between large foreign companies operating in the region. (emphasis added)

We therefore observed, in Furtado, an important reflection on the role of the USA in maintaining underdevelopment in the countries of Latin America, since it was a country that collaborated with the civil-military coup in Brazil in 1964, within a framework of stagnation, which, for Furtado, would continue and lead Brazil to a process of economic regression – "pastoralization" – as he states most clearly in the essay Brazil: from the Oligarchic Republic to the Military State (1968b), but which did not occur, as Furtado himself observes from the book Analysis of the Brazilian "Model" (1972), in which industrialization continues, but of a dependent nature and subordinated to the hegemonic interests of the capitalist center, especially in the USA, with the permanence of underdevelopment.

1.2   *Dependency Theory and the Formation of a Controversy with*
        Furtado

Within DT, we first analyze Weberian Dependency Theory (WDT),[11] composed by Fernando Henrique Cardoso and Enzo Faletto (main references),
who question the stagnationist theses of the period (including Furtado's in his
works from 1966 to 1968), but predict a dependent and associated development as a way out for underdevelopment. In their view, exposed in the book
Dependency and Development in Latin America (first published in 1970),[12]
dependency within an industrialized peripheral economy is characterized by
direct industrial investments made by central economies in peripheral countries, which lead to partial development within a framework of heteronomy
and cause division among wage sectors, that is, between those linked to the
advanced capitalist sector (who benefit from development) and the traditional
(or backward) capitalist sector.

For Cardoso and Faletto, this dependency has a new character, different
from that which characterized the countries of Latin America at the stage
when their economies were predominantly primary export-led, since industrialization occurs (mainly in Brazil, Argentina and Mexico), in a process without autonomous decision about ways to overcome underdevelopment for the
countries of that region, as it started to be commanded by foreign investment
(from transnational companies in central countries). However, although the
situation of dependency persists, the authors observe opportunities for development. According to Cardoso and Faletto (1984, pp. 141–142):

> The novelty of the hypothesis is not in the recognition of the existence
> of external domination – an obvious process – but in the characteri-
> zation of the form it takes and the distinct effects, with reference to
> past situations, of this type of dependency on classes and the State. We
> emphasize that the current situation of dependent development not
> only overcomes the traditional opposition between the terms develop-
> ment and dependency, allowing to increase development and maintain,
> by redefining them, the bonds of dependency, as it is politically sup-
> ported in a system of alliances different from that in which past assured

---

11   We call WDT dependent and associated development strand of DT because Cardoso and
      Faletto use a theoretical eclecticism that includes, in addition to Marxism, instruments
      of Weberian analysis (with even more emphasis) when analyzing Latin American indus-
      trialization through application of Weber's ideal types for the countries of that region. For
      ideal types, see Weber ([1925] 2002).
12   We used the 1984 edition.

external hegemony. It is no longer exporting interests that subordinate solidarity interests with the domestic market, nor rural interests that oppose urban ones as an expression of a type of economic domination. Instead, the specificity of the current situation of dependency is that "external interests" are increasingly rooted in the production sector for the domestic market (without undoing, of course, previous forms of domination) and, consequently, are based on political alliances that find support in urban populations. On the other hand, the formation of an industrial economy on the periphery of the international capitalist system minimizes the effects of the typically colonialist exploitation and seeks solidarity not only in the dominant classes, but in the group of social groups linked to modern capitalist production (wage workers, technicians, entrepreneurs, bureaucrats, etc. previous forms of domination) and, consequently, are based on political alliances that find support in urban populations..

We can affirm that Furtado approaches WDT as from 1970 with regard to the analysis of the new situation of dependency, but he distances himself from it by stating that dependent peripheral industrialization does not overcome underdevelopment (approaching, at this point, Marxist Dependency Theory (MDT)).

We now analyze MDT,[13] composed by André Gunder Frank, Ruy Mauro Marini, Theotonio dos Santos and Vânia Bambirra (main authors) who criticize the thesis of stagnation defended by Furtado and understand a new phase of underdevelopment, that is, of dependency in an industrialization context (different from the phase of dependency of a primary export-led economy on the periphery in relation to the central industrialized economies).[14] According to Dos Santos (2000, p. 134):

> In 1964, I fought all the stagnationist theses that saw in the monetary stabilization policy of Roberto Campos the destruction of Brazilian industry. On the contrary, I stated that the stabilization policy should lead to a new phase of growth, based however on a higher level of productivity, economic concentration, monopolization and nationalization (...).

---

13   For more details on an overview of MDT, see Dos Santos (2000), Martins (2011) and Bichir (2012).

14   According to Marini in Dialectic of Dependency (2000 [1973]: 109), dependency can only be understood in a relationship between independent nations, unlike a colonial economy. We work on this point in more detail ahead.

We can see this criticism of Furtado's stagnationist thesis in Marini's essay, Underdevelopment and Revolution (first published in 1967),[15] in which he affirms that the economic reforms implemented in Brazil in the first years of the civil-military dictatorship (1964–1967) through the Government Economic Action Plan (PAEG), opened a new phase that would materialize with the Brazilian economic "miracle" (1968–1973), that is, of economic development with industrialization, but of a dependent character, denoting the success of the advance of US imperialism in subordinating the Brazilian market to its transnational corporations.

In another essay by Marini, Dialectic of Capitalist Development in Brazil (first published in 1965),[16] we highlight from his reflection the fact that the imperialist expansion of Brazil after the 1964 civil-military coup was, in fact, a Brazilian sub-imperialism or an indirect extension of US imperialism. In Underdevelopment and Revolution we see a precise definition of sub-imperialism. In the words of Marini (2014, p. 40):

> Subimperialism is defined by, therefore:
> a)   from the restructuring of the world capitalist system that derives from the new international division of labor; and
> b)   based on the laws of the dependent economy, essentially: the over-exploitation of work; the divorce between the phases of the capital cycle; extreme monopolization in favor of the consumer goods industry; the integration of national capital with foreign capital or, what is the same, the integration of production systems (and not simply the internationalization of the domestic market, as some authors say).

Still on this theme, Marini (1992, pp. 137–138) states:

> Sub-imperialism corresponds to the perverse expression of the differentiation suffered by the world economy, as a result of capitalist internationalization, which contrasted with the simple scheme of division of labor – crystallized in the center-periphery relationship, which concerned ECLAC – a much more complex system of relations. In it, the

---

15   This article was first published in Spanish in 1967. We used the Brazilian translation published in 2014 in the book Subdesenvolvimento e Revolução.

16   This article was first published in Spanish in 1965. We used the Brazilian translation published in the book Dialética da Dependência (2000), anthology of the main articles by Ruy Mauro Marini, organized and presented by Emir Sader.

diffusion of the manufacturing industry, raising the national average organic composition of capital, that is, the existing relationship between means of production and the labor force, gives rise to economic (and political) sub-centers, endowed with relative autonomy, although they remain subordinate the global dynamics imposed by large centers.[17]

We also highlight Marini's essay Dialectic of Dependency (first published in 1973),[18] in which it deepens the meaning of dependency, that is, of the situation in which peripheral countries (as in the case of Latin American countries), even if they come to industrialize, as occurred from the 1930s (and with more intensity from 1950s), continue to be dependent on the capitalist center, and more: the situation of stagnation experienced by the countries of Latin America (and especially Brazil in the period 1962–1967) was nothing more than a reorganization of the productive forces in dependent capitalism, allowing such a situation to last (and even worsen), as seen in the example of the Brazilian economic "miracle" (1968–1973 period). In this view, in the dependent industrial economy, capital accumulation would also be characterized by the overexploitation of labor (as it was characteristic in the export-base economy), defined as follows by Marini (2000, p. 126):

> It is necessary to observe (...) that, in the three mechanisms considered [the intensification of work, the extension of the working day and the expropriation of part of the work necessary for the worker to replace his work force], the essential characteristic is given by the fact that the worker is denied the necessary conditions to replace the wear and tear on his workforce: in the first two cases because he is obliged to spend more work than he normally should, thus causing his premature exhaustion; in the latter, because it excludes even the possibility of consuming what is strictly necessary to preserve its workforce in a normal state. In capitalist terms, these mechanisms (which in addition can and usually do occur

---

17   Regarding this reflection by Marini, it is worth mentioning Luce's comment (2014: 48–49), complementing our exposition: "The perverse meaning to which Marini refers is the fact that relative autonomy cannot escape the global dynamics imposed by large centers . When one or more dependent economies ascend to a new level in the hierarchy of world capitalism, it is to assume a new character of dependency and to become, also, extractors of surplus value, appropriating part of the value produced by the peripheries – but without raising the standard of living of its working class ".

18   This article was first published in Spanish in 1973. We used the Portuguese version published in the book Dialética da Dependência (2000).

simutaneouslly) mean that workers receive under their value and it correspond to a overexploitation of workforce."

And given the overexploitation of work, technological development has faced serious problems of realization, as the market for sumptuous goods has ended up being very restricted internally, given the existence of an abyss between the standard of living of workers and that of the sectors that feed the high sphere of circulation, in addition to generating a strong division between workers in industrial sectors linked to the production of sumptuous goods, workers linked to industrial sectors linked to the production of non-durable consumer goods (traditional industries with low capital use), in addition to strong underemployment presence.[19] According to Marini (2000, p. 148):

> In this measure, given that they do not represent goods that intervene in the consumption of workers, the increase in productivity induced by the technique in these branches of production could not translate into greater profits by raising the rate of surplus value, but only through the increase in the mass of realized value. The diffusion of technical progress in the dependent economy will then go hand in hand with greater exploitation of the worker, precisely because *accumulation continues to depend essentially on the increase in the value mass – and as a result of surplus value – rather than on the rate of surplus value.* (emphasis added)

The "solutions" found for such a situation were the following, according to Marini (2000, p. 148):

> The resource used to solve them was to involve the State (through the expansion of the bureaucratic apparatus, subsidies to producers and financing for sumptuous consumption), as well as inflation, with the purpose of transferring the purchasing power of the sphere low to the high sphere of circulation; this implied further lowering real wages, in order to have sufficient surpluses to effect the cash transfer. However, insofar

---

19   On this issue, Dos Santos (2000, pp. 135–136) states: "[The] mass of underemployed competes not only with the unskilled employed worker. It also affects the bargaining power of qualified workers, who accept wages in our countries that are much lower than the international standard, due to the fear of going back to the situation of misery that they observe around them. Therefore, the introduction of more sophisticated technologies in our countries is unable to eliminate the conditions of *over-exploitation* [emphasis added] by our workers".

as the consumption capacity of workers is thus compressed, any possibility of stimulating technological investment in the production sector destined to meet popular consumption is closed.

Another "solution" found, according to Marini (2000, p. 150), was (as can be seen from the mid-1960s) the expansion abroad, that is, exports of manufactures of both essential goods and sumptuous goods, which can be seen both in the projects of regional and sub-regional economic integration and in the design of aggressive policies of international competition, denoting the resurrection of the old export-led economy model (only with a new guise) throughout Latin America.

In this process, Latin American industrialization therefore constituted a new international division of labor, since the lower stages of industrial production were transferred to the dependent countries.

Theotonio dos Santos, in *Imperialism and Multinational Corporations* (1977), draws attention to the role of the multinational corporation in capitalism in the second half of the 20th century: element, cell of modern imperialism, reinforcing the situation of underdevelopment and dependency on peripheral countries.

From the exposure of WDT and MDT, we can make a systematization that presents the convergent and divergent points between these aspects of DT.

With regard to convergences, both sides criticize the thesis of Furtado's stagnation and affirm that dependency is not overcome by industrialization and that in this process the presence of transnational companies is increasingly strong, denoting the process of expansion of world capitalism in the center to the periphery, in which the internal bourgeoisies of the Latin American countries that industrialized became associated with the capital coming from the central countries. According to Dos Santos (2000: 129): "One could clearly conclude that this bourgeoisie was historically unable to sustain an economic program of independence and autonomy that would guarantee control over the economic surplus generated in the region".

As for the divergences, we observe:

1) WDT emphasizes a Weberian analysis of Latin America's dependency and underdevelopment process (even if it also uses Marxist analysis) and, despite the continued dependency of Latin America in a situation where its economies are industrialized, there is the possibility of achieving development, associating peripheral Latin American economies with central economies, characterizing dependent and associated development.

2) MDT does not see the possibility of overcoming underdevelopment in a situation in which the dependent countries are industrialized, given the

framework of overexploitation of the workforce, of an industrialization based on the technology adopted in the center and coming from its companies that install their industrial plants in peripheral countries within the advance of imperialism and which, in cases such as Brazil, leads to a situation of sub-imperialism, in order to be able to expand its production to the other countries in the region, given the limited demand in the domestic market. In other words, there is, in fact, not overcoming a situation of underdevelopment and dependency, but, on the contrary, the maintenance of both, with the continued overexploitation of workers, underemployment, marginality and social exclusion.

It is also worth stating here that both in the other countries of Latin America and in other continents, contrary to what happened in Brazil, the two aspects of DT participated in an intense debate in the period we analyzed. In the Brazilian case, in the 1970s and 1980s, there was a "non-debate", according to Prado (2011, p. 69):

> Here, in fact, there was a non-debate, and in its place, there was a unilateral reading in relation to contributions linked to Marxism and the Latin American revolutionary struggle. Such contributions, in addition to being the target of censorship and political persecution, underwent a systematic work of intellectual misrepresentation, in which the ex-president and sociologist Fernando Henrique Cardoso played a central role, also counting on the collusion of several important and important intellectuals. with tenacious intellectual inertia, which has only recently been broken. In Brazil, a kind of "unique thought" was being built on the subject of dependency, centered largely on the perspective defended by Cardoso, in such a way that a relative lack of knowledge – and even deformation – of the contributions inscribed in the Marxist tradition was established,

A striking example of this non-debate can be seen when Fernando Henrique Cardoso and José Serra published the article as *As desventuras da Dialética da Dependência* (*Misadventures of the Dialectic of Dependency,*1978), in which they criticized Marini's reflections in *A Dialética da Dependência* without having published in Brazil the essay object of this criticism and also its reply to that criticism.[20]

---

20   The entire debate, including Marini's reply – The Reasons of Neodevelopmentism (Response to Fernando Henrique Cardoso and José Serra) -, together with Dialectic of Dependency and The Misfortunes of the Dialectic of Dependency was published by Marini in 1978 (when he was professor at National Autonomous University of Mexico) in

From what was exposed about Celso Furtado and DT, we can list the elements with which Furtado approaches this theory:

1) Industrialization in the periphery does not overcome underdevelopment, on the contrary, it contributes to its maintenance, given the adoption of technology imported from the center, collaborating to aggravate the picture of structural heterogeneity.

2) Peripheral industrialization, when it started to produce sumptuous goods that were previously imported, adopts productive methods with high capital density, creating conditions for real wages to remain close to the subsistence level, that is, there is an increase in the rate of exploitation, following a line of reflection close to Marini's over-exploitation of the workforce, especially when he affirms that there is a double process of concentration of income: for the benefit of the central countries and, within each peripheral country, for the benefit of the minority that reproduces the center's lifestyle (which he called "modernization").

3) "Modernization" determines the type of industrialization in the periphery, since the production of goods and services seeks to meet the demand for sumptuous goods from the middle classes and local elites that mimic the consumption pattern of their counterparts in the central countries, characterizing a picture of cultural dependency (going beyond economic, as DT puts it). In other words, Furtado agrees with the dependency thesis in a context of industrialization but takes its own path by emphasizing the cultural dimension of this dependency.

4) Furtado agrees with MDT in defending the impossibility of overcoming underdevelopment within a framework of dependency, unlike WDT, which defends the possibility of overcoming underdevelopment through dependent and associated development.

5) Latin America has a relationship of dependency and submission in relation to the USA, denoting its hegemony towards this region. Furtado does not use the expression imperialism, adopted by MDT, but his reflection is very close to that aspect of DT.

We observed that Furtado's approach to MDT is greater than traditionally indicated, however, it is necessary to point out that Furtado is following his own path.

---

extra number of Revista Mexicana de Sociologia. It is also worth mentioning the article by Bambirra (1978) that responds to MDT's critics.

2   Underdevelopment and Dependency in the Face of Globalization:
        Developments of Celso Furtado's Reflections and Dependency
        Theory

From the studies of DT and its debate with Furtadian thinking, we observed
different developments in its two aspects that deserve to be highlighted.

At WDT, we observed an update of the theory by embracing the theses of
globalization and continuing to defend dependent and associated development, but within the movement towards adhering to globalization with neoliberal cutting policies. We can see an approximation between the reflections
of Fernando Henrique Cardoso (and also his actions as President between 1995
and 2002) and Manuel Castells.[21] However, what we see as a result of the proposals put forward is the permanence of underdevelopment, dependency, and
an ever-decreasing margin of maneuver for peripheral countries, given the situation of continuity of imperialism, but under a new guise.

When analyzing the reflections of Fernando Henrique Cardoso[22] and
his performance in the Presidency of Brazil, Dos Santos (2000, pp. 143–144)
explains how such an update took place in the following points:

1)   A certain degree of absorption of the workforce in the growth and
      adoption phases of social policies contributes to mitigate the destruc-
      tive effects of the contradictions created by dependency on the world
      economy, that is, concentration of income and power and social
      marginalization.

2)   Dependent capitalist accumulation is not necessarily more contradic-
      tory than that of central capitalist countries and nothing obliges it to
      continue to be based on overexploitation of labor.

3)   Dependent or associated capitalist development can be reconciled with
      liberal and democratic political regimes.

4)   The enemies of development are populism and corporatism, whether
      from the state or from civil society institutions, in a view in which the
      issue of underdevelopment is a consequence of the backwardness
      of our traditional societies and not of the character of our capitalist
      development.

According to Dos Santos (2000, p. 144): "These are the theses that underlie
Fernando Henrique Cardoso's political activities in our day [period when he
was President of the Republic, 1995–2002] and he exhibited them in a clear

---

21   In the book A Sociedade em Rede (1999), we observed this proximity more clearly.
22   Dos Santos bases his analysis mainly on the following books: Dependency and
      Development in Latin America (1970) and As Ideias e Seu Lugar (1993).

and diaphanous way in your presidential campaigns and in your government program ".

We can say, therefore, that WDT deepens its defense of dependent and associated development in times of neoliberal globalization.

At MDT, the analysis of the globalization process also takes place, as we can see in the book *World Economy, Regional Integration and Sustainable Development* (1999), by Theotonio dos Santos. However, for our analysis in this work, we use the article by Marini, *Process and Trends of Capitalist Globalization* (2000),[23] because it analyzes the consequences of globalization[24] for dependent countries in a more specific way, meeting the objectives of this work, as we can see in the points of the text that we highlight below, according to Marini (2000, p. 282–284):

1) Developed countries have an immense superiority in terms of research and development, which is what makes technical innovation possible, thus constituting a technological monopoly and, therefore, a factor of aggravation of the dependent condition of peripheral countries.

2) Central countries exercise control over the transfer of industrial activities over peripheral countries, both due to their technological and investment capacity, acting in two ways: a) through priority transfer to countries dependent on less knowledge-intensive industries; b) by the dispersion between the different peripheral countries of the stages of the production of goods in order to prevent the emergence of nationally integrated economies.

3) The result of these actions by the central countries can be seen in the international division of labor at the production level, causing dependent countries to return to the place of the international division of labor they occupied in the 19th century, that is, in which they sold primary

---

23 This article was first published in Spanish in 1997. We used the Portuguese version published in the book Dialética da Dependência (2000).

24 According to Marini (2000, p. 269): "The world process that we have entered since the 1980s and which has become known as globalization is characterized by the progressive overcoming of national borders within the framework of the world market, with regard to structures for the production, circulation and consumption of goods and services, as well as for altering political geography and international relations, social organization, value scales and ideological configurations specific to each country ". The author also states that there are four aspects to be highlighted in this process (Marini, 2000, pp. 270–272): a) the great magnitude of the population involved; b) the acceleration of historical time; c) the enormous production capacity at stake; d) the depth and speed that these transformations are beginning to show.

goods to the center and from there they bought manufactured goods, but now with the use of fully capitalist management methods.

4)   Globalization also produces, with this "new" international division of labor, increasing gaps in terms of knowledge and technical training in the workforce and contributes to the worsening of dependency.

From these points, Marini (2000, pp. 291–292) puts some perspectives on this process:

> We are, therefore, reaching a point where, just as in the 19th century, the central issue becomes the workers' struggle to impose limits on the orgy to which capital is given (to employ an expression of Marx) and submit to their control the new social and technical conditions in which they can develop their production activity. It is not a matter, of course, of stopping the increase in labor productivity and not even its natural corollary, the increase in intensity, but of distributing the production effort more equitably, which implies reducing the workday by a proportion compatible with the advance of the general productive capacity. But, even if it is that simple, it implies placing the content and forms of world economic development on radically different bases.
>
> This is the main reason why the solution to the problems currently facing the peoples of the world must necessarily pass through the class struggle and, in particular, the willingness they have to take the reins of economic policy in their hands, which means to say: assume the direction of the State. The only answer that the problem of globalization involves today is to set in motion a radical democratic revolution.

And this struggle of the peoples goes through a wide alliance of workers from central and dependent countries, according to Marini (2000, pp. 294–295):

> As the globalization process advances, it is inevitable that the objectives of the workers are more clearly defined and mechanisms are created that allow them to act in an orderly manner in the scenario that capital itself is designing, that of the fully constituted world market. Even in the preceding phase, corresponding to large-scale internationalization, which prepared the conditions for what is now underway, there have already been movements of solidarity that, in addition to any ideology, reflected common interests among workers in the center and the dependent world. The progressive constitution of a true international proletariat, which is the necessary counterpart of capitalist globalization, will make

it possible to put the peoples' struggle for higher forms of social organization on new bases.

Another development of the Marxist side of dependency theory can be seen in the growing approximation with the political economy of the world-system,[25] as Dos Santos (2000, p. 55) states:

> Dependency theory continued and perfected a global approach that sought to understand the formation and evolution of capitalism as a world economy. In the 1950s, Prebisch spoke about the existence of a world center and periphery, a thesis that he will perfect in the 1970s under the influence of the debate on dependency (...). Dependency theory sought to refine this scheme by reviewing the theory of imperialism since its formation, with Hilferding, Rosa Luxemburg, Hobson, Lenin and Bukharin. André Gunder Frank (1991) draws attention to this search for an analysis of the world system that is drawn mainly in the early 1970s with Amin (1974), Frank (1978,1980 and 1981), Dos Santos (1970 and 1978), but it gains a great boost with the work of Immanuel Wallerstein (1974, 1980, 1989), which develops the tradition of Fernand Braudel (1979).

Celso Furtado, from his theoretical elaborations in the 1970s, would continue to reflect, in later works, on the alternatives for Brazil in the face of the challenges that were emerging for the Brazilian nation: the economic crisis and the enormous foreign debt in the 1980s, as we observed in *O Brasil Pós-"Milagre"* (Brazil After the "Miracle", 1981) and in *A Nova Dependência: Dívida Externa e Monetarismo* (The New Dependency: External Debt and Monetarism, 1982), in addition to the risks of adherence to neoliberalism, as we observed in *Brasil; A Construção Interrompida* (Brazil: The Interrupted Construction, 1992).

In the book Global Capitalism (1998), Furtado analyzes the effects of globalization in peripheral countries (especially in Brazil), which lead to increased dependency (continuing the situation of underdevelopment) and proposes alternatives to face this situation, as we can observe in the following paragraphs.

---

25   According to Dos Santos (2000, p. 57): "The world-system approach seeks to analyze the formation and evolution of the capitalist mode of production as a system of economic-social, political and cultural relations that was born at the end of the European Middle Ages and evolves to become a planetary system and blend in with the world economy. This approach, still in development, highlights the existence of a center, a periphery and a semiperiphery, in addition to distinguishing, between the central economies, a hegemonic economy that articulates the system as a whole".

We first highlight the following observation from Furtado's analysis (1998, p. 21):

> The social groups that commanded the fantastic wealth accumulation process conformed the model of corporate organization, but within limits dictated by the salaried classes. These acquired increasing importance as merchants absorbing the flow of production.

However, with globalization, there is a new phase of this struggle, according to Furtado (1998, p. 22):

> The planetary political integration in an advanced course of realization is reducing the scope of the regulatory action of the national States in which the union organizations were supported. As a result, the organization of productive activity tends to be planned on a multinational and even global scale, to the detriment of the bargaining power of the working masses. Hence, the double process of unemployment and social exclusion, on the one hand, and, on the other, income concentration has intensified on all sides.

With globalization, the author continues in his reflection, there is a disarticulation of the forces that guaranteed the dynamism of national economic systems. According to Furtado (1998, p. 29):

> The more companies are globalized, the more they escape the State's regulatory action, the more they tend to rely on foreign markets to grow. At the same time, entrepreneurs' initiatives tend to escape the control of political bodies. We thus return to the model of original capitalism, whose dynamics was based on exports and investments abroad.

The consequences, then, of adherence to this model by the periphery are negative, since the most serious problems in both poor and wealthy societies stem from the orientation assumed by technological progress and by the indirect incorporation into the productive system of poorly paid labor in the countries of delayed industrialization (in the foreground, Asians), causing the social exclusion of growing portions of the population, as a result of the high concentration of income.

In short, the new challenges are of a social nature and not basically economic, thus requiring political imagination and utopia. Therefore, in the view

of Furtado (1998, p. 54), to overcome underdevelopment in a context of globalization, certain conditions must be met by any peripheral country:

1) Degree of autonomy in the decisions that limit as much as possible the
   drainage to the outside of the investment potential.

2) Power structures must make it difficult to reproduce the consumption
   pattern of rich countries and ensure a relatively high level of investment
   in the human factor, paving the way for social homogenization.

3) A certain degree of decentralization of business decisions so that an
   incentive system capable of ensuring the use of productive potential can
   be adopted.

4) According to Furtado (1998, p. 54): "social structures that open space for
   creativity in a wide cultural horizon and generate preventive and correc-
   tive forces in the processes of excessive concentration of power".

However, for these objectives to be successful, it is essential to exercise a strong
political will supported by broad social consensus.

Finally, it is worth highlighting, as a way of systematizing this reflection by
Furtado, his statement that the challenge posed at the beginning of the 21st
century is to change the course of civilization, to shift its axis from the logic of
the means to the service of accumulation in a short time horizon for a logic of
ends in function of social well-being, the exercise of freedom and cooperation
between peoples, ecological preservation and with a strong participation of
civil societies (Furtado, 1998, p. 64)

Brazil would face this change as follows, according to Furtado (1998, p. 67):

> This change of course, as far as we are concerned, requires that we aban-
> don many illusions, that we exorcise the ghosts of a modernity that
> condemns us to sterilizing cultural mimicry. We must recognize our his-
> torical situation and pave the way for the future from the knowledge of
> our reality. The first condition for getting rid of underdevelopment is to
> escape the obsession to reproduce the profile of those who call them-
> selves developed. It is to assume one's own identity. In the crisis of civili-
> zation that we are experiencing, only confidence in ourselves can restore
> our hope of reaching a successful outcome.

3   Final Considerations

We can affirm, based on what was analyzed in this work, that Celso Furtado's
thought about underdevelopment and dependency is close to DT (especially
MDT), as we observed during our analysis, denoting a process in which these

reflections can be understood from the economic structure of capitalism in the periphery and in the center (as Marx's Historical-Dialectic Materialism puts it), creating a new lange in the parole, that is, in Pocock's Theory of Political Language, innovating in the theoretical debate through expressions such as dependency, cultural dependency, modernization, sub-imperialism.

We observed that Celso Furtado, even approaching DT, maintains its own path of reflection, by emphasizing cultural dependency and "modernization" as factors for maintaining underdevelopment.

In the unfolding of the reflections of Celso Furtado and DT in the face of globalization, the approach also occurs more clearly with MDT, by continuing to affirm the impossibility of achieving development in a dependent and associated way.

Bibliographic References

Bambirra, Vânia. Teoría de la dependência: una anticrítica. México: Era, 1978.

Bichir, Maíra Machado. A problemática da dependência: um estudo sobre a vertente marxista da dependência. Dissertação de mestrado, Universidade Estadual de Campinas (UNICAMP), 2012.

Borja, Bruno. Para a crítica da economia do desenvolvimento: a inserção de Celso Furtado na controvérsia internacional. In: Mello, Maria Mello de (coord.). Ecos do desenvolvimento: uma história do pensamento econômico brasileiro. Rio de Janeiro: IPEA, Centro Internacional Celso Furtado de Políticas para o Desenvolvimento, 2011, p. 79–124.

Cardoso, Fernando Henrique; Faletto, Enzo. Dependência e desenvolvimento na América Latina: ensaio de interpretação sociológica. 7ª ed. Rio de Janeiro: Zahar, [1970] 1984.

Cardoso, Fernando Henrique. As ideias e seu lugar: ensaio sobre as teorias do desenvolvimento. Petrópolis: Vozes, 1993.

Castells, Manuel. A sociedade em rede. São Paulo, Paz e Terra, 1999.

Curty, Carla; Malta, Maria. Elementos metodológicos para a organização da história do pensamento econômico brasileiro: a abordagem das controvérsias. In: Malta, Maria; León, Jaime; Curty, Carla; Borja, Bruno. Controvérsias sobre história, desenvolvimento e revolução no Brasil: pensamento econômico em interpretação crítica. In this book, 2021.

Dos Santos, Theotonio. Imperialismo e corporações multinacionais. Rio de Janeiro: Paz e Terra, 1977.

Dos Santos, Theotonio. A teoria da dependência: balanço e perspectivas. Rio de Janeiro: Civilização Brasileira, 2000.

Furtado, Celso. Subdesenvolvimento e estagnação na América Latina. Rio de Janeiro: Civilização Brasileira, [1966] 1968.

Furtado, Celso. Um Projeto para o Brasil. Rio de Janeiro: Saga, 1968a.

Furtado, Celso. Brasil: da República oligárquica ao Estado militar. *In*: Furtado, Celso. (org.). Brasil: tempos modernos. Rio de Janeiro: Paz e Terra, 1968b.

Furtado, Celso. Análise do "modelo" brasileiro. Rio de Janeiro: Civilização Brasileira, [1972] 1982.

Furtado, Celso. A hegemonia dos Estados Unidos e o subdesenvolvimento da América Latina. Rio de Janeiro: Civilização Brasileira, 1973.

Furtado, Celso. O mito do desenvolvimento econômico. Rio de Janeiro: Paz e Terra, 1974.

Furtado, Celso. Prefácio a nova economia política. Rio de Janeiro: Paz e Terra, 1976.

Furtado, Celso. Criatividade e dependência na civilização industrial. Rio de Janeiro: Paz e Terra, 1978.

Furtado, Celso. O Brasil pós-"milagre". Rio de Janeiro: Paz e Terra, 1981.

Furtado, Celso. A nova dependência: dívida externa e monetarismo. Rio de Janeiro: Paz e Terra, 1982.

Furtado, Celso. A fantasia organizada. Rio de Janeiro: Paz e Terra, 1985.

Furtado, Celso. Brasil: A construção interrompida. Rio de Janeiro: Paz e Terra, 1992.

Furtado, Celso. O capitalismo global. São Paulo: Paz e Terra, 1998.

Luce, Mathias Seibel. O subimperialismo, etapa superior do capitalismo dependente. Tensões Mundiais. Fortaleza, v. 10, n. 18, 19, p. 43–65, 2014.

Mannheim, Karl. Ideologia e utopia. Rio de Janeiro: Zahar Editores, [1936] 1972.

Marini, Ruy Mauro. Dialética do desenvolvimento capitalista no Brasil. *In*: Marini, Ruy Mauro. Dialética da dependência. Petrópolis: Vozes; Buenos Aires: CLACSO, [1965] 2000.

Marini, Ruy Mauro. Subdesenvolvimento e revolução. *In*: Marini, Ruy Mauro. Subdesenvolvimento e revolução. 5ª ed. Florianópolis: Insular, [1967] 2014.

Marini, Ruy Mauro. Dialética da dependência. *In*: Marini, Ruy Mauro. Dialética da dependência. Petrópolis: Vozes; Buenos Aires: CLACSO, [1973] 2000.

Marini, Ruy Mauro. As razões do neodesenvolvimentismo: resposta a Fernando Henrique Cardoso e a José Serra. *In*: Marini, Ruy Mauro. Dialética da dependência. Petrópolis: Vozes; Buenos Aires: CLACSO, [1978] 2000.

Marini, Ruy Mauro. América Latina. Dependência e integração. São Paulo: Brasil Urgente, 1992.

Marini, Ruy Mauro. Processo e tendências da globalização capitalista. In: Marini, Ruy Mauro. Dialética da dependência. Petrópolis: Vozes; Buenos Aires: CLACSO, [1997] 2000.

Martins, Carlos Eduardo. Globalização, dependência e neoliberalismo na América Latina. São Paulo: Boitempo, 2011.

Marx, Karl. Grundrisse. São Paulo: Boitempo, [1857–1859] 2011.

Marx, Karl. Contribuição à crítica da economia política. 2ª ed. São Paulo: Expressão Popular, [1859] 2008.

Marx, Karl. O capital. Teorias da mais-valia: história crítica do pensamento econômico. 2 ed. Rio de Janeiro: Bertrand Brasil, [1906–1910] 1987.

Mazucato, Thiago. Ideologia e utopia de Karl Mannheim: o autor e a obra. São Paulo: Ideias & Letras, 2014.

Millikan, Max F ; Blackmer, Donald L. M. (orgs.). Nações em desenvolvimento: a sua evolução e a política americana. Rio de Janeiro: Fundo de Cultura, 1963.

Pocock, John. Linguagens do ideário político. São Paulo: Editora da USP, 2003.

Prado, Fernando Correa. História de um não-debate: a trajetória da teoria marxista da dependência no Brasil. Comunicação & Política, v. 22, p. 68–94, 2011.

Prebisch, Raúl. El desarrollo económico de la América Latina y algunos de sus principales problemas. In: Cepal, Estudio Económico de la América Latina 1948 . Santiago do Chile: CEPAL, 1949.

Prebisch, Raúl. Dinâmica do desenvolvimento latino-americano. Rio de Janeiro: Fundo de Cultura, 1964.

Rostow, Walt Whitman. Etapas do desenvolvimento econômico: um manifesto não comunista. Rio de Janeiro: Zahar, 1961.

Serra, José; Cardoso, Fernando Henrique. As desventuras da dialética da dependência. Estudos CEBRAP. São Paulo, n. 23, p. 35–80, 1978.

Tavares, Maria da Conceição; Serra, José. Além da estagnação. In: Tavares, Maria da Conceição. Da substituição de importações ao capitalismo financeiro. Rio de Janeiro: Zahar editores, 1972.

Weber, Max. Conceitos básicos de sociologia. São Paulo: Centauro, [1925] 2002.

CHAPTER 7

Seeds of Brazilian Underdevelopment

A Controversy on Property, Labor Force and Production

Larissa Mazolli Veiga and Maria Malta

1   Introduction

This chapter intends to present the view of four interpreters who contributed to the controversy on the issue of limits to development, especially when the planning of the Brazilian economy put the focus again on the agricultural sector as the "bottleneck" to be overcome to accelerate production, that is, in the 1960s and 1970s, particularly during the Brazilian civil-military dictatorship. This was the last moment in which the agricultural question was formulated in an articulated manner with a historical-political reflection typical of Brazilian interpreters. From this, the recovery of this controversy has a political sense of bringing forward the centrality of the choice of the agricultural development model and its structural impacts. The structure of the property on the land, the organization and use of the social work force and the form of international insertion of nations are links of this option with the pattern of development underway in each society. In this way, the current silencing of this debate and its transformation into a discussion that boils down to the evolution of productivity in the sector is revealing, at the same time, a choice for a certain accumulation model and an attempt to erase the contradictions present in it.

We argue that Brazilian underdevelopment has always found its most complete and complex expression in its agricultural sector, both from an economic and a political point of view. The Brazilian economic and social formation is intertwined with the way of productive organization of this sector, from the predominant form of the workforce used to the ordering of property on the land. The way of producing food and agricultural surplus in Brazil always defined its history. In this sense, this sector has been the subject of many analyzes and controversies, especially since its importance is great for the country's economic dynamics. It was agriculture that engendered the first economic cycles and characterized the export-led external insertion of Brazil, providing foreign exchange to make it possible to trade with the rest of the world throughout its history, in addition to being the sector responsible to produce a good part of the economy's wage-goods. We realized, then, that it was from the form of development of the agricultural sector that the Brazilian economy and its underdevelopment were born, so its understanding is fundamental in the interpretations about the country.

From our point of view, an understanding of the debates that have arisen, both in relation to the internal dynamics of the agricultural sector, and about its interaction with the rest of the economy, is essential to identify the reason why the Brazilian economy has been for a long time caracterized as backward, archaic, of low productivity, with an excess of employed labor force and, because of that, would present serious obstacles to development.

We have no doubt that studies on underdevelopment are broader than the exclusive analysis of the dynamics of the agricultural sector, however the frequently found way of diagnosing the issue of Brazilian underdevelopment points to its association with low agricultural productivity. This, in turn, would be the result of a backward productive structure (form of land ownership, work organization and form of capital financing), unable to respond to demand increases, even the simple demand related to the domestic production of foods. This inefficiency in the supply expansion process would present a mismatch with the industrial sector, generating an increase in the prices of agricultural products, which would directly influence the real wages of the economy, by changing the relative prices, considering that it is in the agricultural sector that most of the basic products of the economy are found. This is a fundamental point of the controversy on screen.

This relationship between the agricultural sector and the rest of the economy is not, however, an exclusive concern of Brazilian authors or of underdeveloped economies, in fact it is a question that permeates the history of economic thought in a broad way, and we can find the beginning of this debate in the work classic authors (with emphasis on the works of Quesnay, Adam Smith and David Ricardo). An important moment for resuming this concern and influencing Brazilian thought is with the debates on development that took place at the end of the Second World War, but mainly with the creation of the Economic Commission for Development in Latin America and the Caribbean (ECLAC). Brazilian economic thought in general, and the controversy that we will deal with, in particular, is part of this debate.

Therefore, this chapter will outline the path to revisit the controversy over limits to development and the agricultural question, organizing it in three moments and spaces: initially the perspective of limits to development brought by classical economists, when they approach the agricultural question, focusing in its impact on the production of the social surplus, on prices, on the balance between sectors and on the international competitiveness of each national economy; later, in studies on Latin American underdevelopment, dualist models and criticism of this view brought about by analyzing the structural heterogeneity contained in structuralist models, highlighting the political issue of choosing the uses of agricultural surplus, the different forms of productive organization within the sector itself and its social dimension and; finally, in the Brazilian debate under which the perspective of social formation and a policy of agricultural "modernization" for agriculture-industry interaction and for overcoming underdevelopment gain centrality.

2   Limits to Development and Agricultural Surplus: The Thought of the Classics

The first discussions about the importance of the agricultural sector for economic development can be found in classical economists. The physiocrats were the pioneers and put agriculture as the central sector for the dynamics of the economy, since, according to these authors, it would be the only one to produce value.

Thinkers like Smith (1723–1790) and Ricardo (1772–1823), who analyzed the economy using a theory of value based on work and a theory of distribution that determined production of the surplus without locating it exclusively in a sector, began to displace agriculture from the central role of the dynamics of the economy. These authors were concerned with increasing the economy's productivity, as they focused on increasing surplus production as a key to the accumulation and development process.

The perspective of accumulation is that which addresses the questioning of the agricultural issue. For them, this sector could present itself as an obstacle to the development process, since its production would provide diminishing returns because land, an essential natural resource for its execution, is a finite resource. Therefore, to overcome this physical limit of the finitude of the land, it was essential that there was an agriculture that would serve a growing population and production.

Thus, the agricultural question, unlike the agrarian question, deals with what are the productive conditions of agriculture that support the other sectors of the economy. In this way, this view is directly related to the issue of economic development, since it identifies which are the roles that agriculture should fulfill in the development process. For Quesnay (1694–1774), the main exponent of the physiocratic school, agriculture would be the only productive sector of the economy, because it would be the only sector that had the capacity to generate an economic surplus, because as the land the only factor could generate several new fruits from a single seed, he concluded that it was from it that the new value originated.

Quesnay identified the net product (produit net), the surplus, and characterizes it as that which is produced beyond what is necessary to reestablish production at the same level. The author also pointed out that the net product could only be produced within agriculture and that only landowners would be entitled to this surplus, which would be transferred to them in the form of land rent. For him it is this agricultural surplus, the excess production over immediate needs, which would allow the development of trade, the existence of artisans and governmental organization, so it would be agriculture, with its surplus, that would sustain the economy.

As agriculture would be the only sector responsible for creating a surplus, it is this sector that would give the dynamics of the economy, that is, the greater the surplus generated by agriculture, the greater the capacity of this economy to develop. Because of this, the economy as a whole would be organized around this sector and all government efforts should be directed towards it, since economic development depended on the development of agriculture. In this rationale for orienting economic policy towards development, the author reveals to which class he would serve and what interests he defended with his theory, that is, to landowners.

Smith, unlike physiocrats, extended the notion of productive work to all sectors of the economy. For this author, productive work is that capable of generating surplus, that is, all work that is subject to the division of labor and specialization would be capable of producing a surplus regardless of the sector in which it is exercised. In this way, the dynamics of an economy would be determined by the capital accumulation of the economy, and no longer just by the dynamics of agriculture.

In Smith's view, work in agriculture would be more productive than the work of merchants and artisans, because agricultural workers would not only produce for their subsistence but would also generate surplus for their employers and landowners. However, industrial labor would be more productive than agricultural labor because it would be a sector in which the highest productivity per worker could be obtained due to greater specialization and division of labor.

Smith's argument was that increased productivity of any activity would arise from the division of labor, due to the specialization of tasks and the increased efficiency of the worker in carrying out each specialized task and the encouragement of his ingenuity to create specific instruments for each one of them. In its conception, the work in agriculture did not allow a great specialization and, therefore, this work would be destined to a low productivity. Thus, the author concludes that there is no way to increase productivity in the agricultural sector indefinitely, as it happens in other sectors, making it a sector that in a way would slow growth, as its potential productivity is extremely low compared to the industrial sector and is not able to expand for very long.

In this new way of presenting the economic dynamics, agriculture would leave the dynamic center of the economy. However, it would still play an important role, since as it is a supplier of food and raw materials for the industry, its dynamics would affect the rest of the economy, as the increase in demand for agricultural products depends on demographic growth, but also on economic growth.

For Ricardo, the importance of the agricultural sector gains another dimension because, when organizing and developing Smith's reasoning, he presents a theory in which this sector appears regulating the rate of profit of the economy, since it was the dynamics of land income that would guide the profit rate.[1] The land rent would be the result of different levels of fertility. Its determination would depend on the dynamics by which the increased demand for agricultural products would force the cultivation of less fertile lands, and consequently less productive. Thus, the price of these products made using poorer quality land would be higher and, due to the principle of competition, all land should remunerate the capital employed on it at the same rate of profit, so the difference in productivity between the lands would be reverted to a higher income. to the most fertile lands in the exact hierarchy of their fertility. Ricardo looked at the question of the distribution of the product of the economy between social classes and would be distributed among capitalists, workers and landowners. Thus, in its scheme, an increase in the price of food (agricultural products) would generate an increase in wages for the entire economy, as well as an increase in the share received by the owners, which would result in a fall in the rate of profit obtained by the capitalists. A fall in the rate of profit would reduce investments, both because of a lower availability of capital and because of the lesser possibility of making a profit, causing the capital accumulation of this economy to lose its dynamism.

At the heart of the agricultural problem for Ricardo was that diminishing returns from land productivity, or from the use of less productive land, would hinder the growth of the entire economy. This process would occur through the increase in land rent, which would bring down profit rates, and with it profits, which, from Ricardo's point of view, are the fund for capital accumulation. Low agricultural productivity would become detrimental to the rest of the economy.

---

1   See "The essay on the influence of the low price of cereal on the profits of capital" (Ricardo, 1815).

In both Smith and Ricardo, economic policy recommendations for the purpose of increasing the pace of accumulation were aimed at maintaining high rates of profit. Smith still had some contradiction in his reasoning, as he assumed that an excessive increase in capital could generate a fall in the rate of profits, given the competition between capitalists to invest capital, but Ricardo had no doubts about the need to focus efforts on industrial production in England and moving the agricultural frontier outside the territory in order to keep the English rate of profit high. These authors also revealed their class position when making their recommendations for development and also their reflection from the capitalist center.

Thus, in a general way we can say that the classical economics theorists were concerned with the production and distribution of the social product and about what would be the factors that would stimulate or retract the economic growth. In this way, for them, the agricultural sector would influence economic development through their productivity, but also considering how the variation in costs that their products would affect the reproduction costs of the entire economy, revealing that their management was fundamental, even if in the service of an economy in favor of capitalists as a class.

This view of classical economists had a great influence on Latin American structuralist thinking and from it on Brazilian economic thinking on underdevelopment, however it is still necessary to understand the steps of this movement and the centrality of understanding the agricultural issue in this process. The authors who will put at the center of the debate the essentiality of understanding the role of the structure of the agricultural sector for underdeveloped training are influenced by the formulation of the works of several authors related to the post-World War II development debate. Among these authors, the work of Arthur Lewis and Raúl Prebisch deserves attention, in order to understand the thoughts of Brazilian authors and the controversy on screen.

3   Limits to Development Outside the Classical Liberal Perspective: Structural Surplus of "labor[2]", Productivity and Structural Heterogeneity

3.1   *Arthur Lewis and the Structural Surplus of Labor*
The interpretation of the question of the limits of development of Arthur Lewis (1915–1991) starts from the perception of the existence of a structural

---

2   It is important to highlight that the authors have chosen to keep the expression manpower, whenever it was originally used by the authors or in a section that refers to the authors' own

surplus of labor in the agricultural sector, which would be reflected in the low productivity of labor in that sector, would allow a supply response highly elastic workforce, or that would meet a rapid need for job expansion due to industrial growth, without on the other hand resulting in loss of production in the agricultural sector. What is discussed from this observation is how this transfer of workforce will occur and how it will influence variables such as employment, productivity in both sectors and, finally, wages.

Arthur Lewis's work falls within the scope of the models, which have a connection with the dual models of economics. A possible reading[3] of the duality pointed out is related to dynamics of different functioning between parts of the economy, considering that only one of them is exclusively the capitalist logic. Thus, in this dual logic, there is a main sector, capitalist or industrial, and the agricultural sector would not obey the logic of capitalism in its productive organization. In other words, to a large extent this analysis focuses on how the agricultural sector interacts – and often ends up promoting – with the development of the other sectors adapting or limiting the growth of the economy as a whole.

The main problems raised about the interaction of agriculture with other sectors of the economy and its correlation with economic development are the issue of intersectoral demand, the supply of labor, normally referred to as "labor" by these authors, and food supply. All of these components can affect the rest of the economy very intensely. Regarding intersectoral demand, the point is also raised that with the growth of agricultural activity, there is an increase in demand for industrialized products by this sector.

The supply of food, as well as raw materials, is equally important for the development of the industrial sector, since, if agriculture did not respond to increases in demand, the price of food would rise and inflate the rest of the economy.

The above assumptions have direct implications for the economy's wages. Wages in other sectors of the economy would be influenced both by the prices of agricultural products, which depend on the productivity of the sector, and

---

ideas. However, with regard to the moments in the text in which the authors themselves express their voice on the thought presented, they preferred to use the expression labor power to refer to the commodity in capitalism that is the sole property of the free worker.

3   We will present here a different reading from that originally presented by Lewis (1954), in his article the non-capitalized sector would not necessarily be the agricultural sector, although in several economies in the world there was a reasonable correspondence between the two. This view is linked to neoclassical readings that followed the line opened by Lewis, who emphasized more the direct relationship between the non-capitalized or low-productivity sector with subsistence agriculture. or low productivity with subsistence agriculture.

by the supply of labor, which would react to the need for expanding demand for labor by other sectors, or specifically in higher capitalization sectors.

From these two problems there is a concern with the modernization of agriculture. For some authors, the modernization of agriculture would be extremely necessary so that it could accompany and provide the necessary bases for the industrial sector to have an accelerated growth rate. Thus, in dual models, the heart of the discussion about the sector is around how agricultural development would influence the development of the other sectors and what are the consequences of the mismatch between these sectors for the economy as a whole.

Lewis (1954) begins his argument by exploring the classic assumption of the existence of a supply of labor, which led to the issue of capital accumulation, explained from the distribution of income. This return to the classic assumption was a reaction to the neoclassicals who came to assume a limited supply of labor in their models.

Arthur Lewis, however, pointed out that there were still countries in which the supply of labor was still in excess. For him, in densely populated economies there was a situation of abundance of work and scarcity of capital, thus characterizing an "economy with unlimited supply of labor".

This excess supply of labor power would be veiled over low productivity jobs, which were found, although not exclusively, in the agricultural sector. In this sector, as well as in others with low capitalization, the marginal productivity of labor would be less or less than the subsistence wage, which allowed them to employ idle workers, thus there would be no surplus that paid the capital that could be reinvested and, therefore, not producing economic expansion, which would characterize non-reproducible capital.

Unlike the capitalist sector, where reproducible capital prevails, where a current wage is equal to the marginal productivity of the worker, it allows capital to generate a surplus that can be reinvested, generating an economic expansion. This division between the use of reproducible and non-reproducible capital in the sectors is what characterizes Lewis' dual model.

The salary in the agricultural sector would be defined only by its level of subsistence. The wages of the industrial sector of this economy, on the other hand, would be defined either by social conventions, or by the minimum necessary for the subsistence of an agricultural employee plus an additional, also socially defined, which is consistent with the fact that they are working in the cities.

What will foster this increase in the level of employment is the accumulation of capital in the industrial sector, that is, in the capitalized sector. The greater this capital accumulation, the more employment will be generated, because of this movement, there will be an increase in the productivity of the entire economy, since workers will be employed in more productive sectors.

This absorption happens at constant wages because as the marginal productivity of the agricultural sector is very small, this transfer of labor will force the sector to have its productivity increased, which would not reduce agricultural production, keeping the level of subsistence constant. This also contributes to industrial growth, since the increase in agricultural productivity would guarantee the supply for expanding demand in this sector.

Staying at wages at a constant level allows the economy's profit rate to increase, increasing the savings rate, which, consequently, would increase the economy's investment rate, driving the economy's growth.

The displacement of surplus labor from the agricultural sector to the capitalist sector will take place until the level of employment is where the marginal productivity of labor is equal to the subsistence wage of the industrial sector. At this point the surplus of labor will be exhausted.

For Lewis, the agricultural sector would play an important role in the development of the economy. The excess supply of labor and the supply of subsistence products would be extremely necessary for industrial expansion to take place without real wages increasing, allowing profits to increase so that there could be reinvestment, increasing capital accumulation, causing what the economy develops.

Thus, Lewis's dual model ended up revealing that the issue of low productivity in the sector has a much greater relationship with the social issue of joblessness and land concentration than effectively a technological backwardness, therefore overcoming the heterogeneity of use of capital and labor power between sectors, which is a fundamental condition for overcoming underdevelopment as it is perceived as an indication between a movement to increase productivity in the agricultural sector and a more articulated productive interrelation between the industrial and agricultural sectors in dual models. .

It is worth a dive in Prebisch's reasoning to understand how the structuralists arrive at this issue.

3.2   Prebisch's Structuralist Model

The central theme of the study of structuralism was the issue of underdevelopment, here represented by the ideas of Raúl Prebisch (1901–1986). For these theorists, underdevelopment is due to the historical form of construction of these economies. As a result, according to the structure created historically, the international insertion of underdeveloped countries would occur only through their agro-export production, which would bring production concentrated in large estates and would present low productivity.

This type of international insertion would place the underdeveloped countries in a position of inferiority in terms of GDP per capita in relation to the already industrialized countries and mainly generating a structurally heterogeneous domestic socioeconomic composition. Overcoming this dilemma would only occur with industrialization, which, in turn, would only be achieved through state induction. If such a movement did not occur, the pattern of external insertion would be perpetuated and, in fact, would even widen the distance between developed and underdeveloped countries.

This position was opposed to the current of liberal thought, in which the agricultural vocation was defended, in addition to specialization, since the fruits of international technical progress would be equally distributed through the fall in the relative prices of industrialized goods in which there would be an incorporation faster pace of technical progress. However, structuralist criticism emphasized the fact that the benefits of increased productivity did not reach the periphery due to the inability to incorporate such gains reflected in a real increase in the worker's wage, a fact that occurred in the center.

In this way, the industrialization of the periphery would have a central role, because this would be the only way to appropriate these benefits, only through industrialization that a process of homogenization of the labor market could be achieved. Thus, the center-periphery relationship was a historical result of the way in which the benefits generated by technical progress would spread unevenly in the world economy.

The heart of the criticism elaborated by Prebisch addressed what were the bottlenecks of backward economies, mainly Latin American ones, which hindered the industrialization process and hindered their development. For the author, specialization in the export of primary products was bound to generate a loss of terms of trade.

With this intense concern about industrialization and opposing the specialization of exports outside the agricultural sector, he analyzed what would be the role played by agriculture for economic development. Due to the historical formation of the agrarian structure of the peripheral countries, agricultural supply would be inelastic, and this inelasticity would reside in the fact that the productive structure would be delayed, of low productivity, unable to respond to the demand pressures of economic growth. As a result of this process, there would be an increase in inflation, which would harm the rest of the economy.

According to Prebisch, the only way out of this bottleneck would be to modernize the agricultural production structure, aiming to increase the productivity of this sector through technical progress and the mechanization of production. However, the excess of labor, resulting from the agrarian structure and low productivity, which would be released in this modernization process, could not be fully absorbed by urban areas, since the capital in these areas would not be enough to absorb this surplus of labor.

However, this modernization could be prevented by the current agrarian structure. With an abundance of land allocated to large estates and an excess of labor, investment in technology to increase the productivity of the workforce would be seen as unnecessary, so, in addition to agricultural modernization, agrarian restructuring was necessary in order to encourage technical progress.

In addition to the question of the different trajectories of productivity and real wages in the center and periphery, Prebisch also highlighted the fact, which is also linked to structural inequality, that commodity cycles are much more intense, due to the movement of prices and the inelasticity of demand of these products, than those of industrialized goods, accentuating the economic instability in the periphery. Thus, the deterioration in terms of trade would occur because, as commodity price fluctuations are more pronounced, the net result of the upward and downward phases of the cycle would be that there would be a net loss in terms of the relative prices of commodities vis-à-vis industrialized goods.

Therefore, for the author, specializing in the agro-export sector, based on monoculture, and mainly on tropical products, with low wages, would only reaffirm the peripheral position of underdeveloped economies. To circumvent this situation, the only solution would be to induce industrialization through a promotion via the State, since it would not be in the interest of "market forces" to carry out this task.

Prebisch's structuralist model and the policy associated with it had a major influence on the formation of Brazilian developmentalist thinking. In this sense, the controversy that we will portray below is theoretically and politically dependent on its formulation.

4   The Controversy of the Agricultural Issue in Brazilian Economic Thought: Politics, Underdevelopment, and Structural Heterogeneity

4.1   *Celso Furtado: Underdevelopment as the Center of the Debate*
Celso Furtado (1920–2004), through his work, always showed a concern with the issue of underdevelopment and how to overcome it. His analyzes sought to understand the Brazilian economy through the center-periphery relationship and emphasized that these relations would be conditioned by the uneven distribution of technical progress, which was concentrated in the central countries and that this contributed to further increase the gap between these and

the peripheral economies. This tendency to increase the difference between the economies of the center and the periphery was due to the historical process of social and economic formation.[4] Therefore, for the author, underdevelopment would be a historical process, not a stage towards development, "underdeveloped structures do not develop, they are replaced by others with the ability to develop." (Furtado, [1961] 1963)

Furtado perceived agriculture not only as an economic activity, but he also saw the sector as the basis of social and political organization. The modernization of agricultural activities would be a way of eliminating the archaic structures that contributed to underdevelopment and increasing the agricultural surplus to support industrialization, which for him would be the only way to overcome underdevelopment.

A fundamental feature of the agricultural sector in Brazil pointed out by the author is the coexistence of the latifundium with the abundance of land. For him, it was not the offer of land that conditioned the organization of the agricultural company, but the availability of capital and entrepreneurial capacity. Therefore, the large property has already been created for export and of a capitalist character, with greater productivity.

> In Brazil, agriculture was born in the form of a large commercial company. This predates the country itself, as it did not result from the need for the survival of populations that had settled in the territory. The population emigrated precisely because it was feasible to organize export agriculture.
>
> FURTADO, [1961] 1963, p. 260

The other properties, of smaller size and quality of land, were left over to the rural population, where there is artisanal production, with an excess of labor and low productivity, aimed at domestic supply. From this, it characterized this sector as being marked by a duality, coexisting in it two modes of production, one backward – facing the domestic market – and another with a more advanced production structure – facing the external market (Furtado, [1969] 1975).

Furtado points out that the way in which the agricultural sector in Brazil developed occurred differently from the classic model, in which the growth in demand for agricultural products and the absorption of the surplus labor

---

4 On the concept of Furtado, with regard to the process of historical and social formation of Brazil, see Borja (2020) in this book.

force in this sector by the urban sector occurred simultaneously. In these cases, referred to as "classics", there would be an increase in the cost of the labor force, which would induce agricultural entrepreneurs to invest in technical progress, leading to the use of labor-saving techniques.

In the Brazilian case, and at this point in the argument Furtado reveals the influence of Lewis in his thinking, there is a large surplus of labor, with low wages, and an abundant supply of land available for cultivation. However, during industrialization, this surplus cannot be absorbed by the urban sector (an element brought about by Prebisch's reflection), which further depresses wages in the agricultural sector and together with the great abundance of land. Thus, due to an extremely cheap labor force, the incentive for investment in the mechanization of production in agriculture does not happen. Thus, the author concludes that the growth of the industrial sector of the economy could take place without any pressure on rural wages, and that the low cost of the labor force would discourage agricultural modernization.

Another reason for the difficulty of agriculture to "modernize" in Brazil, according to Furtado's analysis, is that the center-periphery relationship consisted of a historical result of the way in which the benefits generated by technical progress, understood here as techniques that increase productivity of labor, have spread unevenly in the world economy. The benefits of increased productivity did not reach the periphery, due to the inability to incorporate such gains into the real increase in the worker's wages, as occurred in the center, creating difficulties for technical progress to reach the agricultural sector. Furtado then realized that there is a structural tendency towards heterogeneous absorption of labor-saving technologies across sectors in underdeveloped economies.

In the texts written in the 1960s, Furtado was still very marked by a vision, which was later described as stagnationist, but which essentially observed the distribution of income as the main limit to growth in underdeveloped countries and participated in the controversy of the agrarian issue, seeking demonstrate the great responsibility that the structure of this sector had on such dynamics. This author was also concerned with the fact that the country's external insertion is given by the agricultural sector, promoting a peripheral insertion, since the exported products would suffer deterioration of the terms of trade, as pointed out by Prebisch, which would further stimulate the structural heterogeneity of the Brazilian economy and contribute to its underdevelopment.

In his chapter "Industrialization and Inflation" of the 1969 book, the author is dedicated to explaining why industrialization is necessary, but not enough to overcome underdevelopment, and for that he must resort to investigating the agricultural issue. In his conclusions he states that "as a result of the exhaustion of the import substitution process, development would have to open its way as an alternative to the growing social tensions" (Furtado, 1969, p.266). The Paraiba economist was convinced that the possible directions would be two; 1) the increase in industrial productivity with the transfer of these gains to wages, including impacting wages in the rural sector, which would make room for greater capitalization in agriculture with the adoption of technologies that save labor force; or 2) the direct transformation of the agrarian structure, which according to the author "would allow the rational use of factors, particularly labor, it would be possible to reduce the costs of the agricultural surplus and expand it, with higher wages inside and outside agriculture." (Op. cit p.267). In both cases, Furtado evidenced that the issue involved a political perception of the need to take these directions, which would give a "direction for a more rational use of factors and a less unequal distribution of social income" (op.cit p.267).

Later in his work, his perception of the impossibility of economic growth without the proper distribution of income changes, in the same movement in which he realizes that dual models are not sufficient to represent the complexity of underdeveloped structures. In this reflection, Furtado stressed that agriculture would preserve its traditional structures and would not modernize even though industrialization and urbanization happening relatively quickly, as underdeveloped structures are marked by structural heterogeneity and this does not prevent its growth, but its development. In any case, the notion that:

> The lack of an objective perception of these problems was due, in the past, to ideologies aimed at restoring an oudtated economic structure. In the immediate future, it may result from the fear of loss of privileges that are the counterpart of the high social cost of recent development.
>
> FURTADO, 1969, p. 268

Furtado recognizes, therefore, from this before the full maturation of his dynamic model of underdevelopment, that the questions related to structural changes, mainly regarding the elements that would impact the income distribution would imply a necessary disposition on the part of the "privileged" by underdeveloped social formation, to give up this status in the name of reducing the gigantic social cost of its reproduction.

4.2 Caio Prado Junior: Regressive Modernization without Changing the Ownership Structure

Caio Prado (1907–1990), in his 1966 book "A revolução Brasileira", unlike Furtado, does not put the center in the debate on the issue of agricultural productivity and its impact on prices and income distribution. Its bottom line was land reform. This author analyzes the agricultural issue to counter the feudal theses,[5] wanting to meet the idea that the social relations engendered within Brazilian agriculture would present remnants of feudalism, along European lines. To this end, it sought to begin its analysis of the agricultural sector through production relations in the field.

For the author, the Brazilian agricultural sector was structured on the large slaveholding exploitation property turned to the foreign market, which determined the mercantile nature of the sector. Thus, the Brazilian agricultural sector would have been born with a capitalist sense, the dynamics installed here in colony Brazil intended to serve the interests of the metropolis, thus the agricultural sector emerges as an agro-export company meeting the needs of the international market, totally different from the European servile agrarian construction.[6] The author characterized this sector as organic. However, he acknowledged that related to this sector it is born and totally dependent on it, but that it also supports basic food products, an inorganic agricultural sector is born, which follows a different organizational logic, even if submitted to that of the organic sector.

Another strong characteristic of the agricultural sector in Brazil is that the dimension of the organic and inorganic relationship, pointed out by the author, and the type of production relationships that take place within it. Even with the abolition of slave labor and the adoption of a free labor force, certain practices of using the labor force remained, maintaining a low-productivity and extremely low-paying job, thus signaling a conservation of the traits of the slave tradition. Caio Prado points out that this situation of permanence of colonial characteristics remains through the development of this sector, because, in addition to the production relations, the structure of the large-scale latifundium has remained practically intact.

The author recognizes that the Brazilian economy has undergone major transformations and, thus, also the agricultural sector. However, despite the advance and modernization seen in some segments of agriculture, as he himself mentions, for example, the sugar cane sector that concentrated its production and became mechanized, it was not able to overcome some of its main characteristics that revealed relations regressive social production processes. From his point of view, this issue is revealed by the fact that the Brazilian economy has not managed to get rid of the way in which it is inserted internationally and by remaining dependent and subordinated to the international

5 This debate is extensively explored in the text by Borja, Curty and León (2020) in this volume.
6 This reasoning has been present in his work since his 1933 book, Political Evolution of Brazil, with the concept of the meaning of colonization.

economic and financial system, continuing to participate in it in a peripheral and marginal position. At the same time, by not forming a national economy, in the sense of an effective internal market,

In this way, Caio Prado will point to the fact that technical progress can happen from a structure seen as backward. This is the legacy of the colonial period, without being feudal remains, which will shape, in the Brazilian economy, capitalism and its contradictions. For him, the low remuneration of rural workers is necessary for low-cost production of exported primary products, however this fact would present itself as an obstacle to the formation of the domestic consumer market, becoming incompatible with industrialization and, consequently, of the country's economic development. Although incompatible, they are fully capitalist relations of production.

> We have just noted that the pre-capitalist survivals in the labor relations of Brazilian agriculture, far from generating obstacles and contradictions opposed to capitalist development, have on the contrary contributed to it. The agriculture business – and it is on this basis that the major and main part of the Brazilian rural economy is structured – often does not maintain itself thanks precisely to the low living standards of workers, and, therefore, to the low cost of labor that employs.
>
> PRADO, [1966] 1987, p. 97

Therefore, Caio Prado concludes that, unless there is an active political intervention towards a new model of social and productive organization, Brazilian agriculture would modernize, in line with the development model of the rest of the economy, but would maintain its colonial structures and its production relations inherited from the process of social historical formation that created an organic and an inorganic sector in the country. For him, agrarian reform would not be necessary for modernization in agriculture, it would be necessary to create what he called the national economy, to solve the social problems that existed in rural areas, which were not the result of productive backwardness, but of social relations built there and all the implications that these remained had for Brazilian society and economy.

4.3   *Ignácio Rangel: From Feudal Latifundio to Capitalist Latifundio*
Ignacio Rangel (1914–1994) had a different view than Caio Prado on the question of the relationship between the form of ownership and the effectiveness of agricultural production for the Brazilian development model. The Maranhão's author has always sought to analyze the Brazilian reality from what he himself calls the basic duality of the Brazilian economy, trying to understand it

through the interaction of the process of economic formation in Brazil with the social classes and their economic and social roles. different economic and social structures. For him, duality would represent the Brazilian mode of production, complex, which combines different modes of production working internally in a contemporary way. Because of that,

The development of the productive forces would take place from the stimuli given by the movements of the Kondratiev cycle on the external side of the external pole, that is, it came from outside the country. In this way, it analyzed the Brazilian economy from two poles, one internal and one external, interpreting economic development through duality, the relationship between these two poles, which does not occur in a harmonious way, resulting from the relationship between contradictions inside and outside from the country. This double determination did not only happen in the economy as a whole, but also within each sector of it – agricultural, industrial or commerce – in this way, the agricultural sector would also be marked by these contradictions.

Thus, economic development, a theme addressed throughout his work, but in a dedicated way in his 1954 book "The economic development in Brazil", for the author meant the transfer of capital and resources from agriculture to industry. Therefore, in order to have industrialization, there would necessarily be a dismantling of the agricultural sector, transferring resources to the mercantile sector of the economy. Thus, Rangel argues that the contribution that the agricultural sector should provide to industrialization – in addition to the transfer of resources – would be to supply the demand for agricultural goods and to control, in a certain way, the labor market, releasing, retaining, or reabsorbing strength. of work, according to the need in other sectors of the economic system.

Rangel characterized the Brazilian agricultural sector as having two poles, which would be complementary and antagonistic, one of them would present itself as backward and archaic, characterized by still feudal relations, aimed at the domestic market, and the other representing the agricultural producer, capitalist and connected. to the foreign market. The backwardness of the Brazilian agricultural sector lay in the fact that there was no division of labor, and a consequent specialization of it, which could generate an increase in productivity. In the agricultural family unit, workers were busy with lower productivity jobs, causing wasted work, further lowering rural productivity.

However, the other pole of the agricultural sector, in its relationship with the industrial pole, which was given by industrialization, dissolved the agricultural productive structure so that resources were installed in the industrial sector. The transformations in the agricultural sector would happen at the same time as industrialization, due to the duality movement. As a result, the agricultural sector has modernized and mechanized, increasing its productivity and producing more to meet the demands of the industrial sector. However, this modernization has led to a major release of labor for the industrial sector, flattening wages as a whole.

This process, despite launching a large industrial reserve army in the economy, would help to develop the capitalist productive forces and would represent a productive restructuring in the country. Thus, Rangel points out that capital formation destroys and creates jobs, on the one hand the increase in investments creates jobs, on the other hand the implementation of new technologies from it does not require manpower, showing here, once again, the movement of duality and the transformation of one duality into another, in the third duality, that which was outlined in Brazil between 1922–1973.

Thus, Rangel argued that the dissolution of the rural complex and the consequent industrialization took place without the need for land restructuring. In this process, driven by industrial capital itself, the feudal latifundium was replaced by the capitalist latifundium and allowed to give this industrialization a great boost. However, industrialization without agrarian reform, promoted an unequal distribution of income by accumulating wealth in one pole of society and accumulating misery in the other, with large contingents of labor force liberated from agriculture forming a huge industrial reserve army. The solution that Rangel presents, however, is both creative and controversial. It does not propose an agrarian reform with the restoration of a peasant economy that never existed in Brazil. In its conception, it is necessary to facilitate capitalist development in the countryside, encouraging the capitalist use of land to break the historical speculation that the latifundium exercises over land prices and centennial marketing schemes. The author believed that making the restructuring of the "rural complex" viable would be accompanied by a generalization of wage relations in the Brazilian economy, which could also generate a greater settlement of families in the countryside, given the improvement of working conditions resulting from this process in the sector. At the same time, this salaried rural population would contribute in a more structured way to the formation of an internal market for industrial goods. However, Rangel never saw this process take place.

4.4 Antônio Barros de Castro: The Role of Agriculture in the Development of Underdevelopment

Antônio Barros de Castro (1938–2011), in his book "Seven essays on the Brazilian economy", dedicated more than one of his essays to agriculture, but one of them was especially dedicated to the controversy on which we are concerned. In this essay the author sought to investigate what the functions of agrarian dynamics would be and how they influenced the process of economic development. This analysis of agriculture aimed to meet the arguments of the discussions at the time, including an overview of this discussion in the first part of the essay, which attributed to this sector a fundamental obstacle to the industrialization process, but also raises the fact that several of these authors see agriculture as a matrix for the type of industrialization that had developed in Brazil (Castro, 1969).

Castro points out that the literature he had taken as a reference had multiple issues under discussion and that he wished to focus the debate on the question "has agriculture been fulfilling its functions in Brazilian development" (Castro, 1969, p.92). In order to define these functions, the author uses a scheme that generically brings together four roles, although considering that there are differences in their hierarchy and adaptations depending on the historicity of each national experience: 1) to provide a permanent growth of the agricultural surplus, the in order to provide food and raw materials; 2) free up the workforce for other sectors; 3) create markets for industrial products and; 4) transferring capital to the urban sector. In his work, Castro argues that agriculture did not hamper industrialization,

Regarding the generation of surplus in agriculture, Castro shows that whenever there was a need to increase agricultural supply, production was able to respond to this increase. It also points out that this type of surplus, in countries with an agrarian vocation such as Brazil, already existed even before industrialization was established and would be destined for the work employed in the agro-export sector.

It points out that in the cycles of urban expansion analyzed, the supply of agricultural products met this demand because there was no increase in food imports, nor a general increase in the prices of these products. Another important factor that would prove the supply of the need for agricultural products would be that agriculture grew at a much slower pace than the growth of industry.

As for the release of labor for the industrial sector, Castro notes that the surplus of labor released by the agricultural sector, plus the vegetative growth of the population, were more than sufficient to meet the demand for workers in the industrial sector.

In fact, in the course of industrialization, there was an inability to absorb all this labor from the countryside, creating a chronic imbalance in the labor market, which constantly pushed wages down. These low wages added to the rapid increase in the productivity of industrialization, gave industrial entrepreneurs an extremely high rate of profit.

Even with this low wage and low jobs in agriculture, which would under-mine the creation of an internal market that would support industrialization, Castro argued that since industrialization was initially promoted through an import substitution, it did not depend on the growth of an internal agricultural market, since it already had the market for buyers of imported products, members of the higher income classes with a much higher purchasing power than the majority of the population.

The only exception to this model was the coffee culture, which through wages of its workers managed to foster a consumer market. Thus, it concludes that industrial growth was independent of the counterpart of the creation of a rural mass consumer market, due to growth with concentration of income.

The transfer of capital between agriculture and the other sectors would be mainly the responsibility of the fixed exchange rate policy, which ended up making this transfer viable through indirect subsidies. With the internal devaluation of the currency and the fixed exchange rate, that is, the real appre-ciation of the exchange rate, imports became cheaper, thus, it is possible to import inputs for the industry such as fuels, equipment, raw materials, etc. But this was only possible due to the resources of exporting agriculture, which would aim for a more devalued real exchange rate to obtain a higher amount of revenue in domestic currency for the same amount exported.

There were other mechanisms for transferring resources that, however, according to Castro, would be difficult to measure or had less weight in this process. Taxation on income from agriculture and the fall in relative prices of agricultural products also contributed to the transfer of resources, however their effects on industry were difficult to measure. Capitals only seeking a higher remuneration, due to the crisis of 1929, transferring voluntarily to other sectors, were not as important as transfers via fixed exchange rate.

Thus, when carrying out his analysis on the role of agriculture for Brazilian development and as a possible limit for it, Castro did not see agriculture as an obstacle to Brazilian economic development, on the contrary, even with its underdeveloped structure it managed to fulfill its role of supplying the neces-sary inputs for industrialization. It also highlights that the way industrializa-tion occurred in Brazil did not require major efforts for agricultural growth as it did with other countries.

However, in his reflection, the author does not fail to emphasize, and resume questions posed by his predecessors because he states that:

Once the determinant role of agriculture in the premolding of the economic structure is admitted, it is worth asking whether, during industrialization, agriculture continues to exert influence in determining structural characteristics and the directions taken by the development process.

CASTRO, 1969, p. 140

This question is the key to the issue of maintaining Brazilian underdevelopment even in the face of the industrialization of the dimensions experienced in the country. Castro points out how "the rural universe is projected, giving characteristics to the industrial urban development that will be largely made to its image and likeness" (op. cit, p. 141).

5   Conclusion

The controversy over the role of agriculture as a limit to development in Brazil is extremely important to show that Brazilian capitalism has stopped finding solutions to its accumulation process, remaining exclusionary and abandoning the path of overcoming the main issues of underdevelopment. In fact, agriculture has always managed to meet the requirements of industrialization, in the form and intensity that were formulated.

In this sense, Castro's work points to proof of a series of hypotheses raised by his predecessors and deepens them, opening a research agenda that identifies the biggest problems of Brazilian industrialization in maintaining the "deepest deformations originating in our rural universe" (Castro, 1969, p.143). In fact, the controversy on display reveals that agriculture was never a limit to development in Brazil, and that modern Brazilian industrialization simply did not require the performance of functions considered "classic" in the agricultural sector for the process of capital accumulation as imagined by the classical economists from their own historical experiences. In summary,

Exactly due to the strength of this discussion, already in the late 1970s, the whole debate about the land issue is losing ground and the questions about agriculture start to focus on issues that deal with the increase of productivity in the field, as the sector exporters are now seen as the possible lifeline for what was presented as the deepening of the increase in the costs of external indebtedness. This fact deepens with the advent of neoliberalism and neoclassical theories, which further remove the perspectives of economic theories from analyzes of the surplus, further displacing political issues from academic and economic debate.

The authors of the structuralist field, however, no matter how divergent they may be, will not be able to have their conceptions considered, insofar as they challenge, albeit in a different way, the neoliberal paradigm that throughout the 1970s was built to end, from 1979, in the "there is no alternative" of the Reagan-Thatcher era.

The bibliography found since the 1980s presents itself as being highly specialized, focusing only on the sector's productivity, which makes it difficult to have a more general view of the agricultural sector and how it interacts with other sectors of the economy, and, as a consequence, they remove the political character of this discussion (or define it from a specific side). It is in this period that the concept of agribusiness or agro-industry begins to appear, emphasizing the interaction between agriculture and industry, in the formation of an integrated productive block. It is also the moment when overcoming underdevelopment leaves the country's agenda, being replaced by the question of stability. A country project is opened in which there is food for all and overcoming structural heterogeneity and underdevelopment.

Bibliographic References

Arbage, Alessando Porporatti. Agricultura e desenvolvimento econômico na visão dos clássicos – Uma Perspectiva Histórica. Extensão Rural, n. 4, p. 15, 1997.

Balsadi, Otavio Valentim. Evolução das Ocupações e do Emprego na Agricultura Brasileira no Período 1992 a 2006. Emprego e Trabalho na Agricultura Brasileira. IICA, Brasília, 2009

Castro, Antônio Barros. Sete ensaios sobre a economia brasileira. Forense, 1975.

Corazza, Gentil; Martinelli Júnior, Orlando. Agricultura e questão agrária na história do pensamento econômico. Teoria & Evidência Econômica, Passo Fundo, v. 10, n. 19, p. 9–36, 2002.

De Mera, Claudia Maria Prudêncio. A Questão Agrária no Brasil: as contribuições de Caio Prado Junior e Ignácio Rangel. In: Anais do XI Encontro Regional de Economia – ANPEC – Sul. Universidade Federal do Paraná, Curitiba, 2008.

De Oliveira Lima, Rodne. Caio Prado Júnior e a questão agrária no Brasil. GEOGRAFIA (Londrina), v. 8, n. 2, p. 123–134, 1999.

Ferreira, Francisco Marcelo; Sant'anna, André Albuquerque. Crédito Rural: da especulação à produção. Revista Visão do Desenvolvimento, v.11, BNDES, 2006.

Furtado, Celso. Teoria e política do desenvolvimento econômico. 5a. ed. São Paulo: Nacional, [1969] 1975.

Furtado, Celso. Desenvolvimento e subdesenvolvimento. Rio de Janeiro: Fundo de Cultura, [1961] 1963.

Garcia, Álvaro Antonio Louzada. Agricultura e desenvolvimento econômico no Brasil: os debates nas décadas de 50 a 70. Ensaios FEE, v. 11, n. 1, p. 198–222, 1990.

Hoffmann, Rodolfo; Ney, Marlon. Estrutura fundiária e propriedade agrícola no Brasil. Brasília: NEAD/MDA, 2010.

Johnston, Bruce F.; Mellor, John W. The role of agriculture in economic development. The American Economic Review, v. 51, n. 4, p. 566–593, 1961.

Leite, Sérgio Pereira. Estado, padrão de desenvolvimento e agricultura: o caso brasileiro. Estudos Sociedade e Agricultura, v. 13, n. 2, p. 280–232, 2005.

Lewis, W. Arthur. O desenvolvimento econômico com oferta ilimitada de mão-de-obra. In: Agarwala, Amar Narain; Singh, S. (orgs.). A economia do subdesenvolvimento. Rio de Janeiro: Forense, p. 406–456, 1969.

Nicholls, William H. A agricultura e o desenvolvimento econômico do Brasil. Revista brasileira de economia, v. 26, n. 4, p. 169–206, 1972.

Prado Júnior, Caio. A revolução brasileira. Editora brasiliense, [1966] 1987.

Prebisch, Raúl. O desenvolvimento econômico da América Latina e seus principais problemas. Revista Brasileira de Economia, v. 3, n. 3, p. 47–111, 1949.

Rangel, Ignácio. O desenvolvimento econômico. In: Rangel, Ignácio; Obras reunidas. Vol. 1 Rio de Janeiro: Contraponto, [1954] 2005, p. 39–128.

Rangel, Ignácio. Industrialização e agricultura. In: Rangel, Ignácio; Obras reunidas. Vol. 2 Rio de Janeiro: Contraponto, [1955] 2005, p. 16–19.

Rangel, Ignácio. Industrialização e economia natural. In: Rangel, Ignácio; Obras reunidas. Vol. 2 Rio de Janeiro: Contraponto, [1957] 2005, p. 19–23.

Rangel, Ignácio. A questão agrária brasileira. In: Rangel, Ignácio; Obras reunidas. Vol. 2 Rio de Janeiro: Contraponto, [1962] 2005, p. 23–80.

Rangel, Ignácio. Recapitulando a questão agrária brasileira. In: Rangel, Ignácio; Obras reunidas. Vol. 2 Rio de Janeiro: Contraponto, [1977] 2005, p. 81–87.

Rangel, Ignácio. Estrutura agrária, sociedade e Estado. In: Rangel, Ignácio; Obras reunidas. Vol. 2 Rio de Janeiro: Contraponto, [1978] 2005, p. 87–95.

Rangel, Ignácio. Questão agrária e agricultura. In: Rangel, Ignácio; Obras reunidas. Vol. 2 Rio de Janeiro: Contraponto, [1979] 2005, p. 95–114.

Rangel, Ignácio. Revisitando a "questão nacional". In: Rangel, Ignácio; Obras reunidas. Vol. 2 Rio de Janeiro: Contraponto, [1980] 2005, p. 115–125.

Rangel, Ignácio. III PND e agricultura. In: Rangel, Ignácio; Obras reunidas. Vol. 2 Rio de Janeiro: Contraponto, [1981] 2005, p. 405–408.

Rangel, Ignácio. Problemas da reforma agrária. In: Rangel, Ignácio; Obras reunidas. Vol. 2 Rio de Janeiro: Contraponto, [1985] 2005, p. 125–128.

Rangel, Ignácio. A questão agrária e o ciclo longo. In: Rangel, Ignácio; Obras reunidas. Vol. 2 Rio de Janeiro: Contraponto, [1986a] 2005, p. 129–141.

Rangel, Ignácio. A questão da terra. In: Rangel, Ignácio; Obras reunidas. Vol. 2 Rio de Janeiro: Contraponto, [1986b] 2005, p. 141–149.

Rangel, Ignácio. Crise agrária e metrópole. In: Rangel, Ignácio; Obras reunidas. Vol. 2 Rio de Janeiro: Contraponto, [1986c] 2005, p. 149–155.

Rangel, Ignácio. Fim de linha. *In*: Rangel, Ignácio; Obras reunidas. Vol. 2 Rio de Janeiro: Contraponto, [1988] 2005, p. 155–157.

Rangel, Ignácio. A queimada e a ecologia. *In*: Rangel, Ignácio; Obras reunidas. Vol. 2 de Janeiro: Contraponto, [1989] 2005, p. 157–161.

CHAPTER 8

Restricted Democracy, Mass Democracy and the Crisis of the New Republic

Jaime León and Maria Malta

1   Introduction

The transition from the civil-military dictatorship (1964–1985) to a republican regime, also known as re-democratization, refers to the "Diretas Já" movement in the early 1980s and went through a diffuse phase between 1985, with the departure of the military of the head of the executive, and 1988, with the foundation of a democratic State of law. Thus, the institution that was born at that time, the New Republic, is a recent historical period of Brazilian society that began with the promulgation of the 1988 Constitution, which formally values the rights of the Brazilian "citizen", but that was born, paradoxically, together the spread of neoliberalism[1]in the world. We argue that, as a result of the current crisis in world neoliberalism and the internal contradictions of the articulation of forces between capital and labour, the New Republic entered into crisis in 2013 with the popular manifestations known as "Jornadas de Junho" and that this crisis gains contours of a terminal crisis from the 2016 legal-parliamentary coup.

This chapter aims to critically analyse the process of construction, development and decline of the New Brazilian Republic. For that, we will do the assembly and analysis, in the light of the method presented in Curty & Malta (2021), in this book, of a possible controversy of democracy in the period of re-democratization taking into account our socioeconomic formation. The cut of this historical analysis is focused on the contributions of two authors representing the theory of dependent capitalism: Florestan Fernandes and Carlos Nelson Coutinho. The choice of these two authors, in the context of the large number

---

[1] We understand neoliberalism as the unitary group that became hegemonic in the late eighties and with the end of the Cold War of i) a set of economic policies that value the reduction of state intervention in the economy; ii) a set of ideas that place the individual and freedom as the center of analysis of the economy to the detriment of society and equality; iii) the cooling of the class struggle tending towards the capital side, as stated by Saad-Filho and Boffo (2018).

of contributions in the field of theories of dependent capitalism,[2] has a special connection with our perception that also, during this period, the Partido dos Trabalhadores (PT) – Workers' Party –, born from the crisis of the civil-military regime, would play a crucial role in the composition and limits of the class struggle and in the current democracy in the country. Both authors will have a fundamental role in the construction of the political debate that will provide the basis for PT's political action in the 1980s and 1990s. It is also worth noting that both assume a growing critical position in relation to party politics, reaching a break with it in the course of the 1990s, in the case of Florestan, and in the early 2000s, in the case of Coutinho. Next, we set up our analysis of the New Republic in the light of the historical facts relevant to the debate.

The working hypothesis is that in the almost thirty years of the New Republic, a type of democracy born in the crisis of the dictatorship, co-optation democracy, could mature and complete its development during the PT governments (2003–2016). In this period, great contradictions of this form of democracy developed, which started to boil with the socioeconomic and political crisis that started in 2013 and which, since the legal-parliamentary coup of 2016, have caused the New Republic to be in its apparent final collapse.

We point out that the level of development that brought co-optation democracy to its peak was only possible due to a double articulation of factors: an external factor of the international economic conjuncture favourable to income growth, which internally enabled a new round of modernization of consumption patterns under the principles of neoliberalism, associated with a longer-lasting internal process of "transformism" suffered by PT. This party commanded the State between 2003 and 2016 and was able to open the arc of alliances in order to guarantee the passing of the class struggle in what we are characterizing as the final phase of the New Republic.

In this way, we also bring the hypothesis that the change in the current scenario is related to the reversal of the global conjuncture, starting from the global financial crisis of 2008, which revealed the moment of structural crisis of capital and thus destabilized the internal economy, exposing its dependent

---

2   There are many theories and groups of authors that can be listed among the Brazilian theories of dependent capitalism: Marxist dependency theories such as Theotônio dos Santos, André Gunder Frank and Vania Bambirra. Structuralist Dependency Theory as of Fernando Henrique Cardoso, Enzo Faletto and José Serra, Theories of Dependent Capitalism as of Florestan Fernandes, Octávio Ianni and Carlos Nelson Coutinho, Theories of late capitalism as of João Manoel Cardoso de Mello and Maria da Conceição Tavares or Celso Furtado's theory of underdevelopment. Thus, we want to make it clear that we have deliberately chosen one of the aspects because we see in it the most striking ability to explain our socioeconomic reality,

and peripheral character and opened the possibility of questioning the political form of co-optation democracy, pointing to the emergence of political organizations with authoritarian ideological characteristics associated with a neoliberal economic vision, both combined with a form of social organization commonly found in Pentecostal churches created in the 20th century in Brazil based on the theology of prosperity.[3]

2 Bourgeois Consensus on Capitalist Domination and Transformation: Basic Notions of a "restricted Democracy" or a Dictatorship in the Name of Democracy

Florestan Fernandes is our author of reference to interpret Brazil under the civil-military dictatorship. It is worth highlighting, as presented in Curty & Malta (2021), in this book, that the controversy over Latin American socio-economic formation as dependent capitalism, of which Florestan is an important participant, finds its synthesis in Brazil. Despite having already completed their bourgeois revolutions through processes of dependent industrialization and the formation of class societies, Latin American countries have institutions and values of power of colonial origin that continue to be reproduced in these societies within the state apparatus of the political society, closely linked to the economic interests of the dominant sectors.

One of the major consensus of this controversy is that with the beginning of the bourgeois revolution in Brazil in the so-called Vargas Era (1930–1945), such institutions would not have consolidated the same type of democratic integration in force in the countries of the capitalist center, on the contrary, they would have established an authoritarian character in the democratic culture of Latin American countries: this is the restricted democracy, according to Florestan Fernandes. In it, coup d'état attempts are usual whenever bourgeois power is threatened and only those who are considered integrated into the civil society, those who manage to formally enter the labour market or hold goods and assets, have a voice in political society.[4]

---

3 It is the theology that preaches individual material prosperity as a sign of God's blessing and argues that faith, positive speech and donations to Christian ministries will always increase the material wealth of the faithful. Two important texts of this theological view are Roberts' Oral Formula for Success and Prosperity's God's Formula; Montgomery, GH (1966) and God's Master Key to Prosperity by Lindsay, Gordon (1960).

4 Regarding this conception, it is worth highlighting the quote by Octavio Ianni: "In Latin America, the bourgeois revolution comprises a historical process of wide scope, with outbreaks, discontinuities, setbacks. Depending on the country, it has developed broadly and

According to Florestan, the coup that gave rise to the civil-military dictatorship that ruled Brazil for 21 years since 1964 was the result of what the Brazilian bourgeoisie saw as a solution to their crisis in the 1960s and would serve as the conclusion of the process of bourgeois revolution started in 1930. These class fractions came together compositely, like a patchwork quilt, for a solidarity based on the defence of their common interest: their maintenance as a ruling class. Therefore, the bourgeoisie and the bourgeois class fractions, in the context of dependent capitalism marked by the articulation between internal social segregation and external dependence, made, with the 1964 civil-military coup, an option that swept any possibility of solution of the dependent structure to which Florestan Fernandes (1972) called it a double articulation:

Such articulation reproduces underdevelopment and dependence indefinitely and acts as a barrier that prevents the control of the means of social change in an autonomous way by the majority of the population (which is the working class) and makes it impossible to achieve its ends according to their interests. We can even say, due to the way in which external indebtedness was established (see table 8.1) and the violence that characterized the relations of social control via the "Institutional Acts" of the dictatorship, that this double articulation intensified in the years of the dictatorship.

On the one hand, the bourgeoisies joined their main ally – the international capital – to reproduce themselves as a class; to enter the world economic space more widely; and to take control of a State that made possible achievements that were beyond the private sphere of bourgeois action. On the other hand, they were able to act openly, oppressively and repressively against their main enemy – the popular classes. This combination of actions that Fernandes (1975) called a bourgeois consensus. At that moment in history, this presented itself as the only viable way for the bourgeoisies and their class fractions to remain in political command within the framework of dependent capitalism, so they had no doubt in taking it.

The context was at the peak of the Cold War, in which the defence of the capitalist order was at the heart of policies across the continent. The dominant ideas of the center were those of the dominant classes of the hegemonic

---

adversaly, since the independence revolutions and entering the 20th century. There are cases in which its main developments take place in a few decades. Naturally, the national conditions under which the bourgeois revolution takes place are diverse and very peculiar. But it is possible to say that these conditions, in each and every country in Latin America, did not produce the consolidation of democracy. On the contrary, the strong, comprehensive, authoritarian state was consolidated, closely coupled with economic power, closely linked to foreign interests" (Ianni, 1988, p. 2).

TABLE 8.1   Evolution of the Brazilian external debt
             (1971–1987)

Year	% GDP	Year	% GDP
1971	16.8	1980	27.0
1972	19.5	1981	28.6
1973	17.7	1982	31.5
1974	18.1	1983	49.5
1975	19.3	1984	53.8
1976	20.9	1985	49.8
1977	21.4	1986	43.1
1978	25.9	1987	42.9
1979	25.0		

SOURCE: PREPARED BY THE CENTRAL BANK OF BRAZIL / BP

country of the world order and were imported mimetically by the dominant classes of the countries of the periphery. It is not for nothing that abstract values such as "solidarity of the hemisphere" or "defence of the Western Christian civilization" were defended even though they overlapped the interests of each country in particular as a nation. Nation being the majority of the people. It meant the submission of national interests and, therefore, the overcoming of democracy as something liberating (Fernandes, 1975; Netto, 2014).

In assuming such a reactionary stance, the Brazilian bourgeoisies and their class fractions abandoned, for they did not need, the bourgeois ideology and utopia as established in the classic cases of English, French and American bourgeois revolutions. These revolutions were formed in a distinct historical and social reality,[5] in which the bourgeoisie was the revolutionary class and not the class that sought to remain in power. The Brazilian bourgeoisies opted for a solution that reinforced the character of restricted democracy, establishing two antagonistic revolutions in the Brazilian society: one which intend to accelerate the historical time by promoting the modernization of the economy, indispensable for the legitimation of their domination; another one with a counterrevolutionary character, as it made economic, social, cultural and political

---

5   It is worth remembering that the Brazilian bourgeois fractions were born from colonial oligarchies and not from a break with them.

contradictions permanent within the bourgeois society through a "preventive class dictatorship" (Fernandes, 1975). In general, the formation of the nation in a democratic, national or popular way was removed from the order of the day by the dependent bourgeoisies and, because it is not something simple to erase in the history of a country, this continues to have consequences.

In a complex way, the bourgeois domination was camouflaged, appearing to coincide with the interests of the nation, this was an assumption of the bourgeois ideology from the dependent capitalism: great prominence to productive modernization and economic growth through the expansion of agribusiness and a precarious industry, but sweeping under the carpet the intensification of social inequalities and the intense popular oppression and repression. According to Florestan, there was a clear separation between "civil society" and "nation" – which in the sociologist's view was the majority of the people – and a clear identification of the "bourgeois class" with the "nation". The gravitational axis of the political relationship between the ruling classes.

Florestan Fernandes elucidated how the intensification of the bourgeois domination increased the military and technocratic impregnation in the State as processes of preservation and consolidation of the order, including excessive demonstrations of brute force. During the dictatorship, the State, in addition to being police-military, was legal and political, and its main function was to subdue the need for political articulation between the classes, since it itself determined the order that should be respected: the bourgeois order. The State, therefore, became a very strong political entity that centralized the controls of political and legal domination and promoted the economic acceleration of society. A syncretic national State was born in Brazil, for it apparently defended the order as though it were democratic, representative and pluralistic, but in reality, it was an instrument of the authoritarian oligarchies fully permeated with contradictions.

In Florestan's perspective, however, the bourgeois autocratic model, in its violent form, was inexorably transitory. The international conjuncture of the late 1970s implied substantial changes in the external dimension of the double articulation, since the rise in American interest rates, together with the second shock of international oil prices, created an unprecedented crisis for Brazil, highly indebted internationally. The debt crisis together with the years of extreme violence and internal social oppression brought to light the deepest contradictions of the restricted democracy in its autocratic model and made its permanence unsustainable. Large movements of workers' organizations have emerged, even though they are illegal, demonstrations against famine and denounces of political and social violence have spread. It was necessary to formulate, progressively, a way out of that context.

It is at this juncture that the controversy over the possibilities of a democratic exit for Brazil is established by its left. Florestan Fernandes and Carlos Nelson Coutinho are fundamental participants in that debate. These authors deserve special mention both for the importance of their interpretation of Brazil from this period and as theoretical formulators of the base that was used by the PT to guide its political action.

3   The Controversy of Democratic Perspectives at the Birth of the New Republic: Co-optation Democracy and Mass Democracy

Florestan Fernandes observed that a fundamental element of the contradictory character of democracy in Brazil was that the very option for bourgeois consensus (the restricted democracy in its autocratic form) contained the seeds of its destruction, or at least its weakening and replacement with a new form of democracy. In his view, even though this agreement gave the bourgeois class fractions the possibility of openly managing new forms of class struggle with an autocratic State, it did not give it autonomy to the outside and limited the very internal horizon of solidarity between the bourgeoisie and the other classes.

The option for consensus meant giving up the material basis of self-propelled development, as it increased external dependence and deepened social segregation by considering the dispossessed classes as mere irreconcilable enemies or social sectors that should be protected. The only by-product was increasing that double articulation.

After the first phases of repression, the 1964 reforms[6] and the political hardening in 1968 with the Institutional Act no.5,[7] the various and conflicting bourgeois interests were able to return to the political scene, implying the inevitable internal tension of the system of power. The economic recovery (see Table 8.2

---

6   The 1964 reforms were brought together in the Plano de Ação Econômica do Governo (PAEG), which included a diagnosis for inflation as it were of demand and costs, and which proposed a gradualist prognosis with fiscal and monetary reforms, the practice of exchange rate realism and the establishment a wage rule, based on its previous squeeze.

7   Institutional act n.5, of December 13th, 1968, was the most violent institution of coercion of the dictatorship with the loss of mandate of parliamentarians against the regime, the closure of the National Congress until October 21th, 1969, intervention in states and municipalities that gave extraordinary power to the governors, the institutionalization of torture through the suspension of constitutional guarantees, the control of demonstrations, the censorship of the press and the intensification of censorship by revoking the political rights of several Brazilians. All of these measures broadened the bases of State repression and oppression.

TABLE 8.2   GDP growth rate (%) 1964–1973

Year	Brazil	Year	Brazil
1964	3.4	1969	9.5
1965	2.4	1970	10.4
1966	6.7	1971	11.34
1967	4.2	1972	11.94
1968	9.8	1973	13.97

SOURCE: OWN ELABORATION BASED ON IBGE DATA /
NATIONAL ACCOUNTS SYSTEM

below) opened the door for internal disputes over the direction of the development process. It is in this context that Florestan Fernandes points to the emergence of the transformed form of restricted democracy, the co-optation.

Co-optation democracy is nothing more than a specific and elaborate form of restricted democracy. It consists of the temporary passivation of the class struggle and presupposes the corruption of the economic agents involved and of the system of power, since the permanent character of the class struggle cannot be eliminated from the capitalist mode of production, since it is based on exploitation of labour and the existence of private property and the legal and political institutions that guarantee its existence. Co-optation democracy can also be called a policy of class conciliation. The way co-optation works is varied and results from a slow and gradual process that demands the study of its specificities. In summary, in Fernandes' conception, co-optation democracy is an evolution of the form of bourgeois domination that has adapted to the new historical times in which the dictatorship can no longer be used as a preponderant form of political order. Its existence, however, depended on certain conditions of the double articulation.

The co-optation of the civil-military period consisted of the systematic and generalized aggregation of bourgeois interests, both Brazilian and foreign, and served as a facilitating link to produce privileges among the "most equal". It was not a process restricted to the upper fractions of the bourgeoisie, but also to the middle (or petty bourgeoisie) fractions that were able to take advantage of the technocratic and military apparatus of the State. Finally, the dominant interests imposed themselves from top to bottom, forming a true bourgeois paradise. This space, however, was only opened by the positive economic situation of the "economic miracle" of 1968–1973, under comfortable economic growth rates this process of sharing the economic gains would be done politically in a concerted manner through the upper and middle classes. In addition, the dynamics of productive modernization had a strong impact on the working class that suffered from repression.

In this scenario of peak of bourgeois regeneration through the economic miracle, the dynamics of the emergency of monopolistic capitalism, externally, and the dependent industrialization, internally, put the interests of the bourgeoisie and workers increasingly in conflict during a period of certain stability within the military regime of the early seventies. However, the scenario would change at the end of the decade, workers' organizations were able to get out of illegality and started to return to the scene and, with them, demonstrations and strikes were being increasingly organized. Within the neighbourhood associations and ecclesial communities based in the Catholic Church, discussions and demonstrations were also held on issues of human rights, hunger and violence. It is necessary to emphasize that the activation of those repressed forces was insufficient for a socialist revolution, but it inexorably imposed changes on the dependent society. It was for this reason that the political distension of the civil-military regime started to be desired by the very fractions of the ruling class, leaving its flagrant contradictions.

From this transition movement that started in the seventies, the PT would be founded in 1980, and all the basic discussion that will give rise to the founding movement of this party was taking place across the country and outside. Florestan was part of this movement and his interpretation of the current situation was very influential in the debate. From the author's point of view, the bourgeois task in that period of early political opening would be twofold: to reinforce the bourgeois autocracy by expanding co-optation downwards, creating ways of connecting with the rest of civil society, the working class, in order to camouflage the bourgeois privileges, and establishing the constitutional and legal scope of the autocratic State more broadly. It would not be a question of returning to a supposed "democracy", but of returning to safe conditions for the continuation of the social order from before 1964.

The sociologist was precise in formulating that the ruling classes would have to find new coercive State forms and that a possible expansion of the co-optation democracy would imply the benefit of classes other than the upper and middle classes. However, he understood that the possibility of vertical social mobility would have two consequences: i) it would increase the horizon of bourgeois conscience by converting these dispossessed classes into possessors, generating protests within the order; ii) it would generate a growing organization of pressures against the order, since the contradictions of class society would be exposed.

In this sense, Florestan believed that the democracy of open co-optation would be born weak, since in the perspective of the tutored classes it would offer very little, while in the view of the dominants it would have a very high price. It was as though the political form of co-optation democracy was a second option for everyone who participated in it. Florestan points out that the Brazilian bourgeoisies would not be able to cope with co-optation on such precarious bases with an autocratic State, because in a country of extreme concentration of income and power there would be little left for the purchase of alliances or loyalties (Fernandes, 1975, p. 424). If this was the task open to the bourgeoisie, the future task of the Brazilian working class kept uncertain.

It is in this context of the emergence of a co-optation democracy still under an autocratic State that Florestan proposes that the PT, a party born in 1980 arising from the 1978 workers' strikes, would have to decide whether or not to choose to become a revolutionary proletarian party (Fernandes, 1981) . Florestan brings an important reflection on the role of workers at the forefront of the revolutionary process. In highlighting this, he makes a statement that seems to be confirmed today as a prophecy:

> The proletarian revolution focuses on the collective emancipation of workers by the workers themselves. Either the PT decipher the correct solution of this historical need on the Brazilian scene or it will join the ranks of the reforming parties magnetized to the "capitalist reform of capitalism", to "improved capitalism" or to "capitalism of social welfare".
>
> FERNANDES, 1981, p. 241

At the same time that Florestan remained convinced of the idea that the horizon of the working class was the socialist horizon, he understood that a process of democratic transition was necessary, with the establishment of a new constitution for the organization of the class. There were no conditions for an immediate revolution yet, but the party should establish itself with this strategic objective. In his understanding of the real political situation in Brazil in the 1980s, the author would be a constituent deputy between 1987 and 1991 and will exercise, through the PT, the position of federal representative, for which he exercised between 1991 and 1995.

Florestan Fernandes' interpretation of the consolidation of the bourgeois revolution in Brazil was a milestone for thinking Brazil as a nation and the democratic and revolutionary possibilities in the country. However, his political analysis was far from consensual. In particular, regarding the democratic perspectives and the organizational form under which the new party and the political action of workers in the 1980s should be constituted.

It can be said that Carlos Nelson Coutinho, an intellectual from the Brazilian Communist Party and exiled in Italy, where he had received a strong influence from Enrico Berlinguer's Gramscian thought and Eurocommunism, had a different vision for the perspectives of Brazilian democracy than that presented by Florestan Fernandes. More precisely, at the time of the amnesty law, 1979, Coutinho's *A democracia como um valor universal* (Democracy as a universal value)[8] came out. He bet more strongly in the democratization process as a great support for the task that he considered competent to the left forces in the country: the struggle for the end of the regime of exception implemented in 1964 and the implantation of socialism.

Coutinho would be responsible for introducing one of Gramsci's readings in Brazil,[9] aligned with the view of the State as a representation of the superstructure, which led him to affirm in the late seventies, in a movement of criticism of Soviet Stalinism and the bourgeois social democracy, that the transition to

---

8   His work is marked by the strong connection between democracy and revolution and is strongly influenced by the search for a "third way" between Stalinist socialism and European social democracy. In order to understand the title of Coutinho's (1979) text, we have to believe that such a democratization process on new bases presupposed the denial of the false identity between the genesis and validity of democracy. The explanation of the expression "democracy as a universal value" comes from the fact that the concept of democracy, formally, does not depend on the moment and the society where it originated. The quality that the democratic system imposes in the intensification of the political life of the masses would be to make democracy universal, valid in different social formations as a principle to be reached. A critical view of the author's Gramsci reading was that of Edmundo Dias, a professor at Unicamp, that defended the dialectic unity of infrastructure and superstructure. Faced with this criticism, Carlos Nelson Coutinho would review his position of the State as a representation of the superstructure.

9   The controversy that we are mounting over the perspectives that were open in the period of democratic transition between the interpretations of Florestan Fernandes and Carlos Nelson Coutinho are permeated by a series of other views. To stay only in the left field, we could say, according to Duriguetto (2007), that there was a debate at this time about the relationship of civil society and its role in relation to democracy. For Iasi (2014), on the one hand, the interpretations of Wanderley Guilherme do Santos, Fernando Henrique Cardoso and Bolívar Lamounier could be aligned. Despite being different from each other, they can be synthesized by criticizing the concentration of power, economic and political, opposing it a liberalization of the market and advocating in favor of strengthening civil society – which for them, it would be a space of freedom for social organization of the diverse interests existing in society. What these interpretations do is to empty the class struggle character of civil society, reducing it as a channel for negotiation with the State and not as a space for confrontation with the State; on the other hand, the ideas that took into account the participation of movements and social struggles would be synthesized. Among the main interpretations of this area are those of Carlos Nelson Coutinho, Francisco Weffort and Marilena Chauí. For a more in-depth look at each of these proposals, see Duriguetto (2007).

socialist democracy would be something likely and of long transition, neces-
sitating the creation of "ideological, economic and political assumptions"
(Coutinho, 1979). So the democratization task put to the left was a strategy, not
a tactic,[10] to put an end to Prussian solutions – or "passive revolution" solutions,[11] according to the vocabulary seen in Coutinho (1989) – responding to
the insufficiencies of the bourgeois revolution in Brazil.

Carlos Nelson's interpretation of Brazil points out that the capitalist system,
which at that time had recently reached the state monopoly phase, inexorably
brings in its dynamics the elements that could make the transition from liberal
democracy to socialist democracy viable. The transition from liberal democracy to socialist democracy would therefore be the dialectical overcoming of
liberal democracy, as elaborated by liberal authors since the 17th century. This
would happen with the continuation of old traits, with the incorporation of
new elements and the denial of elements incompatible with the new historical
moment of human emancipation, an opening possible thanks to the incipient
creation of those ideological, economic and political assumptions.

Socialist democracy would be founded on the participation and control of
the masses in the political process and by reversing the passive revolution solution. For this democracy to be achieved, it would have to be built by a process
of "democratic renewal" that would end political alienation – the result of the
authoritarianism of the exception regime – and the tendency for State bureaucratization. This would be due to the strengthening of trends that recently
emerged in that context. Namely: the emergence of new mechanisms of
direct democracy relatively dissociated from the State (business commissions,
unions, religious associations, neighbourhood groups, etc.), bringing together,

---

10   When we refer to tactics and strategy, we are referring to Gramsci's theoretical frame-
      work, used by Carlos Nelson Coutinho. In general, tactics and strategy have the meaning
      of rational action aiming at the achievement of a certain final objective, therefore they
      encompass the idea of the final objective and the way to do so. However, the field of tac-
      tics refers to actions that are taken to deal with situations of the moment, it is the theory
      to deal with episodic class clashes. The strategy, on the other hand, would be a planned
      action aimed at obtaining future advantages or interests of classes or fractions of class
      with respect to domination over the opponent over whom one wants to establish a posi-
      tion. These concepts refer respectively to the Gramscian concepts of "war of position" and
      "war of movement".

11   For Lenin, the "Prussian way" that had taken place in Prussia was different from the
      molds of American revolution, English and French, on the one hand, and Russian and
      Chinese on the other. In Coutinho (1979) the term "via Prussian" appears to determine
      the Brazilian social formation, but from Coutinho (1989) this term is replaced by passive
      revolution, in order to incorporate the Bahian author's interpretation of the use of this
      category used in the work of Antonio Gramsci.

in one unit, plural interests, mainly of the working class, in an organized way from the bottom up, which would make up a "collective political subject"; it would also reinforce the forms of indirect democracy (parliament and partisan political scene), in order to constitute a "political synthesis of collective subjects" (Coutinho, 1979).

In this sense, the party would also be a collective political subject built from this process of democratization and even for this reason a warning is made: these mechanisms of direct and indirect democracy could not result in the "proletarian bureaucratization of the State", because the idea of a "regulated society" defended by Coutinho was to have a self-government of producers associated with the end of political alienation.

This, theoretically, would give the possibility of the dialectical overcoming of liberal democracy by socialist democracy. Therefore, socialist democracy requires more than the socialization of the means of production, but a real socialization of politics with the overcoming of the antinomy between those who are rulers and those who are ruled, a fundamental element of politics according to Gramsci (Coutinho, 2011).

The point of Coutinho's propositional analysis that generated much controversy was his belief that the possibilities for the transformation of democracy back in the period of political distension of the civil-military regime would, at first, be limited to the restraints of liberal democracy, since the process of democratic renewal it would be slow and gradual. The roots of this lie in the fact that the source of Brazilian democratic weakness lies in the tradition of passive revolutions, which, together with the mark of anti-democracy, would generate a temporary barrier to the "democratic renewal" at the level of the masses, mentioned above. This renewal would remain for some time under the hegemony of national and international bourgeois monopolies.

Coutinho came up with the following formulation about an imminent bifurcation for the opening of the civil-military regime:

> Although in the context of a permanent search for the maximum possible unity, it is certain that the nature and extent of the alliances targeted by popular forces will change – depending on the concrete tasks. In a schematic way, we could say that the tasks of democratic renewal unfold on two main levels. First, logically and chronologically, it is a question of first conquering and then consolidating a regime of fundamental freedoms, for which a unity with all the forces interested in this conquest and the permanence of the "rules of the game" to be implemented is necessary by a Constituent Assembly endowed with legitimacy.

And, secondly, it is a question of building the alliances necessary to deepen democracy in the sense of an organized mass democracy, with increasing popular participation; and the search for unity, at this level, will aim to achieve the necessary consensus to undertake measures of an anti-monopoly and anti-imperialist character and, at a later stage, for the construction in our country of a socialist society founded on political democracy.

COUTINHO, 1979, pp. 45–46

The first opening, that of searching for unity of the forces that sought the end of the regime of exception, was important to achieve the set of freedoms mentioned for the guarantee of a regime established by the Constituent Assembly after the civil-military regime ended. Therefore, the first objective was to supersede the civil-military regime.

Up to this point, even with different nuances in the analysis Florestan and Coutinho tend to converge in politics, but as for the second movement suggested by Coutinho, which is exactly the one that Florestan would identify as favourable to the deepening of co-optation democracy, the divergence regarding the tactic arises of action of the bourgeoisie and its implications for the class struggle in the country.

In this way, the second path, of building alliances that would set the course for mass democracy, is what seems to emerge as the point of greatest controversy in the text. If both for critical political economy and for critical political theory, on which the Bahian author is based, the contradictions of capitalist society are set in the irreconcilable class struggles, both economic and political, the building of alliances to guide liberal democracy towards democracy of masses would be a task full of difficulties and did not pointed to a criticism of the existence of private property.

For Coutinho, the passage through the democratic-popular agenda was a necessity for the arrival in Gramsci's regulated society or, simply, in socialist democracy: democracy was a process.[12]

---

12 "There is still a long way to go in the struggle to expand the socialization of politics, to build an effective role for the masses, capable of definitively consolidating Brazilian civil society. The outcome of the current transition process started with the so-called 'New Republic' will depend on the outcome of this struggle: to the extent that this transition was the result of a combination of popular pressures 'from below' and transformational operations 'from above', its point of arrival may be either the creation of a real mass democracy, open to the advance towards socialism, or the restoration of the old elitist and exclusionary liberalism, now in the 'modern' form of liberal corporatism. But also, in this case, the empirically verifiable data (membership of unions, growth of grassroots

This discussion of the perspectives on Brazilian democracy would find in the creation of the PT the materiality of party representation, insofar as it already existed in the political spaces that formed the basis of what came to be this party. It is within the PT that much of the discussion on the political action necessary to effectively establish a democratic process that, as Fernandes had already stated, would decipher the correct solution to the historical need for collective emancipation of workers on the Brazilian scene. There was no space in the 1980s, at the base of the PT, to think outside the democratic or socialist horizon, but the interpretation that such a party would make.

4   Transformism: Democracy as an Instrument of Accommodation to Bourgeois Order in the New Republic

Transformism for Gramsci is a process of gradual and continuous absorption of allied and enemy sectors, apparently irreconcilable, through various techniques within a given organization or political movement. And we have the hypothesis that this was the process through which the PT constituted itself as the greatest political force in the Brazilian congress in the early 2000s. However, it is necessary to construct this hypothesis historically.

The PT is a party of currents, without democratic centralism, but built from its congressional theses, like the parties of the left tradition. At their 5th National Meeting in 1987, PT leaders made it clear that, in their formulations, they would dismiss the national character of their political strategy as central, indicating that the alliance with the Brazilian bourgeoisie would be spurious, insofar as it would in no way contribute to the achievement of the party's final goal: the introduction of socialism in Brazil (Iasi, 2013).

It is interesting to see how the PT's policy aimed to share the socialist strategic horizon with the communist tradition, but it indicated a break with the strategy of the Brazilian Communist Party (PCB) that advocated a necessary national stage, while maintaining the prospect of democratization with accumulation of forces between various classes to carry out the "transition to the transition" just like the Democratic-National Strategy of the PCB before it. The PT program was known as popular-democratic precisely because it did not incorporate the national dimension in its strategy.

---

communities, reinforcement of left-wing political parties, especially PT), they do not deauthorize optimism (Coutinho, 1989, p. 134).

Consistent with the prospect of democratization as an accumulation of forces, in the 1980s and 1990s the party contested majoritarian and proportional elections forming important seats and winning some city governments and state governments. In order to achieve its governments, in the bourgeois State, the PT joined the alliance processes. In these processes of alliances, local agreements were superimposed on the programmatic elements and the general orientation of the party's actions changed shape.

At the same time that this occurred in some parts of the country, internally, during the governments of José Sarney (1985–1990), Fernando Collor (1990–1992), Itamar Franco (1992–1995) and Fernando Henrique Cardoso – FHC – (1995–2003) the party still retained some of its founding principles, its congressional bench was the greatest force antagonistic to the neoliberalism that was implemented in that context of two consecutive decades of low growth (Prado & Leopoldi, 2018). At the same time, the party still did not meet the objective conditions for taking power and was assisting in the congress the practice of the so-called coalition presidentialism.

If we consider the perspective of Fernandes (1975), co-optation democracy at new levels was not yet possible, either because of the Brazilian socioeconomic situation or even because of the global economic situation at the time. The 1980s was the readjustment of the gold-dollar standard, with a strong dollar policy[13] and geopolitics of "Star Wars[14]" followed by the overthrow of the communist world, while the 1990s were a decade of financial crises in Asia, Russia and Latin America.

It is worth remembering that the Latin American scenario was of a foreign debt crisis and there was intense instability in the region. Sarney, on the one hand, ruled under strong popular pressure after the Constituent Assembly and, on the other, had the mission of continuing the legacy of the dependent bourgeois revolution that began to turn to neoliberalism at the end of the Cold War and promoted the beginning of restructuring productive; Collor was the one who started to implement neoliberal economic measures in Brazil and his government would be troubled by social, economic and, mainly, political crises; Itamar Franco and FHC focused their efforts on monetary stabilization and

---

13   Policy developed by the North American government under the Reagan administration of increasing domestic interest rates by attracting international capital to American financial markets and guaranteeing the appreciation of the dollar against other national currencies in the world.

14   It was the American military program proposed by President Ronald Reagan in 1983 to build a defensive system of missiles and artificial space satellites capable of preventing a nuclear attack against the territory of the United States.

TABLE 8.3   GDP growth rate (%) Brazil v world

Year	Brazil	World
1980–89	3.02	3.27
1990–99	1.75	3.15
2000–08	3.78	4.32

SOURCE: OWN ELABORATION BASED ON DATA FROM
IBGE AND IMF

on what effectively consolidated neoliberalism to Brazil: the Real Plan with its
monetary tripod that consisted of fiscal adjustment, austere monetary policy
and floating exchange rate.[15]

In view of these troubled circumstances, it can be concluded that there was
no space, within the democratic game, for the conciliation of divergent interests and to meet the demands of the poor, not even in a palliative way. These
conditions were not on the agenda at that time. The lost decade of the eighties
and the decade of the nineties meant the prolongation of the compression
of the living conditions of the workers, although after August 1994 there was
monetary stabilization and immediate reduction of poverty

After the instability of the turn of the century, the 2000s opened up with
new possibilities. The advancement of China's growth has significantly favored
Brazil, in addition to the specific situation of elections for Latin American
center-left presidents. In order to come to power, PT had to count on a more
favorable international context; the internal monetary stabilization; a candidate with Lula's origins and his popular appeal. Moreover, PT considered that
a (subservient) agreement with the dominant bourgeoisies was necessary to
reach the requirements to take to power. It is worth noting that the program
that emanated from the PT Congress in 2002, when the presidential elections
were held, in which they elected their first president, the word socialism was
no longer in the text, much less in the field of the strategic horizon (Iasi, 2017).
Impacts on Growth can be seen at table 3 above.

By assuming the line of least resistance of conciliation and passivation of the
class struggle and by surrendering to the neoliberal principles of the monetary
stabilization plan, the PT completed its transformation process and became a

---

15   This "foot" started as a "foreign exchange anchor", that is, a fixed exchange rate policy,
      but after the Asian (1997–1999) and Russian (1998) crises, it was necessary to adjust to a
      flexible exchange rate policy to better fit the standards of the Washington Consensus.

party within the left of the order, reproducing the dependence and underdevelopment typical of dependent capitalism, for acting only on the effects and not on the causes of the social issue (León & Malta, 2017). Then, in Florestan's terminology, it co-opted the tutored classes, providing cyclical solutions to structural dilemmas such as poverty and inequality. It is important, however, to emphasize that the governments previous to those of the PT only achieved an improvement in the living conditions through the new round of modernization of the consumption patterns of the Lula and Dilma governments. In this sense, PT was a milestone in the country's history by incorporating the poorest sectors into the consumerist illusions of capitalism, but without solving the problems of social segregation.

However, we must note that in the specific case of the political construction necessary for the presidential election, the PT not only made use of the policy of alliances in the electoral process, but of coalition presidentialism after being elected with the purchase of political alliances to obtain a parliamentary majority.

In 2005, exposed for being involved in the case of corruption known as "mensalão" in which the party bought votes from parliamentarians through shady negotiations and financing, the PT evidenced the sense of buying alliances as co-optation through corruption and alliance with bourgeois interests, taking Florestan's predictions of what a co-optation democracy would be to its last and harshest consequences. The specific dynamics of the monthly allowance consisted of the monthly and illegal pecuniary payment for some members (Anderson, 2020).

The PT's action strategy, therefore, was to achieve new ways of maintaining the status quo by progressively transforming its original program to meet the expansion of alliances, while maintaining a popular discourse mainly focused on social inclusion through consumption. Ironically, co-option was exercised in its full form, with the opening down by a socially based working party. Fulfilling the characteristics of Gramsci's transformism and Fernandes' co-optation democracy.

Co-optation, that second option that fell to the bourgeois fractions and the working class in re-democratization, would undergo a definite inflection with the so-called Jornadas de Junho de 2013, in which a large part of the population took to the streets to show their dissatisfaction with the promises of the democratic state of São Paulo. Our interpretation is that the year of 2013,[16] exploded

16 A closer look at the economic aspects of the 2013 crisis, the fall in profitability and its origin in the class struggle is a job that deserves greater attention and deserves to be developed in future works.

like a powder keg that the PT's own policies and public opinion organs ignited (Sampaio Jr., 2017). The neglect with the resolution of the social issue and the increasingly evident participation or collusion with cases of corruption, especially those involving Petrobras, point in this direction. An accumulation crisis also became a crisis of representativeness and the youth, showing their dislike of the parties of the order, took to the streets to protest.

Since then, the class struggle in Brazil has taken on some dimensions. A political dimension with the crisis of political representativeness, since a good part of the population started to question the functioning of liberal democracy, even more with the fratricidal dispute between the bourgeois class fractions after the impediment of President Dilma; an economic dimension that came from the eighties with the process of deindustrialization and that the PT has not reversed; a social dimension exposed by the social denunciation of the perception of high levels of inequality and poverty.

The ruling classes did not hesitate to show their intolerance to the use of conflict as a way of resolving social struggles and used public opinion against any demonstration against the order. State apparatus such as the press and the new conservative movements such as Vem Pra Rua and Movimento Brasil Livre (MBL) – which was created in part to counter the similar acronym MPL (Movimento Passe Livre) which has a progressive agenda that fights for zero transport tariff – tried to take the lead in the demonstrations and managed to mobilize a large part of the population against the PT government. At the same time, it is important to pay attention to the fact that conservative organizations such as the neo-Pentecostal churches linked to "prosperity theology" have also been expanding within the scope of the popular classes, strengthening a moralistic discourse. The ruling classes manipulated the situation as if the demonstrations that initially began as specific and clearly political protests, were non-partisan and as if they did not have a clear political flag.

Again, as in so many moments in the history of Brazil, the demands of popular movements have been reduced to the agenda of corruption. It is worth remembering, however, that on the other hand, youth sectors organized themselves to demonstrate against the neo-liberal policies of the Dilma Rousseff government and groups such as the black blocs, a youth movement with an anarchist inspiration and with urban guerrilla tactics that agitated the streets in legitimate expression of dissatisfaction.

After a phase of unique spontaneity, born from the internal contradictions of co-optation democracy, which was followed by an explosion in the number of strikes[17]across the country, street movements were manipulated by conservative movements (Sampaio Jr., 2017). The manipulation of public opinion followed in such a way that the initial multitudinous discontent was transformed into hatred by the middle class against the party that represented, for the dominant classes, the middle sectors and a considerable part of the working class, the social changes of the last years: the PT.

Thus, the crisis of the political form that had reached its peak under the PT had reached its moment of final agony with the impeachment of Dilma in 2016. The advanced agendas against workers' rights in the Temer government and the election of Jair Bolsonaro, who at the time was affiliated to the Social Liberal Party (PSL) in 2018, point to the exhaustion of that political form and with it the imminent end of the New Republic.

The type of democratization after the promulgation of the 1988 Constitution did not generate Coutinho's mass democracy and Florestan's co-optation democracy seems to have been carried out until its exhaustion. Even so, the structural reference of restricted democracy and the double articulation that characterize dependent capitalism seems to remain.

5   Final Considerations

The controversy that we present about the perspectives that were presented for democracy in Brazil during the re-democratization signalled that, on the one hand, for Florestan Fernandes, the real possibility that was drawn far from being an immediate socialist transformation, was a new form of State action bourgeois autocratic from the expansion, for part of the working class, of a bourgeois instrument born during the dictatorship, the co-optation of democracy; on the other hand, for Carlos Nelson Coutinho, the prospect was of a possible re-democratization that, at first, should have favored the accumulation of forces, including with sectors of the bourgeoisie, in the sense of political openness and then building an organised mass democracy.

The New Republic was the period in which the political form of co-optation democracy developed, blossomed and perished. This form is based on the pact and the alliance of classes and between class fractions, a true revolution in the

---

17   Ruy Braga is an author who has critically analyzed the strike movement in Brazil, signaling that strikes had been increasing before 2013, but that from that year the number increases at a faster speed. See more in the rebelliousness of the precariat: work and neoliberalism in the global South, Ruy Braga (2017).

techniques of the counterrevolution. The PT's policy was nothing more than to accommodate itself to the frameworks of bourgeois democracy by co-opting the poor, middle and rich sectors, but, as in the 1964 regime, the co-optation of the PT was also a policy and transitory accumulation.

A contribution of this chapter was to show that it was only under certain conditions of the economic, international and national scenario, and with a government of a party of working origin and with founding proposals of a socialist nature, that co-optation could be exercised in its most developed form. The transformism suffered by this party, which aligned with the bourgeois order, orchestrated the reconciliation of interests that seemed irreconcilable in order to pass the class struggle by superficially incorporating sectors of society into the capitalist logic.

Evidence of the decline in the form of co-optation can be seen in the Jornadas de Junho 2013, when the people spontaneously took to the streets to demand jobs, wages, transport and public education, revealing the limits of the democratic rule of law, the possibility of class conciliation and the contradictions of neoliberalism itself. The post-2016 Brazilian scenario must be seen in the global context of the rise of conservative governments, both in the center of the capitalist world and in its periphery.

By the time this text was finalized, in May 2020, the governments that succeeded Dilma's government had already achieved fiscal, labour, social security reforms and had outlined administrative reform, marking a new accumulation regime in which the withdrawal of rights and exploitation of the working class is the main feature. This movement takes place even under an intense crisis of power and under accusations of not respecting democratic rules and the rights acquired by workers over decades of struggle. This means that the pattern of accumulation and bourgeois domination consolidated in 1964, and which has undergone shape changes since then, today has a common content for the exploitation and repression of workers.

It is interesting the hypothesis of Iasi (2016) that the recent context, of Michel Temer's government, established that of heading towards a new dictatorship. However, not in that civil-military form of preventive counterrevolution with a State of repressive exception, but a new type surrounded by legality and with the appearance of possibilities of political alternation as if the rule of law were preserved, but which actually makes the State of exception a rule. From the conjunction between i) the crisis of power; ii) the dynamics of the class struggle and iii) the degree of risk imposed on order, the institutionalized forms of democracy clashed with the interests of the ruling class, opening space for the State to come to act as the universal form of class interest bourgeois.

We return here to the starting point inscribed in the idea of Ianni (1988) that in Brazil there is an authoritarian political culture that prevents the majority of the population from identifying themselves in the State, not being represented there. With the end of co-optation democracy, the ruling classes resorted to the abuse of the coercive aspect of the state. They criminalize civil society and social claims are again treated as a police matter. The logic of the ongoing movement is to further prohibit Brazilian democracy, relieving the State of its public responsibilities.

As a superficial phenomenon that hides the class struggle substratum of bourgeois society, democracy varies between the co-optation and the crushing of the working classes. If the dilemmas of internal social segregation and external dependence that reproduce underdevelopment are not overcome, Brazilian democracy will continue to alienate the majority of the population from the decision-making spheres of politics, economics and culture, since capital, even in times of more severe crisis, finds new ways to exercise its power of domination. To paraphrase Giuseppe di Lampedusa: "if we want everything to stay as it is, everything has to change".

Bibliographic References

Anderson, Perry. Brasil à parte. São Paulo. Boitempo. 2020.

Boffo, Marco; Saad-Filho, Alfredo; Fine, Ben. Neoliberal Capitalism: the authoritarian turn. *In:* Socialist Register 2019, p. 247–270, 2019.

Coutinho, Carlos Nelson. A democracia como valor universal: notas sobre a questão democrática no Brasil. Revista Encontros com a civilização brasileira. n° 9, p. 33–47, 1979.

Coutinho, Carlos Nelson. Gramsci: um estudo sobre o seu pensamento político. Rio de Janeiro. Campus. 1989.

Coutinho, Carlos Nelson. De Rousseau a Gramsci: ensaios de teoria política. São Paulo: Boitempo editorial. 2011.

Curty, Carla; Malta, Maria. Elementos metodológicos para a organização da história do pensamento econômico brasileiro: a abordagem das controvérsias. *In*: Malta, Maria; León, Jaime; Curty, Carla; Borja, Bruno. Controvérsias sobre história, desenvolvimento e revolução no Brasil: pensamento econômico em interpretação crítica. In this book, 2021.

Fernandes, Florestan. Sociedade de classes e subdesenvolvimento. Rio de Janeiro: Zahar Editores. 1968.

Fernandes, Florestan. Capitalismo dependente e classes sociais na América Latina. Rio de Janeiro: Zahar editores. 1972.

Fernandes, Florestan. A revolução Burguesa no Brasil. Ensaio de interpretação Sociológica. São Paulo: Editora Globo. [1975] 2011.

Fernandes, Florestan. O que é revolução? São Paulo: Editora Brasiliense. 1981.

Fernandes, Florestan. Pensamento e ação: o PT e os rumos do socialismo hoje. São Paulo: Editora Globo. 1984.

Gramsci, Antonio. Cadernos do Cárcere. Rio de Janeiro: Civilização Brasileira. [1934] 2011.

Ianni, Octávio. As raízes da anti-democracia na América Latina. Lua Nova: Revista de Cultura e Política. nº 14, São Paulo, p. 17–22. 1988.

Iasi, Mauro. O PT e a revolução burguesa no Brasil. Marília: Editora Unesp. 2013

Iasi, Mauro. Política, Estado e Ideologia na trama atual. São Paulo: Instituto Caio Prado Júnior. 2017.

León, Jaime; Malta, Maria. Um debate sobre a democracia brasileira: tradição plutocrática e perspectivas de democratização no meio de uma crise de poder e de acumulação. Texto de discussão nº 017 do Instituto de Economia da UFRJ. Available on: https://www.ie.ufrj.br/images/IE/TDS/2017/TD_IE_017_2017_LEON_MALTA.pdf. Access on March 2020, 2017.

Mészáros, István. Para além do Capital. São Paulo: Boitempo Editorial, [1995] 2002.

Netto, José Paulo. Pequena história da ditadura brasileira (1964–1985). São Paulo: Cortez Editora. 2014.

Prado, Luiz; Leopoldi, Maria. O fim do desenvolvimentismo: o governo Sarney e a transição do modelo econômico brasileiro. In O tempo da Nova República: da transição democrática à política de 2016. Coleção O Brasil republicano. Volume 5. Civilização brasileira. Rio de Janeiro. 2018.

Pinto, Eduardo. et al. A guerra de todos contra todos e a Lava Jato: a crise brasileira e a vitória do capitão Jair Bolsonaro. Revista da Sociedade Brasileira de Economia Política nº54 (Setembro – Dezembro 2019), p. 183–215. 2019

Saad-Filho, Alfredo; Morais, Lécio. Brasil: neoliberalismo versus democracia. São Paulo. Boitempo. 2018.

Sampaio Júnior., Plinio. Crônicas de uma crise anunciada: crítica à economia política de Lula e Dilma. São Paulo: SG-Amarante. 2017.

Index

CPSIA information can be obtained
at www.ICGtesting.com
Printed in the USA
JSHW082114041122
32627JS00001B/1

9 781642 598056